Indian Defence Industry: An Agenda for Making in India

Indian Defence Industry
An Agenda for Making in India

Col. (Retd.) S.C. Narang

PRASHANT PUBLISHING HOUSE
DELHI-110094

Published by :
Prashant Publishing House
C-34, 28 Foota Road, Gali-3,
West Karwal Nagar, Delhi-110094
Phone : 011-22963970, Mob. : 9810396373
e-mail.: prashantpublishinghouse@gmail.com

Indian Defence Industry: An Agenda for Making in India

First Published 2017

ISBN 978-93-80565-82-8

PRINTED IN INDIA

Published by Mr. R.K. Jha M/s Prashant Publishing House and Published at H.S. Offset House Press, Delhi.

Contents

Preface

The third largest armed force in the world meets 60% of its requirements through imports. The Government of India is looking to reverse this trend with its 'Make in India' program in the defence sector. At Aero India 2015, when Prime Minister Narendra Modi emphatically said the defence industry was at the heart of the 'Make in India' programme, he conveyed his government's intent to reform an archaic arms production base whose inefficiency has earned India the dubious distinction of being the world's largest arms importer. To be sure, the government has taken a host of measures to incentivise local arms production. Under the 'Make in India' programme, the government has awarded 56 defence manufacturing permits to private sector entities in the past one year compared with 47 granted in the preceding three years.

Being the multi-billion dollar and most lucrative defence market in the world, India provides several opportunities for Indian and foreign corporate entities for defence manufacturing. Thanks to the Make in India campaign, the defence sector has moved from the periphery to the core of Indian manufacturing. Several CII reports have suggested that the sector not only has the potential to augment manufacturing but also add nearly one million direct and indirect jobs. Some of the top industrial houses have already made some inroads into the sector. Several more are waiting for the right opportunity.

"Make in India has become the new mantra in the Indian defence industry and within the industry, private sector is the centre of attraction. This is quite evident from some of the big measures taken so far like hike in the foreign direct investment (FDI) from the earlier 26 pc to 49 pc, streamlining of defence industrial licencing, rationalisation of taxes, etc. Ultimately, private sector is the biggest beneficiary. This book thoroughly probes the Indian Defence industry and the policies pertaining to it. This book predicts that whether our armies are winning or taking a beating, the moment the war touches the Indians who matter (that is, the rich, the beautiful and the powerful), urban India would start buckling.

Collaboration and cooperation between the private sector and Public Sector Defence Units may create synergy in defence production. R&D needs to be taken to private firms and SMEs need to be encouraged to undertake the development and production of critical sub-assemblies through various policy supports. A boost in defence production in India will improve its defence preparedness, boost economy and provide employment apart from changing the technological landscape of India. All the matter is just compiled and edited in nature. Taken from the various sources which are in public domain.

This book thoroughly probes the Indian Defence industry and the policies pertaining to it. This book predicts that whether our armies are winning or taking a beating, the moment the war touches the Indians who matter (that is, the rich, the beautiful and the powerful), urban India would start buckling.

—Editor

1

Introduction

In a significant departure, the Ministry of Defence (MoD) has made public the report of the 10-member Experts Committee that was set up in May 2015 to both evolve a policy framework for facilitating 'Make in India' within the purview of the Defence Procurement Procedure (DPP) and streamline the procurement process. More significantly, the report has been put in the public domain even before the government has taken action on its key recommendations, indicating the keenness to solicit views from the wider public on the vital issue of self-reliance, which has so far dogged policy makers despite several policy announcements in the past decade-and-a-half. This Issue Brief examines the key recommendations of the Experts Committee, especially those that pertain to the defence industry.

STRATEGIC PARTNERSHIP MODEL

The signature recommendation of the Experts Committee pertains to various models for the private sector. After taking into account the unique nature of defence equipment and the configuration of the global defence industry, the Committee has arrived at three models for the Indian set up -- Strategic Partnership, Developmental Partnership and Competitive Partnership. According to the Committee, the choice of the model should be based on "strategic needs, quality criticality and cost competitiveness."

Among the three models, Strategic Partnership is somewhat akin to the Raksha Udyog Ratna (RUR) concept. First suggested by the Kelkar Committee, RUR failed to take off apparently due to objections from trade unions affiliated with public sector defence companies and reservations expressed by some industry players on the manner in which the Prabir Sengupta Committee had identified a dozen or so companies as RURs. Surprisingly, the Dhirendra Singh Committee has neither referred to the RUR concept of the Kelkar Committee nor to the RURs identified by the Sengupta Committee. Nonetheless, like the RUR concept, the strategic partnership model also visualises selective identification of a few big private players and nurturing them through preferential treatment, which would entail co-opting them for 'Buy and Make' and Government-to-Government procurement programmes.

While suggesting the strategic partnership model, the Experts Committee has also identified the following six segments in which Strategic Partners (SP) from the private sector would be identified:

- Aircraft: fighter, transport and helicopter and their major systems.
- Warships of stated displacements, and submarines and their major systems.
- Armoured fighting vehicles and their major systems.
- Complex weapons which rely on guidance systems to achieve precision hits, which may include anti-ship, air defence, air-to-air, air-to-surface, anti-submarine, land attack.
- Command, control, communication and computers, intelligence, surveillance, target acquisition and reconnaissance.
- Critical materials (titanium alloys, aluminium alloys, carbon composites, nickel/cobalt alloys etc.).

It may be noted that while identifying the different segments, the committee has categorically suggested that just one or two private players would be identified in each segment, limiting the number of players to almost the same number of players identified through the RUR selection process. In order to prevent 'conglomerate monopoly', the Committee has further suggested that only one SP should be permitted in one segment, and once it chosen in a particular segment it should not be considered directly or indirectly (through cross holdings in another company) in the other segments. This has apparently not gone down well in the industry, especially the bigger ones which aspire to play a larger role in different segments of defence production. The industry's reservations notwithstanding, the idea of strategic partnership is as relevant as the earlier RUR concept since India cannot afford to have a very large and frequently changing number of players in every segment of major defence platforms. Even in the United States, the biggest defence market in the world, the production of major platforms and weapon systems is consolidated among a few major companies. Having said this, the major challenge for the government now is to select the SP in each segment. Given the earlier experience in the selection of RURs, it would be worth watching how the government proceeds on the SP concept.

Industry Friendly Procurement System

A major focus of the Expert Committee is on streamlining the acquisition process and structure so as to create more opportunities for the local industry. The Committee argues that for 'Make in India' to succeed, the procurement system must recognize the unique and strategic nature of defence equipment, which is characterised by high-technology content, stringent quality standard, limited vendor base, low production rate, rapid obsolescence and restricted mobility across borders. In such a scenario, for the local industry to prosper, there is a need to take it into confidence in every possible procurement step, beginning with the planning process. Highlighting the current weakness whereby the local industry does not have information about the type and nature of the long term equipment requirement of the armed forces, the Committee has suggested that the relevant information as contained in various plans and other documents be shared with the industry with the sole objective of enabling the latter to make a concrete decision on investment or technology partnership. In specific terms, the Committee has suggested the revision of the current Technology Perspective Capability Roadmap (TPCR) so as to reflect the type and nature of the equipment required by the armed forces in the next 15 years. At the same time, the Committee has also suggested that schemes amenable to 'Make' projects be shared with the industry along with the details of other schemes as contained in the 5-year Services Capital Acquisition Plan (SCAP).

The Committee is of the opinion that for the Indian industry to contribute meaningfully to 'Make in India', the procurement system needs to move towards indigenous design, development and production or 'Make' projects. In this regard, the Committee while broadly agreeing with the MoD's revised and simplified 'Make' procedure, also makes some specific suggestions to further strengthen it. It rightly argues that since 'Make' projects involve a long-gestation period, the decision on such projects must precede that of other categories by at least one plan period (five year) or more.

Such pre-positioning of 'Make' projects would give much needed leeway to the industry and the services to iron out any issue that may arise at the developmental stage without significantly disturbing the planned induction schedule. The eligibility criteria for soliciting expression of interest (EoI) from the industry should be liberal to include not only the big players but also all the 'innovative and agile industry' including from the Micro Small & Medium Enterprises (MSME) sector. Moreover, the industry executing the 'Make' project should be given tax incentives by way of allowing their developmental cost (of 20 per cent) as being qualified as R&D expenditure.

The Committee is also of the firm opinion that for the local industry to grow, the current approach of the procurement system towards single vendor situations needs a relook. As the Committee rightly observes, single bid situation is an emerging reality, particularly in cases involving 'Buy and Make' and 'Buy and Make (Indian)' projects. Rejecting such proposals for the sake of competition not only delays acquisition, but hampers the interest of the local industry which is now expected to play a much larger role under the 'Make in India' initiative. Aligning with the concept of strategic partnership, the Committee therefore recommends suitable changes in the DPP to reflect the emerging reality.

REASONS TO INVEST

1. India's current requirements on defence are catered largely by imports. The opening of the defence sector for private sector participation will help foreign original equipment manufacturers to enter into strategic partnerships with Indian companies and leverage the domestic markets as well as aim at global markets. Besides helping in building domestic capabilities, this will also bolster exports in the long term.
2. Contractual offset obligations worth approximately USD 4.53 billion in next 5-6 years
3. The offset policy (which stipulates the mandatory offset requirement of a minimum 30% for procurement of defence equipment in excess of USD 306.69 million) introduced in the capital purchase agreements with foreign defence players. It would also ensure that an eco-system of suppliers is built domestically.
4. Favorable government policy which promotes self-reliance, indigenisation, technology upgradation and achieving economies of scale including development of capabilities for exports in the defence sector.
5. The country's extensive modernisation plans with an increased focus on homeland security and India's growing attractiveness as a defence sourcing hub.

SECTOR POLICY

Procurement Policy:

- The defence procurement is governed by the Defence Procurement Procedure (DPP 2016).
- Latest revision of DPP was released in March 2016.

Offset Policy:

- The key objectives of the defence offset policy is to leverage capital acquisitions to develop the domestic defence industry. Mandatory offset requirements of a minimum of 30% for procurement of defence equipment in excess of USD 307.69 million have been envisaged.

Procedures for the Grant of Industrial Licenses have been streamlined:

- The initial validity period of industrial licenses has been increased from 3 years to 15 years with a provision to grant extension for a period of 3 years.
- Guidelines for the extension of validity of industrial licenses have been issued.
- Partial commencement of production is treated as commencement of production of all the items included in the license.

GREATER TECHNOLOGY TRANSFER AND THRUST ON LOCALISATION

Defence Minister Manohar Parrikar recently said that defence procurement from SMEs will register growth of 6 percent this year over the previous year. "Last year, procurement reached 9 percent, and in the current year, it will reach 15 percent. As the volumes increase from Rs 40,000 crore in 2014, to Rs 52,000 crore in the current year, there is more scope for SMEs. It was unheard before," he said. In addition, the Ministry of Defence (MoD) also aims at 7 percent indigenisation by the year 2027.

There is a context to the statement. India is the world's largest defence importer and has steadily held this position for the previous 5 years. It is also the sixth biggest defence spender internationally and the second largest spender in Asia. There has also been consistent criticism of India's defence offsets policy and the lack of participation of the local industry in the defence sector. For the realisation of key government initiatives such as Make in India, there is need for a robust offsets policy—

one that would aid the flourishing of the local defence enterprises.

India's defence offsets policy

In order to leverage India's huge defence import and bolster the local arms industry, the Ministry of Defence (MoD) has in place an offsets policy, which lays down the ground rules for the implementation of offset agreements—arrangements in which the seller of a defence product or service agrees to buy products or services from its client as an inducement. These agreements are legal trade practices in the aerospace and military industries. The offsets policy was made part of the Defence Procurement Procedure (DPP) in 2005 for the first time and has seen several changes since then. It permits foreign vendors to realise their offset obligations through a blend of two key provisions: Foreign Direct Investment (FDI) in Indian companies and purchase of certain products/services from qualified Indian enterprises.

Criticism of India's defence offsets policy

The offsets policy has often been the target of criticism, with experts saying that it has been inadequate in compensating for India's huge purchasing power and also that its implementation has been woefully insufficient. They also claim that it has not led to any substantial growth of indigenous industries. The criticism is not without reason.

The Comptroller and Auditor General of India (CAG), the body entrusted with auditing the implementation of the offsets arrangements and which has audited several offset contracts, has been unforgiving in its assessment of the policy and its implementation. In a report submitted to Parliament in November 2012, it pinpointed a number of weaknesses in the policy, including zero value addition, equipment transfer, invalid selection of the Indian Offset Partner (IOP), and a weak monitoring mechanism.

Moreover, the Defence Procurement Policy (DPP) 2016 has elevated the offset threshold limit to Rs. 2,000 crore (around

US$ 305 million) from Rs. 300 crore. No reasons have been given for the hike. Industry experts believe that it may have stemmed from the ministry's difficulty in executing the existing offset contracts. Whatever might be the case, the hike is flawed on two main accounts: (a) it goes against global practices followed by other countries and (b) it is self-defeating for initiatives such as 'Make in India'. According to global practices, offset threshold is as low as USD 5–15 million in several countries such as Australia, Brazil, and Israel. Furthermore, states usually tend to lower the threshold overtime as they gain in experience.

The increase in the threshold limit means that a smaller number of arms import contracts would now be qualified for offsets. This translates into a setback for indigenous enterprises, specifically local manufacturers of components that have been exploiting the existing policy for boosting their own exports. In the process, enterprises have been able to set up their own capabilities and bolster initiatives such as 'Make in India'. Although, the DPP has a clear emphasis on "Make in India" and self-reliance, with the introduction of a new category of procurement and increased localisation in the existing categories, the hike in the offsets threshold limit negates the thrust on indigenisation.

"The biggest weakness of the policy is the freedom given to foreign companies to choose offsets they want to deliver. Obviously, they have so far chosen offsets, which do not add to the capability enhancement of the local industry. The policy should clearly focus on technology acquisition and high quality and sustainable manufacturing work for the industry, which would go a long way in strengthening the indigenous capability", said Laxman Kumar Behera, author of the book *Indian Defence Industry: An Agenda for Making in India* and a research fellow at the MoD-funded think-tank Institute for Defence Studies and Analyses (IDSA).

India can learn from Japan and Brazil

The Japanese vision has been fairly simple: there can't be real security unless the nation is self-sufficient with respect to technology and arms production. This has been coupled with the belief that the absorption of defence technology and the creation of indigenous arms production capacity will have significant spill-over effects on the growth of civilian commercial technologies, eventually making Japan an industrial and technological superpower.

During the post-World War II period, Japan used its relationship with the USA to develop its local defence sector. Its industrial policy too has been based on technology transfer from the West—first emulating the techniques and eventually overtaking them. This principle has been key to Japan's quick, resilient and diversified industrialisation. In fact, a major source of the technology inflows into Japan came from defence offsets.

According to defence expert Anuradha Mitra, more than 90 percent of Japan's requirements for military products are now met within the country. There have been a number of important developments in the aerospace sector. For the F1 fighter there was a Japanese fire control design; for the T4 intermediate jet trainer the fuselage and engine were developed in Japan; 80 per cent of the materials and systems for the P3-C Orion are sourced from within the country; the FS-X advanced fighter bomber has been built indigenously with Mitsubishi as the prime contractor in collaboration with General Dynamics (later Lockheed Martin).

Similarly, Brazil always viewed the growth of arms industry as a significant long-term goal. The Brazilian government has been able to leverage its defence buys to get state-of-the-art military technology from outside through licensed production and joint ventures.

"Technology transfer has always been a key requisite in all Brazilian arms procurements. The state has also been willing to invest a good deal of resources in the indigenous projects. Embraer Corporation, the Brazilian aeronautics major proved to be leader in the absorption and indigenisation of technologies. In the early 1970s, Embraer had a technology transfer agreement with Piper of the USA for manufacture of the Piper Seneca light aero-planes. In 1975, when 49 F-5 aircraft were purchased by Brazil from Northrop of the US, Embraer was involved in the manufacture of several fuselage components," explains Mitra.

INDIA'S DEFENCE INDUSTRY: A HISTORICAL OVERVIEW

Looking into the Post-Independence Era

The pre-independence (pre-1947) defence-industrial infrastructure in India was limited. It generally catered to the lowest spectrum of defence production—repair and overhaul of imported weapons systems. The then ruling British followed a policy of retaining strategic capabilities for themselves while allowing the native Indians to assist in the tactical dimensions, confined to minor works in most endeavours. An example of this policy is evident from the fact that while the Royal Air Force retained the strategic elements like the bomber force and used their own formations, the Indian Air Force (IAF) was left with only tactical elements—supporting them with secondary and tertiary roles that mainly included repair and similar minor works. The Walchand Aircraft Factory (WAF) in Bangalore was wholly engaged in repair and maintenance of aircraft at that time. From March 1942 till the end of World War II, it was employed for the servicing of American aircraft and was managed, for part of this period, by the US Air Force.

Mazagaon Docks (Mumbai) and Garden Reach Shipyards (Calcutta) similarly existed prior to India's independence to repair warships. However, apart from such single air or ship industrial units, India's defence-industrial capacity during times of pre-independence mainly consisted of what is known as Ordnance Factories (OFs). These factories had been set up primarily to supplement land-based weapons and equipment produced in Britain. Before 1947, there were 16 OFs, all located on Indian territory.

The gun and shell factory at Cossipore (near Kolkata), established in 1801, an ammunition factory at Kirkee of 1889, a rifle factory at Ishapore of 1901, a gun carriage factory at

Jabalpur of 1904, and others were built mainly to produce for the British forces. During World War II, possible threats to the sea lanes of communication in the Indian Ocean and requirements of the allied forces in the region, made it necessary to double the number of factories during this time. The filling factory at Khamara and the light machine gun factory at Hyderabad were amongst such new factories. In brief, pre-partition Indian defence-industrial capacities were confined only to a supplementary role and were placed at the lowest end of the production spectrum.

Post-independence, the Indian leadership wanted self-sufficiency in every sphere of activity. This objective was obvious because India was never allowed to develop industrial competencies. The same objective was no different in the field of defence production. Right from the first Prime Minister Jawaharlal Nehru, every successive Indian leader sought self-sufficiency in defence production.

The need to establish a comprehensive defence-industrial infrastructure thus constituted a primary objective of the political leadership. Right from the beginning, India's industrial policies emphasised 'core' industries to be taken care of by the central government and others by the states. Defence industries, considered as critical national assets, obviously came under the exclusive control of the central government. The first Industrial Policy Resolution of 1948, consequently revised under the Second Five-Year Plan in 1956, made it clear that core industries, including munitions, aircraft, shipbuilding, iron and steel, heavy machine tools, heavy electrical plants, atomic energy and similar others were to be placed under exclusive central government control. During this period, many industrial units related to these fields were established under the strict supervision of the central government, known as 'basic' (Schedule A) industries. The Defence Science Organisation was also established during this period to take up the challenge of undertaking R&D activities. As demands for defence R&D grew, this organisation paved the way for the creation of the Defence Research and Development Organisation (DRDO) in 1958, which to-date remains the most important contributor to India's defence R&D activities. It has got nearly 50 laboratories, spread all across the country, and other scientific establishments and institutions like the Council of Scientific and Industrial Research (CSIR).

At independence, India's defence-industrial production was mainly coming from the existing 16 OFs. These factories were engaged in the production of low technology items like small arms and ammunition, mines and other explosives. Their cumulative value of production was estimated at roughly US $7-8 million during the time of India's independence. Despite the first India-Pakistan War (1947/48) and the need to boost defence-industrial production, no new factory was built during the first decade (1950s). It was during the late 1950s that the need to construct more factories was contemplated. It is also during this time that peace time civilian production in defence industries was emphasised, especially by the then Defence Minister, V. K. Krishna Menon. The policy of production for civilian markets was primarily aimed at maintaining operational capacities during slack periods of demand as well as keeping the level of productivity high by the manufacturing units. By the end of the 1950s, the number of defence-industrial units almost remained the same. The production from these ordnance factories was still geared to low-technology items.

Apart from OFs, and various defence science and technology establishments, the Indian government also created a number of production establishments to take care of various productions in the field of defence. These, like others, were under the exclusive control of the government although they were created as corporations, commonly known as 'Defence Public Sector Units' (DPSUs). There are eight DPSUs in the country, devoted to the production of different military systems and components. They are: Hindustan Aeronautics Limited (HAL), Bharat Electronics Limited (BEL), Bharat Earth Movers Limited (BEML), Mazagaon Dockyard Limited (MDL), Garden Reach Shipbuilders and Engineers Limited, Goa Shipyard, Bharat Dynamics Limited (BDL) and Mishra Dhatu Nigam Limited (MDNL). Both, DPSUs and OFs, are administered by the

Department of Defence Production under the Ministry of Defence.

Both sets of industries have their own research and development units although the overall R&D activities are met by the DRDO. Bharat Electronics Limited (BEL) was the first DPSU, established in 1954, to manufacture electronic equipment primarily for the defence sector. Over the years, more than half of BEL's overall production has turned into products for the civilian market. And it is not the only production entity that has changed that way.

In the post-independence period, till the war with China in 1962, India's defence-industrial base was too weak to take the responsibility of all defence needs. The self-sufficiency model had been adopted since the beginning but as years passed and demands for security grew, India found it difficult to create an industrial base as it was hit primarily by two important factors – lack of sufficient funding and access to modern defence technologies. The Indian leadership was aware of these two problems but they also had a number of other issues to handle. The country was just independent, had already fought a war with Pakistan, did not even have a rudimentary industrial base, and faced numerous nation-building and socioeconomic problems, independence, found it pragmatic to follow a policy of controlling critical industries, including defence, though this is widely debated now. Although both defence and non-defence critical industries were under exclusive state control, the former—due to their strategic importance—became a 'closed' sector.

The leadership also desired and pursued what is commonly known as comprehensive industrialisation. This meant that more and more big industries emerged to cater to needs that were vast, like steel, coal, mining, etc. Thus, big state-owned companies like the Steel Authority of India Limited (SAIL) was established. This was also evident in the defence sector where large industrial units were created to cater to the demands of the vast armed forces. As mentioned, the two problems of lack of investment and access to technologies became acute as the defence industries expanded, making many units perform below par. Also, investment pattern in this sector was not uniform. Critical establishments like the Hindustan Aeronautics Limited (HAL) and DRDO received more funds than others, such as OFs. The ever-growing demands of the armed forces and the problems in the defence sector in meeting those led many to criticise existing policies followed by the then ruling party. The government, in turn, was hard pressed for funds that were essential and was aware of long-term returns for investment in the defence sector. In brief, policies to maximise production in order to attain self-sufficiency in the defence sector although they were considered far-sighted, did not match expectations, thus leading to further constraints.

From Self-Sufficiency to Self-Reliance

The self-sufficiency in defence production was in fact realised from the beginning, and was complemented by the concept of self-reliance after a few years of persistence and failure. Self-reliance, as far as India was concerned, meant—apart from its own production base for support—a degree of dependence on reliable foreign sources for access to technologies, supply of components and complete systems. This, in turn, was debatable as foreign partners to achieve such long-term self-reliance were not forthcoming during the first few years as the West was considered to be unreliable both for military and political reasons.

India tested self-reliance by meeting urgent and immediate demands through imports from abroad while simultaneously striving for indigenous capabilities in defence production. The west European weapons systems, primarily British, French and Swedish, were considered first choice in the Indian arsenal during the first few years; however, after the 1962 war with China, many western countries along with the United States were reluctant to co-operate with India which made a major adverse impact on India's defence production activities. The post-War scenario witnessed a slow entry of the Soviet Union as a major supplier, the position is still retained by its successor Russia.

The post-1962 scenario was marked by utter confusion in the decision-making circles, which in turn impinged the defence industry. India was humiliated in the war with China and thus started looking into its existent defence-industrial capabilities and found to its horror that all was not well. For example, the Indian Air Force (IAF) needed a high-altitude supersonic interceptor against the threat of the B-57 bomber of Pakistan (supplied by the United States) and the Tu-16 bomber of the Chinese Air Force (supplied by the USSR). The requirement especially assumed a serious dimension after the war with China, when India looked outward and found out that only three fighter aircraft worth-considering were available in the market. India neither wanted to buy the British Lightning nor the Soviet MiG-21, and preferred the American F-104. This system was already supplied by the United States to Pakistan and despite repeated efforts India could not obtain it. India's effort to upgrade the existing HF-24 to supersonic capability was not considered by the Americans, either. It was at this time that the USSR came to India's rescue when they not only decided to supply the MiG-21 and other weapons but also gave a go-ahead for license production. India's quest for self-reliance got a major boost through this license production arrangement. This was indeed a turning point in India's self-reliance activities. The Soviets proved to be a trusted friend whose military supplies constitute more than 70 percent of India's total weapons acquisitions now. This friendship immensely benefited India's defence industry as it improved many notable weapons systems and components from this experience. In brief, India's self-reliance model in defence production was given a life lease by the Soviets.

After 1962, India sought to make up for the lacuna as well as boost defence production to match requirements. New ordnance factories were planned and established during the next three decades. The number of OFs thus grew to thirty-five by the mid-1980s. And, by the mid-1990s, it had reached thirty-nine. The fortieth ordnance factory (at Nalanda, in the state of Bihar), started in 1999/2000. These OFs were established in different parts of the country: Ten of them cater to materials and components, ten for weapons, vehicles and equipment, ten for ammunition and explosives and five for other ordnance items. By the early 1990s, they were producing more than 1500 items of arms, ammunition, equipment and components. By the early 1990s, the OFs collectively reached place 45 on the list of the largest arms producing companies in the world, and were placed at 29 in 2000.

The OFs, with a cumulative work force of 1,75,000, have been engaged in various types of land-based weapons. During the period under examination, the bulk of the production, nonetheless, still constituted of large quantities of relatively low-to medium-technology items. These, among others, included small arms, anti-tank and anti-aircraft guns, mortars, associated ammunition, rocket projectiles, bombs, grenades, mines, transport vehicles, leather items, parachutes and ordnance clothing for the armed forces. The establishment of the Heavy Vehicle Factory at Avadi (in the state of Tamil Nadu) in the early 1960s was crucial for the production of tanks and combat vehicles. This is where the first series of tanks, called 'Vijayanta' were manufactured under license from the British firm Vickers. This was followed by the manufacture of the ex-Soviet T-72 'Ajeya' MBTs. Although this project was taken up during the 1970s, it finally rolled out in 1988. In some projects, however, the level of indigenization has been pretty high, for example, up to about 80 percent in the case of 'Sarath' infantry combat vehicles. The overall performance of the OFs during that period was modest, although a lot could have been done to improve the performance of many factories. Hindustan Aeronautics Limited performed modestly during this period. Created in 1964 through an amalgamation of two aircraft companies, Hindustan Aircraft Limited and Aeronautics India Limited, HAL has become the only major aerospace company. With a total work force of nearly 45,000, it stands as the 57 largest defence company in the world.

During the beginning, it was primarily catering to maintenance and overhaul but over a period of time has slowly developed itself to undertake assembly, license manufacture and indigenous design and development. During the 1960s and well beyond, it was engaged in various license manufacture projects, amongst others the MiG-21 series aircraft, HF-24 Marut transonic fighters, 'Kiran' HJT – 16 jet trainer.. Apart from this, it also undertook to license manufacture 'Cheetah' (Aerospatiale SA 315 B) and 'Chetak' (Aerospatiale SA 316 B) helicopters. Bharat Electronics, set up in 1954 to manufacture electronic equipment, was perhaps the only DPSU which showed positive production results during the same period. Other DPSUs such as BEML, BDL, MDL were engaged in production, which may again be termed as modest. Bharat Dynamics Limited, established in 1970, is the other DPSU, which was engaged in the production of missiles and associated products. Except during the 1990s, it had engaged in the past in license manufacture of some of the low range missile series. To sum up: While the Indian defence industry was expected to raise its production level during the half a century (1960s to mid-1980s), both its objectives of self-reliance through indigenous activity and more active collaborative activity, have brought very limited results. Some analysts even term this phase as an 'era of license-manufacture', nothing more. While plant utilisation capacities remained at the lower end, with around 40 to 50 percent, the quality, range and mode of production was modest and generally confined to low and medium technologies.

Gaps Galore

From the early 1960s till the early and mid-1980s, license production and direct purchase and acquisitions remained the predominant form of supply for the Indian defence forces. Analysts like Ajay Singh argue that there was a gap of nearly three decades in India's effort toward indigenous production. This gap was especially evident in the fields of design and development, which constitutes the upper spectrum of self-reliance. A fighter aircraft between Marut and the Light Combat Aircraft (LCA), a basic trainer aircraft between HT-2 and HPT-32, an intermediate trainer between Kiran and an yet-to-be fully developed Advanced Jet Trainer (AJT) are some of the examples that typify both the technology and production gaps.

Weapons for the army had been manufactured under license with no significant design activities undertaken till the 1980s when a tank and a small arms project commenced. The first was a Main Battle Tank (MBT, named Arjun) while the last is known as the Indian Small Arms Systems (INSAS).

The Situation was a little better for the Indian Navy, where at least some ship platforms were designed indigenously. The period thus witnessed a time gap in the design and development while emphases were more on license production and acquisitions that led to two problems – below par quality performance of the defence industry, although the quantum of production was on expected lines and lack of or little funding for critical and strategic sectors of the defence industry including R&D.

Analysts also argue that given the situation even half the allocation for acquisitions would have been sufficient to ensure delivery on time, if not at the required level of technology.

INDIA'S DEFENCE INDUSTRY IS LARGELY PUBLIC SECTOR

The Indian defence sector is largely dominated by public sector units (PSUs) and ordnance factories, which together make up approximately 90 percent of the indigenous defence manufacturing output.

There is an urgent need for a vibrant SME sector in the defence sector. According to a survey conducted by Deskera, an IT firm working in the SME sector, 65 percent SMEs want a greater role in the defence sector. Greater indigenisation will not only make India self-reliant in the defence sector, it will also help in creating huge employment opportunities for young engineers, operators and the labour force in general.

Although 100 percent localisation could be the ideal aim in a strategic industry such as defence, it is not achievable because of globalisation of the supply chains and issues related to economies of scale. Right now, even 15 percent indigenous content promised for this year looks like a long shot.

RAPIDLY INDIGENIZE INDIAN DEFENSE

India's Ministry of Defense (MoD) is expected to soon come up with a revised Defense Procurement Procedure (DPP). Here are suggestions on what needs to be done in the DPP to encourage Indian firms involved in indigenization and take the 'Make in India' agenda forward:

Buy Indian for Existing Requirements

Make a list of products for which Acceptance of Necessity (AON) has been done. Please find out from the industry (through associations and others) whether there are any indigenously designed and developed products available to match the specifications. If they are available, then please ask them to bring the products for evaluation. If they pass the trials, then order may be placed on the price bid by the firm, as long as the price is less than the internationally bench-marked price. The test for indigenously designed and developed technology is that the software, algorithms, and electronics (that is, key technologies) are all developed in-house and the company has the capability to develop next generation of the same products. And also that there is no outflow of foreign exchange during the production and sale of the equipment.

The minimum indigenous content for such procurement should be 75 per cent. Preference Under Buy Indian or Buy Global In a 'Buy Indian' or a 'Buy Global' procurement, if an Indian company, with indigenous design and with indigenous content of 75 per cent or more, clears the trials successfully but is not the Lowest Bidder (or L1), the order should be split between the L1 and the Indian company and each should get half of the total order, provided the Indian company matches the price of L1. In case, there is more than one Indian company fulfilling such criteria, then the company with the maximum indigenous content in its product shall be allowed to match the L1. Order should not be split to more than two companies as this may violate the principle of commonality of equipment, that is, it will be very difficult to maintain and repair such systems, among other things.

Make Procedure

Please make technical capability the basis for eligibility to bid for any 'Make' project. Five per cent net worth based on the total cost of the project is patently wrong. For example, a Software Defined Radio would cost about Rs.50,000 and for one million soldiers it would mean a project cost of about Rs.5,000 crore.

That means, to get the Expression of Interest (EoI), a firm would need to have about Rs.250 crore of net worth! But we know the development cost of the project will be approximately few crores of Rupees. When someone can develop the project in Rs.4 crore or Rs.5 crore, and the manufacturing cost of the product is going to be few thousand rupees, what is the point in asking Rs.250 crore net worth for the firm to be eligible to submit EoI? In the worst case, the net worth should be a percentage of the development cost. And, manufacturing, which is relatively a dumb task, can be outsourced to companies with adequate infrastructure.

Buy Indian (Indigenously Designed And Developed)

The 'Buy Indian (Indigenously Designed And Developed) category needs to be introduced and should be given the maximum preference. The heart of any weaponry and related system is the technology, the software, the algorithms that run the system. The metal around the technology is dumb. Where Indian companies develop technology that meets the requirements of the Indian forces, these products should be bought from that company at the same international prices (as per standard bench-marking done now) at which they would have been procured from foreign companies. And this should be done even if it is a single vendor situation (which is more than likely as there is only one customer - the Indian armed forces).

Positive Side Effects

Almost 30 per cent of the profits that the Indian companies make will come back as income tax. Almost 20 per cent to 30 per cent of the procurement comes back as sales/excise/service tax. If an Indian company has developed the technology, then they will be spending significant amounts of money in Research and Development (R&D) -- 10 per cent to 20 per cent of the revenues will go back into R&D, which will help the company evolve existing products and develop newer defense products.

This policy will attract talent and ensure that lots of Indian companies get into R&D for military purposes. With so much to gain from buying products that are developed indigenously, it is strange that there is no provision, as on date, to give preference to indigenously developed technology.

Note: It is better to proactively identify technologies that have been developed in India and clearly indicate them as vendors. Companies that are trying to outright buy such technologies or license them from foreign companies should be dissuaded. In fact, foreign companies have started looking for partners financially strong and large Indian companies to transfer technology, wherever it is indigenously available. This will impact the indigenous companies very negatively. To preempt it, MoD should proactively identify indigenously developed technologies and name them as vendors.

Single Vendor Situation

As per DPP, Request for Proposals (RFP) is retracted if it is a single vendor situation at Technical Evaluation Committee (TEC) stage. It is suggested that if such a single vendor is an Indian company and the product has 75 per cent or more indigenous content, procurement process should continue. If the company successfully clears the trials and other evaluations, order should be placed on that company.

Blanket Permission To Export To Certain Countries

Like the 'Most Favored Nation' status in other countries, make a list of countries to which export can be done without any permission. These should include the majority of countries in Africa, Middle-East, Latin America, and South East Asia. Only countries that we perceive as unfriendly should not make into the list. For countries that are not in the list we need to take permission. The permission should be granted automatically within 15 days unless the MoD turns down the request to export.

Procurement Under No Cost Full Commitment (NCFC) Basis

Presently most procurement by the MoD are on 'No Cost No commitment' (NCNC) basis wherein it is not necessary that procurement process will culminate in a contract or supply order. It is proposed that some of the MoD procurement from Indian industry are carried out on NCFC basis.

A suggested methodology for the same is as under: The MoD prepares and publishes a document which lists weapons/equipment/systems that it requires to procure from Indian public or private companies. The document should be comprehensive enough to have project related relevant information such as numbers required, internationally bench-marked price, essential Qualitative Requirements and procurement time frame in. Also, the MoD assures full cooperation in terms of access to equipment (weaponry, etc) and subject-matter experts to help build thedesired products.

The MoD invites proposals from Indian companies, who have the capabilities and competencies to undertake various projects listed in above stated document. This may be done through industrial associations.

Shortlisted Indian companies, thereafter, are provided with all the relevant and necessary information of the envisaged project(s), which will enable these selected Indian companies to design and develop the products as per user's requirement. Vendors should also be given enough time to develop the product keeping their complexity in mind.

After required time frame given to vendors to develop the product, the MoD shall issue RFP/EOI to these selected companies and proceed with trial, evaluations and other procurement processes as given in the DPP.

If even a single vendor qualifies, then they should go ahead with the purchase. If there are still some gaps, the companies should be given more time to fill the gap.

The MoD should finally sign the contract with the lowest bidder. The contract should also be signed in case there is only one vendor left at TEC stage or after trial and evaluations.

Since such a procedure does not exist in present DPP, MoD may consider incorporating suitable changes in the procedures so as to enable such a procurement on NCFC basis.

2

Make in India in Defence Industry

Being the multi-billion dollar and most lucrative defence market in the world, India provides several opportunities for Indian and foreign corporate entities for defence manufacturing. Thanks to the Make in India campaign, the defence sector has moved from the periphery to the core of Indian manufacturing. Several CII reports have suggested that the sector not only has the potential to augment manufacturing but also add nearly one million direct and indirect jobs. Some of the top industrial houses have already made some inroads into the sector. Several more are waiting for the right opportunity.

The CII welcomes the much-awaited release of the Defence Procurement Procedure (DPP 2016) on the inaugural day of Defexpo 2016 by the defence minister. The initial feedback from all stakeholders, including industry and end-users, indicates that many issues have been ironed out to enhance the DPP's efficacy. There has been a clear departure from past practices that often left critical defence procurements in limbo. The revised procedures provide more flexibility to the end-users and the industry to work together, especially on development projects. A new procurement category — Indigenously Designed, Developed and Manufactured (IDDM) — has been introduced and accorded top priority. It essentially means the government is leaving no stone unturned to give a boost to Make in India. The "Make" procedure has been further classified into three types to address the concerns of MSMEs in particular. The defence ministry would fund up to 90 per cent of the Make project's prototype development cost. Adding one more safeguard for the industry, the ministry will reimburse the remaining 10 per cent prototype development cost, if the order is not placed within a stipulated timeframe after the successful test of prototypes.

A few issues, including ensuring a level playing field between public and private and the Foreign Exchange Rate Variation (FERV), were addressed before the DPP's release. For instance, excise and customs duty exemptions available to PSUs/ Ordnance Factory Board (OFB) have been withdrawn. The Union budget also mentions this. FERV is now allowed for the private sector in all contracts, as was available to PSUs/ OFB earlier in nomination cases.

The DPP also addresses issues like incentives to move the Indian defence industry up the value chain. Various provisions remove ambiguities, ensure transparency, offer a level playing field and clearly lay down procedures. It won't be an exaggeration to say that the defence ministry has taken all the right steps to create a conducive environment for the defence industry's growth, as envisaged in the Defence Production Policy. Given the opportunity, this industry has the potential to become a huge foreign exchange earner and also lead India to its professed goal of self-reliance.

Nearly $14 billion worth of defence offset obligations will be discharged by the foreign Original Equipment Manufacturers (OEMs) by 2028. It's heartening to note that the government has taken serious note of the industry's recommendation for further streamlining the Defence Offset Guidelines. These guidelines are part of the DPP and have been revised to add more flexibility and accountability.

DPP 2016 has also opened up several co-development and co-production avenues for Indian as well as foreign companies. The ministry seems to have successfully bridged the gap between intent and implementation. Earlier policies and procedures were often criticised for lacking in implementation despite the best of intent. For the first time, the defence ministry has accepted the industry's longstanding request for linking defence procurement with defence production. This inter-linkage would go a long way in realising Make in India in defence.

End-users will literally have to exhaust all possible options of domestic manufacturing before suggesting "Buy Global" procurements. Interestingly, in the past one-year-plus, most of the "Acceptance of Necessity" for forthcoming defence procurements have been granted for "Buy India" and "Buy and Make (Indian)" category. It means the government is walking the talk.

Indian industry is keen to take on complex hi-tech and more challenging projects. It would be desirable to identify and share more Make projects across the three services to enable Indian industry to prepare their business case. Also, prior intimation would also allow Indian industry to look for and tie up with foreign OEMs as a co-developer/ technology partner.

INDIGENOUS PRODUCTION OF DEFENCE EQUIPMENTS IN INDIA

As India is moving towards transformation from a regional power to a global power, the defence sector is increasingly occupying even bigger space in the country's long term strategic planning. As India is gaining power it is increasing its purchasing power as well with several high-end defence deals either in the pipeline or being envisioned to strengthen India's force structure. Estimates show that the Indian Air Force will have more than 1000 fighter jets and around 60 squadrons by 2030. India will be spending more than USD 80 billion on capital acquisitions in the 2010-2015 timeframe.

The Indian government is very clear and focused in its vision for its defence sector - indigenization of the industry and acquiring advanced technologies which will in turn help to reduce dependence on imports from other countries around the world. In nitty-gritty, it would create a ripple effect that the government is hoping to initiate in this sector. In this evolving

Defence value chain it would be unfair to ignore the role that human resource skills, Research and Development (R&D) and the long standing small and Medium Enterprises (SME) Defence Public Sector Units (DPSUs) suppliers and ordinance boards are going to play.

As an emerging economic superpower, India's spending on defence is on a rapid upward trajectory. The main driver appears to be emerging rivalry with China – especially as Beijing seeks to increase its presence in the Indian Ocean. However, traditional rivalry with Pakistan as well as increasing internal security issues are also factors.

A Brief about the INDIAN Defence Sector

The opening up of the Indian economy during the early nineties heralded an era of unprecedented industrial growth in India. The growth rates matched those of the fastest growing economies. A confident and resurgent Indian Defence Industry is making forays into almost all the sectors of manufacturing. Lately, the huge opportunities for growth within the domestic and global defence and aerospace industries have attracted the attention of Indian industry.

India which is the world's fourth largest fighting has the strength of defence equipments with regards to 'State of the Art', 'Matured' and 'Obsolescent' equipment is 15, 35 and 50 percent respectively. This suggests that the Government will have to make serious efforts towards upgrading its defence resources either by developing or procuring defence equipment and systems. Moreover, modernization, up-gradation and maintenance of the existing equipment will also provide immense opportunities to the industry. India is one of the largest global military spenders too. The defence budget for 2009-10 has increased by 34.19 percent over the previous year's budget estimate (BE) of INR 1,056 Bn.

The Department of Defence Production of the Ministry of Defence is responsible for the indigenous production of equipment used by the Indian Armed Forces. It comprises the 41 Indian Ordnance Factories under control of the Ordnance

Factories Board and 8 Defence PSUs namely, HAL, BEL, BEML, BDL, MDL, GSL, GRSE and Midhani.

The Indian Armed Forces are currently the world's largest arms and ammunitions importer, with Russia, Israel, and to some extent, France and United States being the primary foreign suppliers of military equipment.

The history and development of Indian ordinance factories is directly linked with the British reign in India. The East India Company considered military hardware to be a vital element for securing their economic interest in India and increasing their political power. In 1775 British authorities accepted the establishment of the Board of Ordnance at Fort William, Calcutta. This marks the official beginning of the Army Ordnance in India.

In 1787 a gunpowder factory was established at Ichapore; it began production in 1791, and the site was later used as a rifle factory beginning in 1904. In 1801, Gun Carriage Agency (now known as Gun & Shell Factory, Cossipore) was established at Cossipore, Calcutta, and production began on 18 March 1802. This is the oldest ordinance factory in India still in existence.

The Indian manufacturing industry has been a significant contributor to India's GDP and has displayed impressive growth in the last ten years. However, the sector's 16 percent share in GDP is among the lowest compared to other the rapidly growing developing economies and recently released National Manufacturing Policy has articulated an inspirational objective to increase this share to 25 percent over next ten years.

A vibrant domestic defence manufacturing sector can be a vital nail to help realize to fulfill the vision of becoming a super power in the defence sector. The Defence Production Policy 2011 has reiterated the strategic and economic importance of self–reliance in the area of defence. Developing a strong defence manufacturing sector enhances security as it reduces reliance on foreign suppliers, provides opportunity to create IP and domestic technologies and capabilities which often have significant civil applications, provide a platform to tap export markets. Most importantly it has a potential to create over one million jobs.

Defence spending in India has grown at about 17 percent in the past years, and with this India has came forth as one of the largest arms importer in the world. By 2014, it is expected that India would become the third largest defence spender after the US and China. Despite this huge market, the current policies and structure of the industry has constrained the domestic defence production with only 30 percent of the demand being met internally. The participation of private sector is even lower at about 10 percent that too mostly from Tier II or III suppliers.

Historically, India has always favoured the public sector over the private in the areas of defence production. India's first industrial–policy resolution in 1948 made it clear that a major portion of industrial capacity was to be reserved for the public sector including all arms production.

When this document was revised in 1956, it placed the munitions, aircraft and shipbuilding industries in public sector under central Government control, preventing private sector production.

Major Public & Private Sector Undertakings in Defence Sector

- Hindustan Aeronautics Limited (HAL) - Design, development, manufacture, repair and overhaul of aircraft, helicopters, engines and their accessories.
- Bharat Electronics Limited (BEL) - Design, development and manufacture of sophisticated state-or-the-art electronic equipment components for the use of the defence services, para-military organizations and other government users.
- Bharat Earth Movers Ltd (BEML) - Multi-product Company engaged in the design and manufacture of a wide range of equipment including specialized heavy vehicles for defence and re-engineering solutions in automotive and aeronautics.

- Mazagon Dock Limited (MDL) - Submarines, missile boats, destroyers, frigates and corvettes for the Indian Navy.
- Garden Reach Shipbuilders & Engineers Ltd (GRSE) - Builds and repairs warships and auxiliary vessels for the Indian Navy and the Coast Guard.
- Bharat Dynamics Limited (BDL) - Missiles, torpedo counter measure system, counter measures dispensing system.
- Mishra Dhatu Nigam Limited (MIDHANI) - Aeronautics, space, armaments, atomic energy, navy special products like molybdenum wires and plates, titanium and stainless steel tubes, alloys etc.
- Goa Shipyard Ltd (GSL) - Builds a variety of medium size, special purpose ships for the defence, Indian Coast Gaurd (ICG) and civil sectors.
- Tata Advanced Systems Limited (TAS) - Design, manufacture and supply of composite components, sub-assemblies for applications in aerospace division and solutions for personal armour, vehicle armour and special applications.
- Larsen and Toubro - Design, development and manufacture of integrated land based /naval combat/ missile systems, defence electronics & control systems and integrated naval engineering systems.
- Kirloskar Brothers - Infrastructure projects (water supply, power plants, irrigation), project and engineered pumps, industrial pumps.
- Mahindra Defence Systems - Total solutions for the range of light combat/armoured vehicles, simulators for weapons & weapon systems, sea mines, small arms, variants and associated ammunition.
- Ashok Leyland - Design, development and manufacture of special vehicles, serving Indian Armed Forces and international customers such as US army.

INDIA is planning to set up 12 Development Centers with state of the art CAD/CAM facilities to boost R&D efforts in the ordnance factories which will prove to be a positive initiative. In real battle conditions more than esoteric high end technologies the day to day usable technology and product up-gradation helps the fighting forces more. The DPSUs have also embarked on intensification of their R&D effort – the initiatives taken by HAL (10 R&D Centers), BEL and BDL are particularly encouraging.

In this planning stage and transformed settings the country enjoys advantages like availability of investible capital, accessibility to earlier denied dual technologies, willingness for cooperation and collaboration by defence production giants - particularly from the West in the wake of the economic downturn. India today has a scientific community that is globally competitive and a pool of skilled manpower with long years of experience and knowledge relating to Defence industries.

There is also a new enthusiasm in India's public sector enterprises. For acquiring self reliance – cutting across the barriers of public and private sectors, the Indian Defence Ministry can perhaps take a leaf from the experience of ISRO which outsources components, hardware and sub-systems for its launch vehicles and satellites from the Indian industrial units, both in the private and public sectors.

Vision, convergence, speed and de-bureaucratization of defence production and technology development should be the guiding Mantra of India in the coming decades.

INDIA'S DEFENCE INDUSTRY OPPORTUNITY STRIKES

VISITORS to the Talegaon plant of Larsen & Toubro (L&T), an Indian engineering company, might confuse it for the props department of a film studio. Half-a-dozen hangars spread over 50 acres near Pune, a city in western India, are filled with enough weaponry to thrill a Bond villain: camouflaged track-mounted howitzers, anti-submarine rocket launchers and, particularly appealing should Blofeld share Indians' fondness for trains, a contraption to turn a humble carriage into a ballistic-missile-launcher.

The missile itself is a dummy, but the rest of the kit speaks of India's ambitions to breed world-class makers of defence equipment. Although India now has the world's fourth-biggest military budget, it has been the single biggest arms importer for seven of the past ten years, says SIPRI, a research institute (see chart). The government, tired of this unwanted accolade—and convinced indigenous weapons production can provide jobs, budget savings and technological know-how—puts defence at the heart of its drive to boost domestic manufacturing.

Local conglomerates are salivating at an opportunity they expect could be worth $150 billion-200 billion in the coming decade. Tata, Mahindra and Godrej—as well as L&T—are among those that have piled into weapons manufacturing in recent years. But to succeed they will have to take on foreign importers (which snap up about two-thirds of all procurement by value), a crowd of state-owned companies and the country's bloated defence bureaucracy.

Impatience with familiar suppliers opened the first breach for private contractors over a decade ago. An unconvincing victory in a skirmish with Pakistan, in Kashmir in 1999, exposed the Indian army's lack of capability. Insiders blamed a plethora of corruption scandals, involving foreign firms as well as flabby state-owned arms-makers, for leaving forces ill-equipped. But private-sector enthusiasm faded when promises of contracts did not materialise.

The latest sally slightly preceded the arrival of Narendra Modi in power in May 2014, and has been reinforced by his team's energetic drumming of a "Make in India" theme. Mr Modi has spoken of having 70% indigenous weapons procurement by 2020, roughly double today's figure (the defence ministry is a bit less ambitious), with more of it produced by the private sector. To achieve this, procurement rules overtly favour stuff made locally. Some of the red tape entangling all things industrial has been done away with: for example, foreign groups may now own as much as 49% in Indian ventures, up from 26%. Bosses at private Indian firms are delighted by the new rhetoric: Tata, India's largest conglomerate, identifies defence as one of four core growth areas. Groups with a background in cars (Mahindra) or precision engineering (L&T) have recast themselves as arms-makers, often with the help of Western partners such as Airbus, Boeing or Lockheed Martin.

The pipeline for new defence systems looks appealing. The military budget, some $50 billion a year, is expected to track long-term economic-growth rates of around 7% a year. Press reports suggest the armed forces are short of some 300 fighter jets, at least a dozen submarines, over 1,000 combat helicopters, seven frigates and perhaps 3,000 artillery guns. What gear it has is often of cold-war vintage and from Russia, India's traditional supplier. Even ammunition is in short supply.

Yet in practice the armed forces are lousy customers. Defence bureaucrats are risk-averse. Military spending is growing, but much new money goes towards salaries and pensions. The share of funds for procurement, research, development and testing has slumped from 34% in 2005 to 25% today, says IHS Jane's, a research outfit.

Worse, a fifth of the capital budget typically goes unspent because, in the run up to year-end, the finance ministry usually begs generals to shelve projects so that overall public-spending targets can be met. That leaves just $11 billion-12 billion for procurement, says IHS. And much of this is committed to existing projects, often in the hands of state-run companies good at lobbying for their share.

So those in charge of India's putative defence groups are waiting to see if the opportunity is really as big as it appears. Official rhetoric was enough for investment plans to be drawn up, but not quite enough for big amounts to be spent. "We like the policy; we await the execution," says one firm's defence-division boss. A bureaucrat who misinterprets a single word in a regulation could stymie a billion-dollar project, he adds.

Foreign firms will also seek a chance to profit. Nearly 500 attended a recent defence jamboree in Goa. Some are still hoping to do deals to deliver equipment outright. Dassault has been in talks to sell its Rafale fighter jets for over 15 years ("We are getting closer...we are in the final phase," its chairman said last month, redefining optimism). But if it comes off, this deal would probably be one of many contracts to have the first batch of a weapons system made overseas before shifting manufacturing—and some technology—to India for later orders, assuming the local partner could cope with production demands.

The past year has seen the weaving of a tangled web connecting big Western defence groups and Indian manufacturing counterparts. A recent deal for BAE Systems to supply howitzers uses Mahindra as the local assembler. A track-mounted artillery gun at L&T's facility (part of which is a joint venture with Airbus Defence) was designed by Samsung. Boeing and Tata have a partnership to produce Apache helicopter fuselages, among other things.

Sceptics wonder whether local groups do much more than give existing foreign weapons systems an Indian veneer just thick enough to get contracts. Systems developed abroad (often some time ago) can be assembled in an Indian plant, with both sides claiming the gear has been extensively adapted for the Indian market.

Assembly work is not the lucrative bit of the weapons industry—just as the iPhone brings more profits to Apple (its designer) than to Foxconn (its contract manufacturer). For now, India mostly makes the cheaper bits, especially parts that can benefit from lower labour costs. Pricier systems, which require long development lead-times, are hampered by higher capital costs for Indian firms compared with Western rivals.

All that could change if Indian companies develop expertise to design, not just assemble, equipment. Last month the government said it would give priority to weapons designed and made in India.

It should also let firms export their wares—which, in the long term, is the only way investments in arms-making pay, says Deba Mohanty of Indicia, a consultancy. Countries that spend heavily on armed forces typically have successful arms-making companies. India's ambition, one day, is to stop being an exception to this rule.

DEFENCE PLANNING IN INDIA

Before independence, the defence services worked on a system of contract budget. Defence expenditure was pegged at Rs 55 crore per year, which was more than half of the Central Government's revenue. There was no serious threat from outside (except during World War II, when a fresh agreement was signed) and this amount was more than adequate to maintain the establishment.

The savings were not allowed to lapse but put away in the Defence Reserve Fund that was utilised to finance measures for re-equipment of the Defence Services, thus freeing the Government from having to provide fund money greater than the contract amount. Expenditure on defence rose steeply soon after independence. However, there was no planned effort and defence programmes consisted mainly of outright purchases from abroad, drawing heavily on available Sterling reserves. In the late 1950s, some efforts were made to initiate domestic weapons production by the Ministry of Defence when Mr Krishna Menon was the Defence Minister. The Sino-Indian conflict in 1962 aroused a new defence consciousness in the country. After taking care of immediate post-war requirements, systematic defence planning started in 1964. Defence requirements were assessed on a five-year basis and the First Five Year Defence Plan (1964-69) was drawn up. This plan took into account the resources available and assistance which could be expected from friendly foreign countries. The plan was primarily based on an expansion and modernisation programme considered necessary by each Service in the light of the respective threat perception assessed. It also proposed a defence production base that would gradually reduce the country's external dependence, provide for improvements in border roads and communications, and a modest expansion of DRDO. The Government recognised the imperative need to synergise 'defence' and 'development' instead of planning each on a separate and un-related level. The MoD emphasised the "inevitable need to harness all resources of the country for the country's defence and for the defence effort to derive full sustenance from the country's economic development plans". Thereafter, the National Development Council authorised the Chairman of the Planning Commission to review the needs of both development and defence. A Planning Cell was established in 1965 in the Ministry of Defence 'to deal with the wider aspects of defence planning'. The new system was intended to facilitate medium and long-term defence planning and to maintain constant liaison with the Planning Commission and other ministries.

It was expected that the MoD would derive maximum advantage from the development effort by being able to place its priorities for consideration along with the overall economic and industrial plans drawn up by the Planning Commission. The experience of the First Five Year Defence Plan showed that the development of weapons and equipment was a long drawn out process. The Government realised that there could be no forward movement in attaining self-sufficiency in weapons and equipment unless these requirements were planned over a reasonably long period, long enough to cover the span of development and production of new weapons systems and other fighting tools.

The inadequacy of foreign exchange reserves was another hindrance in planning and implementation. In order to mitigate some of these drawbacks, the Second Five Year Defence Plan (1969-74) was instituted on a "roll-on" basis. After a year, an additional year was added so that the Defence Services would have before them a revised and up-dated five-year plan. In this context, the MoD commented: "Opportunity is taken by this annual exercise to take note of and reflect the change in priorities, the shifts in emphasis and the latest concepts and programmes to reorient the plan within the scheme of resources so that the aims and means are most effectively balanced." This system was expected to facilitate the planning of projects that took five years or more and to revise or eliminate projects, depending on the prevailing foreign exchange situation and availability of domestic resources.

For a period of five years, firm assurances were to be given on the availability of resources. This, unfortunately, never happened. In 1971, it was impossible to adhere to the discipline and the pattern of the roll-on plan. Instead of roll-on annual revisions, immediate requirements dominated the Government's attention that pre-empted plan efforts. In its 1971-72 Annual Report, the MoD acknowledged that having a Planning Cell in the ministry was an insufficient and unsatisfactory method of meeting a crisis.

The Planning Cell was not taken seriously in the crucial stages of economic planning and the argument that defence needs would be adjusted in the over-all allocation of resources was proved wrong. In 1974, an Apex Group headed by the Union Minister for Planning again suggested that steady long-term defence programmes would be more cost effective and economical rather than fluctuating allocations due to periodic economic and security crises. In order to integrate defence planning with the overall economic planning effort, defence and economic development plans were made co-terminus.

The Planning Machinery

Most of the defence planning machinery and planning methodology was developed in the decade 1964-74. The Joint Intelligence Committee (JIC) was established in the Cabinet Secretariat to provide external and internal threat assessments. Inputs for this purpose were to be provided by all Intelligence agencies of the Government. The Service Chiefs were to assess the broad military aims and a strategy, coordinated in the Chiefs of Staff Committee, was to be approved by the Defence Minister. However, this was seldom done. Each Service ended up planning its own force level, choice of weapons and equipment, and build-up of infrastructure. In 1977, the Government formed a Committee for Defence Planning (CDP) to "undertake regular assessments relevant to defence planning in the light of all factors having a bearing on national security and defence". However, this committee could not function smoothly nor meet the desired goals.

Planning units were also established in the Department of Defence Production and DRDO. A Planning and Coordination

Cell was created in the MoD to coordinate and compile various plans into a 'Defence Plan' for Cabinet approval. As the bureaucrats in the ministry had no professional knowledge or background, this cell could only compile different requirements without any analysis. In Army Headquarters, the Deputy Chief of Army Staff was made responsible for preparing the Army plan. A Perspective Planning Directorate was established in the late 1970s. Naval and Air plans were prepared in the respective Planning Directorates. Financial considerations, non-existent at this level earlier, were introduced through Finance Planning Sections attached to these Directorates.

In 1986, the Directorate General of Defence Planning Staff (DGDPS), comprising officers from the three Services, DRDO, and Ministries of Defence and External Affairs, was established under the Chiefs of Staff Committee (COSC) to coordinate and harmonise defence planning. Civilian officers from the Ministries probably did not find the job professionally satisfying and were gradually withdrawn, thus leaving the DGDPS a tri-Service set up. All these measures enabled each Service headquarters to prepare defence plans in a more rational manner. But due to lack of clear political direction and each Service primarily planning for itself, joint planning, coordination between Services and other departmental plans of the MoD, were largely ignored.

After the Kargil conflict in 1999, the Group of Ministers (GoM) and later the Cabinet Committee on Security (CCS) approved several reforms. An Integrated Defence Headquarters (IDH) was established and the DGDPS was merged with it. The creation of the post of Chief of Defence Staff (CDS), whose tasks would include ensuring intra and inter-Services prioritisation of defence plans and improvement in joint functioning of the Defence Services, was recommended.

The reforms also included establishment of a Defence Intelligence Agency and creation of Defence Equipment Production, Research and Planning councils in the IDH and MoD, respectively. Unfortunately, the CDS, who would be the cornerstone of integrated operational planning for defence, has not been appointed.

Analysis of the System

Despite several years of planning efforts, defence planning in India is characterised by seesaw bouts of frenzied activity followed by long periods of relative inaction. Five-year defence plans have rarely been formally approved before commencement. The Tenth Defence Plan, now in its third year, is yet to be accorded formal government approval. Ad-hocism is the order of the day, leading to knee-jerk responses and haphazard planning, making India a reactive rather than pro-active nation in matters pertaining to national security. Whenever India's major adversaries plan a big defence purchase, there is an outcry for similar acquisitions, resulting in piecemeal decisions regardless of long-term impact and overall requirements.

The Defence Forces are forced to follow "a case-by-case" approach to modernisation and procurement of arms, ammunition and equipment to replace obsolescent items, in many cases long after their life cycle is over and they cannot be maintained in a cost effective manner. The Army's Vijayanta tanks, MiG-21s of the IAF, and IL-38 maritime reconnaissance aircraft of the Navy are some examples. Weapons development, procurement and absorption are complex processes. A lead-time of 15-20 years is required to plan and execute major projects. Despite this, for several years, a large amount of the capital acquisition budget has been surrendered.

In the prevailing era of strategic uncertainty, the changing nature of warfare demands a judicious mix of threat and capabilities-based forces that can operate efficiently as combined arms, joint Services teams and components of multi-national coalition forces.

TENDENCIES IN THE GLOBAL DEFENCE INDUSTRY

The global defence industry has undergone profound changes in recent years. Changes in demand for military weapons and equipment, the allocation of resources for national security, national and international security priorities especially by major states, among others, have affected the defence industry in many ways. While the Cold War era witnessed a massive military build-up by many countries, thus fuelling demand for this lucrative sector, the immediate post-Cold War period witnessed just an opposite scenario. Demand for military equipment went down during the late 1980s and early 1990s. Budgetary allocations for security sectors fell. Military downsizing occurred. In just a period of half-a-decade, roughly from 1987 to the early 1990s, the defence industry witnessed a different scenario and shrank considerably. It had to shift priorities to adjust to the new environment. In brief, since the end of the Cold War, the defence industry has faced numerous challenges from all quarters. Most of the decline in the volume of arms production took place during the early and mid-1990s. During this time, significant down-sizing, rationalisation and diversification (primarily into dual-use and civilian production) were witnessed in the defence-industrial sector.

Mergers and acquisitions during the 1990s resulted in the creation of a few giant companies like Boeing, Lockheed Martin, British Aerospace, Northrop Grumman, EADS, and others. This also resulted in many smaller companies either having to merge with big ones or having to shift their priorities toward civilian production, thus leaving the defence sector. Defence industries of major countries like the United States and of Western Europe were affected most during this period although countries like Russia, Israel, South Africa, Brazil, India, and others were also affected. Arms reductions during the 1990s were extensive and fetched a sizeable 'peace dividend'.

It was desirable that such a decade of disarmament should have been extended. However, as evidence suggests, indicators of disarmament and conversion now show stagnation; in many cases even a reverse trend toward a strengthening of military postures are witnessed. A decade of cuts in military expenditure ended in 1998/99 when it went up again. The upward trend in military expenditure is likely to continue in future. The 11 September 2001 terrorist attacks in the United States are likely to result in a major shift in defence-industrial developments because of their impact on security requirements at national and international levels. But this is not to suggest that the upward trend in military expenditure was a product of such an unfortunate event.

This trend had already started in the late 1990s, primarily because of increased military spending by countries like the United States and regions like the Middle East and South and East Asia. In this changed scenario, the defence industry seems to gear up to meet new challenges. As procurement budgets have started to swell again and are likely to stay that way, new opportunities are expected for the defence industry. In fighting terrorism, additional defence programmes initiated by countries like the United States will most likely change the structure of the defence industry. While it is expected that giant weapons producers, especially in the United States, are likely to benefit most from the on-going 'War on Terror', national defence industries elsewhere are also likely to reorient themselves to meet future challenges. In brief, the global defence industry, after a period of significant downsizing and rationalisation, is likely to enter into a phase of renewed attention. Demand for smart weapons, increased emphasis on military technology including investment in R&D, growing demand for aerospace and cutting-edge technology products, are all likely to boost defence-industrial activities in many parts of the world.

Trends of India's Defence Industry

Trends in global defence industry have impinged India in many ways. India's defence industry has witnessed significant changes since the end of the Cold War. In the 1990s, changes in both institutional and policy spheres became more prominent. The most far reaching change that has occurred in recent years in India's defence-industrial sector is related to its opening up to the market. Long protected as a closed sector, India's defence industry has now opened up for private participation. As if this was not enough, it is also showing enough willingness to become an exporter and dares to venture into the competitive global arms market. How far it will succeed in its objectives is examined elsewhere, but changes are certainly a product of and response to the contemporary changes in the global industrial defence scenario. At the same time, it is also showing willingness to diversify its range of products, which not only include modern weapons systems but also technologies for wide and popular civilian uses. The Indian defence-industrial sector targets the national, and even global, civilian market to sell its products, especially in the fields of civilian space, medical, and electronics. Thus conversion through diversification has been witnessed in many areas of defence production in India.

India's defence industry has come a long way from being at the lowest end of the production spectrum, catering to the maintenance and repair and overhaul of imported weapons, to a stage where it can boast of designing and developing a range of state-of-the-art weapons systems. Half a decade of defence-industrial experience in India shows that while it started from scratch, it has been able not only to learn and absorb various stages of production intricacies but also produce complex systems that are primarily an indigenous activities. Another important factor is that the Indian defence industry has produced various weapons systems under licenses acquired from various foreign sources.

Although the first Prime Minister of India, Jawaharlal Nehru, believed in 'self sufficiency' in arms production, which became a policy mantra for subsequent years, it had to be supplemented by what is roughly called 'self-reliance in defence'. Self-reliance does not preclude accessing external sources for technology and systems, or external help in any stage of the production cycle. It is the degree of dependency on external sources that is tested in the case of India's quest for self-reliance.

India opted to choose an incremental path, in which it was necessary to continue to meet urgent requirements through imports while striving hard on achieving indigenous capabilities in defence production. Both policies continued till the late 1980s and many of the components of both still continue till today. The 1990s witnessed a series of far-reaching initiatives in the field of national security, of which defence industry was a critical component.

The creation of six Special Task Forces to reform major aspects of national defence coordination and management, under the Chairmanship of the then Defence Minister in 1994 may effectively be considered as the first major step after a long time to initiate and implement much-desired reforms in the defence-industrial sector. This was followed by a series of intensive interactions between various organs of the armed forces, government departments and institutions like the Confederation of Indian Industries (CII). The 'Army-Industry Partnership', a partnership between CII and the Indian Army to get acquainted with each other's needs and to facilitate channels of communication between the armed forces and the private industry, was a result of this process and, in turn, led to other cooperative initiatives. Events like India's nuclear tests in mid-1998 and the Kargil conflict in mid-1999 provided grounds for an intense debate on various aspects of India's national security. Also, as a by-product of the current disinvestment programme, which is primarily aimed toward lessening or wiping out government control and responsibilities in state-owned public enterprises in India, the debate on a reform of the defence industry got a major boost as demands for a privatisation of and private participation in this hitherto closed sector grew more in tune with the changing times.

In January 2001, the Government of India initiated a series of major initiatives that, among others, included Foreign Direct Investment (FDI) up to about 26 percent and full private participation in certain sectors in the defence industry. This policy indeed marks a critical departure from the past. Followed by this, the Group of Ministers (GoM) Report on 'Reforming the National Security System' was made public in early 2001. This laid stress on reforms in all-encompassing aspects of national security, of which changes sought in higher defence management emphasised the need to create specific institutions like the Defence Acquisitions Board to adapt and facilitate changing needs of the defence industry.

While these far-reaching institutional and policy-oriented changes have been underway for quite some time especially since the early 1990s, the demand for private participation has assumed significance in recent years. In such a scenario, analyses of India's defence-industrial sector and policies have become critically important to understand the complex web of linkages that determine national policies in the defence-industrial sector. This, in turn, needs a closer look into the past performance of the defence industry, lessons learnt and a peep into the likely future course.

Research Objectives

The objectives are primarily four-fold. First, we will examine critical aspects of defence-industrial policies adopted by India in the past and link those to performance. It will examine the factors that have influenced India's defence production and their co-relationship with policies and decision-making in this sector. Second, we will examine the main trends during the 1990s, during which major policy changes occurred.

It will critically examine the impact of such policy changes. Third, we will examine the contemporary scenario. Fourth and last, it will look into future problems and prospects. The last two are essential in understanding the intricacies involved in India's defence-industrial strategies and are expected to give some clues related to the future course of action in this sector.

Some of the major queries that will be examined here are: Why a quest for self-reliance in the past? Has the policy of self-reliance paid off? If not, what are the options for the future? Why the changes in defence-industrial policies during the 1990s? Are the objectives achievable? What are likely options for the future? Does it have scope for more diversion, thus leading to conversion through the increase in civilian production, in future? We will invariably try to find answers to these queries, although not necessarily in the same order.

Methods and Sources

We will follow a general descriptive-analytical approach. The scope is limited somewhat to policy analyses due to constraints in the availability of information. This is because India's defence industry has long been a 'closed' sector and thus been under exclusive government control. It is only in recent times that it has opened up, thus leading to an availability of information in a low to medium scale. We will also follow a historical method whereby it will emphasise linkages at policy- and decision-making levels to performance, and this is important in understanding the nature of development that this sector has undergone for the past half-a-century. Available data on specifics will be evaluated. Emphasis will be on an evaluation and interpretation of data from primary (especially government) sources. In brief, the overall approach will be descriptive and analytical.

Literature on the subject is scarce. At international level, the study of India's defence industry has attracted very little attention. The same is true at national level. Barring a few books, written by scholars like K. Subrahmanyam, Air Marshal Samir Sen, Major General Pratap Narain, Chris Smith, WPS Sidhu, and others, substantial work is not evident on this subject. Occasional research papers by G. Balachandran, Rahul Roy-Choudhury, Ajay Singh and others have also focused on limited themes. Secondary and tertiary sources are scarce. Primary sources, however, constitute the most important component of this study. Annual Reports (published by the Ministry of Defence, Government of India), Annual Reports of major Defence Public Sector Units (published by respective organisations), periodic reports published by the Comptroller and Auditor General of India, Parliament Secretariat and similar other reports constitute primary sources for this endeavour. Select interviews with senior government officers, analysts and industry-watchers have been taken into account.

DEFENCE INDUSTRY OF INDIA

The Defence industry of India is a strategically important sector in India. With strength of over 1.3 million active personnel, it is world's 3rd largest military force and has the world's largest volunteer army. The total budget sanctioned for the

Indian military for the financial year 2015 is 2.47 trillion Indian rupees ($40.07 billion).

Military budget

The military budget of India is about 2.4% for year 2015 of the total GDP as per World Bank statistics. The defence expenditure for Fisical year 2017-18 allotted by Ministry of Finance is,excluding pensions a sum of 2,74,114 crores but including 86,488 crores for Defence capital.

State orders

India has been spending worth nearly $3.5 billion to boost its ageing Soviet era military equipment. It has been pushing for greater indigenisation of the military industry as India imports around 70 per cent of its defence hardware mainly from Russia, Japan Israel and United States.

Organisations

The production of Indian defence equipments prior to 2011 was completely in the hands of the Government of India. The Government of India also opened up the Foreign direct investment to 49% from the existing 26% and thereby increasing flow of funds from foreign countries. With the increase in FDI cap, private players such as companies from many developed countries will also be attracted to the Indian defence economy as they can have share in the Indian defence Companies.

Make in India

The Modi government in its first year cleared 39 capital procurement proposals, of which 32 proposals worth [1] 889 billion (US$13 billion) (or 96% of value of total proposals) were categorized as *Buy (Indian)* and *Buy and Make (Indian)*—the top two prioritized domestic industry-centric procurement categories as per the defence procurement procedure (DPP).

In July 2015, the defence ministry eased export regulations and stopped demanding multiple assurances on end-use from foreign governments even for sale of components by Indian entities.

3

Making 'Make-in-India' Move in Defence Production and Manufacturing

The 'Make-in-India' drive of the government has created a conceptual parallax in so far as the defence manufacturing sector is concerned. Foreign companies, and even governments, seem to view it differently from the way it is being seen by the Indian industry. The lack of clarity about the policy underpinnings of this amphibolous trope lies at the root of this dichotomy.

The Ministry of Defence (MoD) has had its own make-in-India policy in the form of the 'Make' procedure since 2006. Notwithstanding the fact that not a single project has taken off till date under this procedure, its aim is "to ensure Indigenous Research, Design, Development and Production of capabilities sought by the Armed Forces in prescribed timeframe while optimally utilizing the potential of the Indian Industry" as "it would also achieve self reliance in Defence Equipment" (sic).1

The emphasis of the Defence Production Policy of January 2011 is also on the Indian industry as the primary vehicle for achieving self-reliance in defence production. This is evident from its objectives, which are:

to achieve substantive self reliance in the design, development and production of equipment/ weapon systems/ platforms required for defence in as early a time frame as possible; to create conditions conductive for the private industry to take an active role in this endeavour; to enhance potential of SMEs in indigenization and to broaden the defence R&D base of the country."2

In keeping with this policy drift, a new paragraph was added to the Defence Procurement Procedure (DPP) 2013, which states that:

Preference will be given to indigenous design, development and manufacture of defence equipment. Therefore, whenever the required arms, ammunition & equipment are possible to be made by Indian Industry within the time lines required by the Services, the procurement will be made from indigenous sources."3

DPP 2013 also laid down a hierarchy of procurement categories: Buy (Indian), Buy and Make (Indian), Make (Indian), Buy and Make, and Buy (Global). These categories are arranged in a decreasing order of preference.4 As is quite obvious, only Indian entities can compete in the procurement programmes classified under any of the first three categories. Indian companies can also participate in the Buy (Global) tenders. And under the Buy and Make category, foreign companies are required to transfer technology to an Indian entity for manufacturing the equipment under the 'make' portion of the Buy and Make cases.

While seeking approval-in-principal – or Acceptance of Necessity (AoN), to use the official jargon – for placing a procurement programme in a particular category that figures lower down in the hierarchy, it is now necessary to provide justification for not choosing any of the categories that precede the proposed category. The reference to the 'Indian industry' in the DPP and 'private industry', as well as 'SMEs' (small and medium enterprises), in the Defence Production Policy implies Indian companies 'owned and controlled' by Indian citizens and other Indian entities.

All this policy baggage goes to show that the effort so far has been to energize the Indian domestic industry to reduce dependence on imports. The purpose of the 'Make-in-India' initiative, on the other hand, seems to be to invite foreign manufacturers to set up manufacturing bases in India. This was the unmistakable message of the prime minister's maiden Independence Day speech on 15 August 2014.

The official 'Make-in-India' website does not throw much light on the policy underpinning of the campaign. But the general tenor of its content shows that the aim is to attract global companies to undertake the manufacture of their products in India.

The problem, however, is that the exhortation to global firms does not seem to be in tune with the objectives of the defence production policy and the procurement procedure that the MoD has been following for the past several years.

That being the case, the 'Make-in-India' initiative is clearly in conflict with MoD's policy of indigenization of defence production by promoting Indian industry. The question that arises is: how do global companies fit into the scheme of things? What do they make in India and how do they sell what they make?

Global companies and other investors are unlikely to bring in foreign direct investment (FDI) and chip in with transfer of technology only to end up becoming minority stakeholders in some joint venture. It is not clear if this is how the government expects 'Make-in-India' to play out in the defence production sector, but surely this is not how global companies and foreign governments would like it to play out.

Conceptual clarity about 'Make-in-India' is, therefore, the *sine qua non* for the success of the 'Make-in-India' initiative, the core conceptual issue being: what is new that it offers to the Indian industry, global companies and foreign governments? Within the category of the Indian industry, clarity is required as regards the role expected to be played by the big players, the SMEs and the public sector, apart from the Defence Research & Development Organization (DRDO) and how these roles would be synergized.

The second issue concerns the procedure for tapping the defence market. As of now, the only procedure in place is the Defence Procurement Procedure, which is built around five procurement categories, including the 'Make' procedure. This document pre-dates the current 'Make-in-India' initiative and may, therefore, not provide the answer to many new issues that have arisen as regards the role of the Indian industry and foreign companies/governments.

For example, it does not answer the question whether manufacturers, including Indian companies, can take the initiative to make something *on their own volition* or should they wait till the MoD comes out with a Request for Proposal (RFP)? Manufacturing a product *suo moto* is fraught with the risk of being unable to sell it.

These new issues have arisen even as the old ones are yet to be resolved. The Indian industry has been having problems with the procurement procedure laid down in the DPP, including the 'Make' procedure. Foreign and Indian companies have been having problem with the offset guidelines.

All these procedures have been under review for more than two years now. While it is absolutely necessary to complete the review immediately, it is equally important to evolve appropriate procedures to be followed by global companies and foreign governments desirous of entering the defence manufacturing sector in India under the emerging circumstances.

The third issue concerns the creation of an industry-friendly eco-system. This is important for the Indian industry as much as it is for foreign companies. India fares poorly on all parameters that constitute the global index of ease-of-doing business, in which it figures at the 142nd position. Everyone understands that improving the eco-system is a difficult and time-consuming inter-ministerial task, but what is difficult to understand is the absence of a conspicuous roadmap for completing this task.

Lastly, a loosely articulated idea of making India a defence manufacturing hub cannot work unless it is backed by a comprehensive blueprint, efficient procedures, meticulous implementation, trained and responsive manpower, continuous monitoring and quick decision-making. MoD will have to do something about all this, especially its decision-making structures and processes and put in place a system of free and frank dialogue with the industry without whose active support it cannot realize the objectives of 'Make-in-India' in defence.

DEFENCE MANUFACTURING

The Indian tycoon and the founder of conglomerate Reliance Group, Anil Ambani, wants to make missiles, helicopters and submarines. His plan is to turn Reliance into a major defence company and he has already bid for INR 840 billion (EUR 11 billion) in government contracts, as per a recent report by the news agency-Reuters. Though Reliance Group is latest in the race, many defence firms are keen to 'Make in India'. A domestic telecom equipment maker Himachal Futuristic Communications (HFC) is one of the private firms eyeing defence projects. The company has already been granted industrial licences for a range of products which include electronic fuses, electro optical devices and communication equipment along with the permit for assembling electronic warfare systems, radars and design, development and manufacturing of aircraft, including helicopters, says Bela Banerjee, director, HFC.

With more than USD 200 billion (EUR 176 billion) capital expenditure expected in the next 8 to 10 years, and with one of the fastest growing defence budgets in the world at 10 to 11 pc growth rate, India focuses on strengthening defence facilities and building manufacturing capacity. Of late, the government has been on the mission. According to the department of industrial policy and promotion (DIPP), responsible for formulation and implementation of promotional and developmental measures for growth of the industrial sector, the commerce ministry has granted 333 industrial licences to private firms for defence manufacturing, which includes names like Mumbai based Micronel Global Engineers, Kolkata based Naistoco India and OIS Advanced Technology based in New Delhi. There are more familiar names too like, Punj Llyod

Aviation, Bharati Shipyard, Ashok Leyland Defence Systems, AMW Motors and then there are big, established ones such as Bharat Forge, Tata Group, Larsen & Toubro (L&T), Mahindra Group, to name a few.

So, the reason for this rush to be part of the defence sector is mostly the result of Prime Minister Narendra Modi's emphasis on defence manufacturing as part of his 'Make in India' campaign. Last year, Modi said that with 60 pc of India's defence requirements met through imports, local defence production is at the heart of the 'Make in India' programme. Launched on September 25, 2014, the idea of 'Make in India' is now more than 20 months old.

Private players - the real beneficiaries

According to AK Gupta, secretary, department of defence production, ministry of defence, the private sector now has the opportunity to pick up a 25 pc share of defence production. "Around 25 pc of the defence PSUs (public sector undertakings) turnover can be off-loaded to the private sector, and the ministry has already de-licensed 60-70 pc of the production. PSUs in defence sector have a cumulative turnover of about INR 500 billion," he said during a conference at DefExpo which took place in Goa in March 2016.

"Under the 'Make in India' programme, the government has awarded 56 defence manufacturing permits to private sector entities in the past one year compared with 47 granted in the preceding three years," says Anurag Garg, director- strategy and defence leader at professional services network headquartered in London, PwC (PricewaterhouseCoopers), adding, "Make in India has become the new mantra in the Indian defence industry and within the industry, private sector is the centre of attraction.

This is quite evident from some of the big measures taken so far like hike in the foreign direct investment (FDI) from the earlier 26 pc to 49 pc, streamlining of defence industrial licencing, rationalisation of taxes, etc. Ultimately, private sector is the biggest beneficiary."

"In the case of the INR 500 billion (EUR 6.6 billion) P-75I project for procurement of six conventional submarines for the Indian Navy, the Modi government has changed the previous government's decision to import two submarines, followed by four to be licence-manufactured by public sector shipyards, and decided to construct all the submarines in domestic shipyards, with the further provision that the private sector would be given a fair chance to compete to get the contract," says Col K V Kuber, independent consultant, aerospace and defence.

In an interview with a defence news portal, Jan Widerström, country head and chairman of Saab (Swedenbased defence firm), said, "Make in India is definitely on our agenda. Our footprint in India is expanding fast. We now have eight Indian partner companies working with us." Its new fighter jet-Gripen E, which is said to have improved avionics system, is also considered under 'Make in India'. Not only Saab, but other players like America's Boeing and Lockheed Martin have also shown interest in making their aircrafts (F/A-18 and F-16) in the country. The opportunity is not only confined to foreign firms but domestic private firms have a significant opportunity, mentions Garg from PwC, adding, "The major players in the space have been investing for the past decade or more like Bharat Forge, Tata Group or L&T and have built a portfolio in electronics, land systems, missiles and aerospace products. Most of these are either in talks or have already signed the deals with the foreign Original Equipment Manufacturers (OEMs)." There were some similar announcements made during the DefExpo in Goa last March. Bharat Forge has tied up with Israel defence tech firm Rafael Advanced Defence Systems, Elbit Systems and UK-based Rolls Royce. Similarly, Tata Group has tied up with US-based firms Sikorsky Aircraft, Lockheed Martin and Boeing.

For more than 15 years, India has tried to engage the private sector in defence production. But domestic defence manufacturing is still dominated by the defence public sector undertakings (PSUs) and the Ordnance Factories Board (OFB), which together command 80-90 pc share. Of late, however,

Indian private companies have shown interest in the defence equipment business and have applied for industrial licences from the ministry of commerce to locally manufacture military equipment, including airplanes and warships.

A report by domestic brokerage ICICI Securities, published in January 2016, stated that imports contribute almost 75 pc of the defence equipment needs, while public sector and domestic private sector players contribute only 20 pc and 5 pc respectively. "While the growth of the defence sector will follow along its strategic and technological requirements, the domestic defence industry is still in its infancy—which translates into a huge opportunity for investors and Indian enterprises," the report by the brokerage firm said.

DPP - to boost 'Make in India'

In April this year, Defence Procurement Policy (DPP) 2016 was unveiled, in which 'Make in India' was the key highlight. A new procurement category — Indigenously Designed, Developed and Manufactured (IDDM) — has been introduced and accorded top priority, which means the government is leaving no stone unturned to give a boost to Make in India. The Make in India category has been divided into two categories — 'Buy (Indian)', with 40 pc indigenous content, and 'Buy and Make (Indian)' having an overall indigenous content of 50 pc, whereas DPP 2013 laid down minimum percentage of indigenous content for each acquisition route, which was 30 pc. "The IDDM and Buy and Make Indian categories will help global OEMs and Indian companies forge partnership for co-development and co-production. The integration of Indian companies in the global supply chain will help the establishment of defence manufacturing," says Garg from PwC.

The 'Make' procedure is divided into two categories – projects under Make I category will involve government funding of 90 pc, released in a phased manner, and based on the progress of the scheme, as per terms agreed between ministry of defence and the vendor. While, projects under Make II category will involve prototype development of equipment or system or platform or their upgrades, or their sub-systems or sub-assembly or assemblies or components with a focus on import substitution, for which no government funding will be provided for prototype development purposes. And it has considered the interests of Micro, Small and Medium Enterprises (MSMEs) too. To bring the MSMEs into the loop, projects with an estimated cost of development of up to INR 100 million (EUR 1.3 million) under the first category and INR 30 million (EUR 395,000) under the second category will be earmarked for them. These projects will be opened to others only if MSMEs do not evince any interest.

"The prioritisation of Buy (IDDM) in procurement category and 'Make' project is aimed to provide handholding to 'Make in India' initiative and has the potential to increase the contribution of manufacturing output to 25 pc of country's GDP," says Col Kuber, adding, "With the DPP 2016 in place, it has become increasingly apparent to all concerned that the defence manufacturing capability cannot be built in isolation and requires the active involvement of the private sector." Boston Consulting Group (BCG) estimates that the defence sector has a potential of increasing the defence-manufacturing workforce by one million people within five years. Every million directed job created in defence manufacturing will create additional 0.5 million in indirect jobs through sub-contracts and vendors.

Looking forward

The government is doing its bit with programmes like Make in India to enhance the industrial capacity and manufacturing facilities of the companies – both Indian and foreign – need to respond to the changes. Garg from PwC says, "To be able to qualify and continue to play in most defence programmes in India, it would be important for foreign companies to have some local presence via transfer of technology, co-development, manufacturing, and for Indian companies to enhance their capabilities to locally design and manufacture. And global OEMs (Original Equipment Manufacturers) need to respond to these changes, by forging relations with large players in Make in India. Though it is happening but still it is not sufficient." It is envisaged that under the Make In India programme, at least half of total India's weapon and equipment needs in the next 10 to 12 years worth more than USD 100 billion (EUR 88 billion) is likely to be produced domestically; so the opportunity is galore.

"The government is taking initiative to encourage greater private participation in the defence sector and emphasis on other local manufacturing requirements, opening up the sector for the foreign investors," adding, "With the global price pressure, India is likely to become a large sourcing base for components and sub-systems thus energising the MSME (micro, small and medium enterprises) sector due to large and relatively low cost engineering talent pool." With initiatives such as Make in India, India's dream to be self-reliant in defence production seems more achievable than before! The Indian aerospace, defence and homeland security sector has emerged as an gorgeous investment occasion for global and domestic players, SMEs and defence public sector undertakings (DPSUs). Increased FDI will enable the domestic industry to advantage in areas of design, modernism and state-of-the-art manufacturing, all critical for India's national safety. A vibrant defence developed base, through increased indigenisation, will provide additional impetus to Make in India, creating service, self-reliance and geo-political stability.

RISING DEFENCE EXPENDITURE IN INDIA

The Government of India has been investing heavily into its Defence industry due to strained relations with its neighboring countries and growth in international terrorism. The Defence budget for the year 2005 was $17.80 billion, a growth of 7.6 percent from the budget allocation of 2000. Typically 5.0 percent to 10.0 percent of the Defence budget is allocated for modernization and weapon induction. The larger share is allocated for payment, allowances, and for maintenance of aging military equipment. The Government of India expects its Defence expenditure to exceed $20.00 billion by 2008.

Private Investments on the Rise in the Indian Defence Industry

The Defence industry in the past has been dominated by the government-run public sector undertakings (PSU). This scenario has changed significantly with the Ministry of Defence providing license to private companies to manufacture select aerospace and Defence products. In 2001, the country opened for up to 100 percent Indian private sector investments in the Defence industry and allowed foreign direct investment (FDI) of up to 26.0 percent in select areas of the Defence industry. Some of the key non-PSU industry participants supplying Defence equipment and services include Mahindra & Mahindra, Tata Group, Kirloskar Brothers, Larsen & Toubro, Ashok Leyland, Jindal, Max Aerospace & Aviation, and Ramoss India.

Increasing Public-Private Collaborations

The Defence industry is gradually liberalizing and the public sector is facilitating greater private sector participation in the area of Defence goods production. There are about 5,100 companies supplying around 20.0 percent to 25.0 percent of components and subassemblies to state-owned contractors and the market size is expected to be around $6.20 billion in 2005. Of India's current Defence procurement of capital items, more than 30 percent is imported, however, this is expected to change with the creation of more public-private partnerships. The Indian Space Research Organization (ISRO) has a strong partnership with the Indian industrial sector for space programs execution. Over 500 small, medium, and large-scale enterprises work with ISRO, supplying hardware, undertaking fabrication jobs, and establishing fabrication and test facilities. The Indian industrial sector provides all raw materials and high-tech electronic items required by ISRO and has also contributed toward developing systems for launch vehicle spacecraft, remote sensing, and ground equipment. Around 231 technologies developed by ISRO were transferred to the Indian industrial sector for commercial use. ISRO also undertakes technical consultancy projects for industries.

DEPARTMENT OF DEFENCE PRODUCTION

The Department of Defence Production was set up in 1962, in the aftermath of the war with China, to create an indigenous defence production base which is self-reliant and self-sufficient. Indigenisation, particularly of armaments, proceeded apace in 1963. In November, 1965, Department of Defence Supplies was created to forge linkages between the civil industries and defence production units. The two departments were merged in December, 1984 to form the Department of Defence Production and Supplies. Since 1962, 16 new ordnance factories have been set up and their capacities have been augmented and modernised selectively keeping in mind the emerging requirements of the Armed Forces. Presently, 39 Ordnance Factories and 8 Defence Public Sector Undertakings (DPSUs) are engaged in the task of manufacture of equipment and stores for Defence Services. In addition, capacities of civil sectors are also utilised for the purpose.

India maintains an extensive Defence industrial base principally owned by the government. At independence, industrialization was viewed to be the engine of growth and jobs for the rest of the economy, and since then the government has owned a large fraction of the industries and also tightly regulated the private sector. India believed that public ownership was necessary to insure developments that would benefit the entire country. India decided early that the Defence industries would be owned by the public sector, and the Indian penchant to establish a "socialist pattern of society" still dominates the Defence industrial base.

India's Defence industrial capacity lies in three main classes of enterprises: the Ordnance Factories (OF), the Defence Public Sector Undertakings (DPSU), and, to a much lesser extent, selected civilian public and private sector manufacturing establishments. The OFs, founded in 1801, are departmentally run government units. There are 39 OFs, grouped into five areas based on the type of armaments they produce: Ammunition and Explosives, Weapons, Vehicles and Equipment, Armoured Vehicles, and Ordnance Equipment. There are eight publicyowned DPSUs: Hindustan Aeronautics Limited; Bharat Electronics; Bharat Earth Movers; Mazagon Dock Ltd; Garden Reach Shipbuilders and Engineers Ltd; Boa Shipyard Ltd; Bharat Dynamics Ltd; and Mishra Dhatu Nigam Ltd. Both the OFs and the DPSU's are trying to move toward greater self-reliance. The government is also trying to promote greater civil sector participation in the armament process.

The indigenisation of defence equipment is an ongoing process and is achieved by transfer of technology and indigenous research. Indigenisation of spares of defence equipment has been undertaken in aircraft, warships, armament, tanks, vehicles and electronic as well as engineering equipment.

While the Ordnance Factories and Defence Public Sector Units (DPSUs) are manufacturing a wide range of products for the defence forces, the private sector has been involved in the supply of raw material, semi-finished products, parts and components of defence equipment. The combined value of the products of Ordnance Factories and Defence PSUs during 2000-2001 has been approximately Rs. 14000 crore as against approximately Rs. 1800 crore on import of stores (which excludes capital equipment) comprising components, spares, overhaul etc.

The Government has recently allowed private sector participation in the defence industry upto 100 per cent and with foreign direct investment permissible upto 26 per cent both subject to licensing, for manufacture of all types of defence equipment within the country. This is expected to add to the investment already made in the public sector.

The Defence industry sector has been opened for participation by Indian Private Sector upto 100 % of equity, with Foreign Direct Investment (FDI), component of it being permissible upto 26 %, both being subject to licensing permissions. This includes all types of defence equipment. Guidelines have been issued by the Department of Industrial Policy & Promotion (DIPP) in consultation with the Ministry of Defence regarding the modalities for consideration of applications for grant of licences. The private companies are allowed to apply either individually or by a partnership firm amongst themselves. The Chief Executive of the company/ partnership will be a resident Indian. The company/partnership firm can have Foreign Direct Investment upto 26 % of the equity. Preference would be given to original equipment manufacturers or design establishments and those having a good track record of supplies. However, there would be a three years lock-in period for transfer of equity from one foreign investor to another foreign investor and such transfer would be subject to prior approval of Foreign Investment Promotion Board (FIPB) and the Government. All applications from the private entrepreneurs will be considered by the Department of Industrial Policy & Promotion in consultation with the Ministry of Defence and the licenses would be granted by the DIPP. The licensees are required to put in place adequate safety and security procedures, which would be subject to verification by authorized Government agencies. The quality of the product will be assured by the Quality Assurance Agencies of the Ministry of Defence. The exports of manufactured items would be subject to policy and guidelines as applicable to Ordnance Factories and Defence Public Sector Undertakings.

The objective of the policy is to attract more investment in the Defence Sector and not to change the ownership of the Ordnance Factory Board and the Defence Public Sector Undertakings. These represent the core strength of Defence Industry in India and their continued growth and full utilisation of capacities would be encouraged by the Government.

INDIA'S OFFSET POLICY TO ENCOURAGE DOMESTIC PRODUCTION

India's offset policy for Defence goods has been designed to leverage the country's position as a large buyer and exporter. India's offset policy for the Defence industry states that any purchase from a foreign supplier in excess of $70.0 million will require a reinvestment of 30.0 percent of the total purchase amount in terms of components and services from India. The offset policy applies to imports by Defence PSU's, ordinance factories, and private participants of the industry. The offset policy is also expected to act as a driver to create market-entry opportunities for mid-rung companies, which are looking at investing in research and development and manufacturing of Defence goods. The proposed offset policy is conducive for the private companies to have a larger presence.

Growth Opportunities in the Indian Defence Industry

The domestic capability of the Indian Defence industry is largely concentrated around the production of the PSUs and ordinance factories. This trend is expected to change with the recent selective liberalization of the Defence industry and a sound offset policy, which are expected to create greater private sector participation and facilitate bigger FDI inflows into the Indian Defence industry. The Government of India has shown keenness in allowing international collaboration for the production of weapon systems, which are purely used for non-lethal purposes. The production of the following weapon systems are expected to be promoted in the future:

- Technologies/equipment for counter terrorism
- Surveillance, communication equipment, and sensors for border management
- Cyber security-synergies in the field of information technology
- Devices to neutralize improvised explosive devices (IEDs)

Suppliers and manufacturers of the above-mentioned weapon systems are expected to be some of the chief beneficiaries of the increased indigenization of the production process in the Indian Defence industry. Key areas of growth identified within the industry are expected to arise from the up gradation of the production capacity expansion, technology transfer, and modernization of Defence infrastructure.

DEVELOPMENT AND MODERNISATION OF INDIAN ARMY

The Indian Army is the largest branch of the armed forces of India and bears responsibility for land-based military operations. Its primary objectives include defending India from external aggression, maintaining peace and security within the country, patrolling borders and conducting counter-terrorist operations.

It also conducts rescue and humanitarian operations during calamities and other disturbances. The President of India is the Commander-in-Chief of the Indian Army. With more than 1,130,000 soldiers in active service and about 1,800,000 reserve troops, the Indian Army is the world's second largest. It is a completely voluntary service and although a provision for military draft exists in the Indian constitution, it has never been imposed.

The Indian Army was formed soon after India gained independence in 1947 and retained most of the regiments of the British Indian Army. The Army is deployed in many of the world's conflict zones as a part of the United Nations Peacekeeping forces. The force is currently headed by the Chief of Army Staff, General Deepak Kapoor. Field Marshal is the highest attainable rank in the Indian Army and is conferred by the President of India, on advice of the Union Government, only in exceptional circumstances. Two officers have attained this rank so far.

Objectives

The Indian Army doctrine defines the role of the Indian Army as-"The Indian Army is the land component of the Indian Armed Forces which exist to uphold the ideals of the Constitution of India." As a major component of national power, along with the Indian Navy and the Indian Air Force, the roles of the Indian Army are as follows :

- Primary: Preserve national interests and safeguard sovereignty, territorial integrity and unity of India against any external threats by deterrence or by waging war.
- Secondary: Assist Government agencies to cope with 'proxy war' and other internal threats and provide aid to civil authority when requisitioned for the purpose."

History

Upon India gaining independence in 1947, the British Indian Army was divided into two parts to serve the newly created nations of Union of India and Islamic Republic of Pakistan. Most units went to India; four Gurkha regiments were transferred to the British Army while the rest went to India.

FIRST KASHMIR WAR (1947)

Almost immediately after independence, tensions between India and Pakistan began to boil over, and the first of three full-scale wars between the two nations broke out over the then princely state of Kashmir. Upon the Maharaja of Kashmir's reluctance to accede to either India or Pakistan, an impatient Pakistan sponsored a 'tribal' invasion of parts of Kashmir. The men included Pakistan army regulars. Soon after, Pakistan sent in more of its troops to annex the State.

The Maharaja, Hari Singh, appealed to India, and to Lord Mountbatten, the Governor General, for help. He signed the Instrument of Accession and Kashmir acceded to India (a decision ratified by Britain). Immediately after, Indian troops were airlifted to Srinagar and repelled the invaders. This contingent included General Thimayya who distinguished himself in the operation and in years that followed, became a Chief of the Indian Army. An intense war was waged across the state and former comrades found themselves fighting each other. Both sides made some territorial gains and also suffered significant losses. An uneasy UN sponsored peace returned by the end of 1948 with Indian and Pakistani soldiers facing each other directly on the Line of Control, which has since divided Indian from Pakistani-held Kashmir. Tensions between India and Pakistan, largely over Kashmir, have never since been entirely eliminated.

FOREIGN DIRECT INVESTMENT (FDI) IN DEFENCE SPHERE

"Direct foreign investment in Indian defence industries for

industrial infrastructure for services, co-development, joint and a production of defence products and components" have been identified by DPP 2008 as a method to discharge defence offset obligations. But in order to encourage investment and transfer of technology to India, it will be important to give foreign defence firms the confidence that they will have greater share in the profits and larger say in the management of the entities they create. Larger stakes should be allowed to foreign firms in such entities whose creation would not have been possible but for these foreign companies. Ironically, Foreign Investment Promotion Board (FIPB) guidelines do not encourage this.

According to the FIPB guidelines, foreign firms that may tie up with Indian entities are allowed only 26 per cent equity in such ventures. The remaining equity has to be owned by Indian entities. The ceiling of 26 per cent is a major impediment to the success of the offset policy. First, foreign firms are reluctant collaborators in any mandatory offset arrangement. Otherwise, these firms would have tied up with Indian entities for the production of defence equipment without any compulsion. But as offsets have been made mandatory in cases involving acquisition over Rs 300 crore, foreign firms can nevertheless be expected to collaborate with Indian firms, as otherwise they will lose the opportunity to profit from the contract that can only be signed with the offset obligation.

But, if the created entity has to survive on a long-term basis, the collaborating foreign firm should have a stake in it. This can only come through the creation of attractive prospects for the foreign firms to make greater profit than investments made elsewhere. Therefore, there is a need to make them, not reluctant parties, but willing and enthusiastic partners in JVs by increasing their stake in such collaborations. An example of how higher stakes in companies can help add value to the offset policy is the Boeing purchase of 34 per cent of Aero Vodochody, a Czech firm, as an offset deal. Boeing's subsidiary Ayers bought LET Kunovice, a Czech plane manufacturing firm, with plans to move part of the production line for its own planes to LET.

Second, if the balance of the 26 per cent that a foreign company brings has to be raised by Indian partners, it can lead to many difficulties. Since 26 per cent equity is the upper ceiling that a foreign vendor can invest in India, it has to find an Indian firm that is willing to raise the balance 74 per cent. This raises two difficulties. First, it has to find an Indian partner willing to find resources for this high level of investment. Second, if the foreign firm decides to use a JV as the sole means of fulfilling its 30 per cent obligation under offset, then it will have to find an Indian partner or partners willing to invest more in terms of equity. To illustrate, if a company X enters into a contract for Rs 1,000 crore, it will have to invest Rs 300 crore to discharge its offset obligations. But since a foreign vendor is only allowed 26 per cent equity, to invest Rs 300 crore, it will have to form a JV that involves a total investment of Rs 1,153.8 crore (Rs 300 crore by the foreign vendor and Rs 853.8 crore by the Indian entity or entities). Both the choices are difficult, as is would not be easy to find Indian entities that can make such high investments.

Conversely, increasing the equity may benefit the nation in several ways. Given the above dampeners (arising from the upper ceiling of 26 per cent), it may encourage greater participation by foreign firms in JVs if they have larger share of the equity. Also, foreign vendors will be reluctant to invest 26 per cent in equity and transfer proprietary technology that may have been developed at high research and development (R&D) cost. There is always a stubborn resistance to transferring technical capability and it can only come at a price as "the transferring country does not simply stand still while its 'beautiful princess' (Williamson, 1983) is shipped abroad and effective competition is created." Therefore, a foreign firm will be less reluctant to grudge competition from an entity established in India in which it has substantial stakes and from whose sales it stands to profit.

Given that comparatively cheap factors of production exist in India, the foreign parent company may even chose to outsource components/items from their Indian JV. Though not in the defence sector, the export performance of Hyundai Motors in India should give India reasons to allow more liberal FDI in the defence sector also. Second, a foreign firm that invests higher equity will have a stake in the success of the project. It will be more willing to outsource items from India to its other holdings to make the project a success.

Otherwise, there is a danger of the interest of the foreign vendor dissipating once the contract is completed, as without a reason to retain their interests, they will shut shop and return. This point can be illustrated with the instance of armoured personnel carriers purchased by the Philippines Army from the UK.

After eight of these were imported from the UK and the remaining 142 were assembled in Philippines, the assembly line was closed, with only minimal offset benefits to the nation. Third, as offset banking has now been allowed, it will give such vendors incentive to accumulate credits for discharging their obligations in future contracts by making value additions and introducing new products.

There should be further transparency in dealing with prospective foreign vendors. At present, GoI does consider higher investments on a case-to-case basis. This concept of case-to-case approach is indeed intriguing to a foreign vendor who in any case finds Indian procedures, bureaucratic control and the penchant for secrecy rather perplexing. The recent reports that the GoI turned down a joint venture proposal of Mahindra and Mahindra with the British defence giant BAE Systems has not helped convey the right message, coming as these did only weeks after the revised offset procedure was announced.

This rejection has even raised doubts on the seriousness with which India is pursuing its policy to attract foreign investment in the defence sector. Perhaps, GoI may have had strong reasons to reject the proposal. But explaining the reasons to the firms may have limited the damage. There should be more transparency in expressing our views and this will result in increased vendor confidence in the nation.

It may also be difficult to argue that increasing the limits of equity participation for foreign firms will impinge on national security. The only danger perhaps is that such foreign firms may end up buying Indian entities (a view expressed by one of the large Indian entities in response to the questionnaire sent by the author). If this is a serious concern, the problem can be addressed by making it a requirement to obtain the approval of GoI before the takeover of any defence establishment by a joint venture.

PARTICIPATION IN UN PEACE-KEEPING OPERATIONS

Presently, the Indian army has dedicated one brigade of troops to the UN's standby arrangements. The large number of sustained troop commitments made by India has been praised for taking part in long and difficult operations. The Indian Army has participated in several UN peace-keeping operations, including the ones in Angola, Cambodia, Cyprus, Congo, El Salvador, Namibia, Lebanon, Liberia, Mozambique, Rwanda, Somalia, Srilanka & Vietnam. The army had also provided a paramedical unit to facilitate the withdrawal of the sick and wounded in Korea.

Inclusion of Hyderabad (1948)

After the partition of India, the State of Hyderabad, a princely-state under the rule of a Nizam, chose to remain independent. The Nizam, refused to accede his state to the Union of India. The following stand-off between the Government of India and the Nizam ended on 12 September 1948 when India's then deputy-Prime Minister Sardar Vallabhai Patel ordered Indian troops to secure the state. Within 5 days of intense fighting, the Indian Army, backed by the Indian Air Force, successfully defeated Hyderabad State forces. The following day, the State of Hyderabad was proclaimed as a part of the Union of India. Major General Joyanto Nath Chaudhuri, who led the Operation Polo was appointed the Military Governor of Hyderabad (1948-1949) to restore law and order.

Goa, Daman and Diu Operation (1961)

Even though the British and French vacated all their colonial possessions in the Indian subcontinent, Goa, Daman and Diu remained under Portuguese control. On 12 December, 1961, after repeated Portuguese refusals to negotiate their leaving, New Delhi launched Operation Vijay and ordered a small contingent of its troops to invade the Portuguese territories and secure them. Unable to withstand the assault that lasted twenty-six hours, Goa, along with Daman and Diu (enclaves lying to the north of Maharashtra) joined India.

Sino-Indian Conflict (1962)

Since 1959, India followed a "forward policy" under which Indian border patrol units continuously pushed their posts forward deep into territory claimed by the People's Republic of China (PRC). Small-scale clashes between the Indian and Chinese forces broke out as India insisted on the disputed McMahon Line being regarded as the international border between the two countries. Despite heavy casualties, Indian troops did not retaliate the cross-border firing by Chinese troops. China's misinterpretation of India's true intentions in Tibet created more rifts between the two countries.

Buoyed by the success of its military operations in Hyderabad and Goa, India took a more aggressive stance towards its border disputes with China. In 1962, the Indian Army was ordered to move to the Thag La ridge located near the border between Bhutan and Arunachal Pradesh and about three miles (5 km) north of the disputed McMahon Line. Meanwhile, Chinese troops too had made incursions into Indian-held territory and tensions between the two reached a new high when Indian forces discovered a road constructed by China in Aksai Chin. After a series of failed negotiations, People's Liberation Army attacked Indian Army positions at the Thag La ridge. This move by China caught India by surprise and by October 12, Nehru gave orders for the Chinese to be expelled from Aksai Chin. However, poor coordination among various divisions of the Indian Army and the late decision to mobilize the Indian Air Force in vast numbers gave China a crucial tactical and strategic advantage over India. On October 20, Chinese soldiers attacked India in both the North-West and North-Eastern parts of the border and captured vast portions of Aksai Chin and Arunachal Pradesh.

As the fighting moved beyond disputed territories, China called on the Indian government to negotiate, however India remained determined to regain lost territory. With no peaceful agreement in sight, China unilaterally withdrew its forces from Arunachal Pradesh. The reasons for the withdrawal are disputed with India claiming various logistical problems for China and diplomatic support to it from the United States, while China stated that it still held territory that it had staked diplomatic claim upon. The dividing line between the Indian and Chinese forces was christened the Line of Actual Control.

The poor decisions made by India's military commanders, and, indeed, its political leadership, raised several questions. The Henderson-Brooks committee was soon set up by the Government of India to determine the causes of the poor performance of the Indian Army. The report of committee apparently faulted much of the command of Indian Armed Forces and severely criticized the executive government for its failures on several fronts. The committee found that the major reason for the defeat was low deployment of troops on India's border with China even after hostilities began and also criticized the decision to not allow the Indian Air Force to target Chinese transport lines out of fear of Chinese aerial counter-attack on Indian civilian areas. Much of the blame was also targeted at the incompetence of then Defense Minister, Krishna Menon who resigned from his post soon after the war ended. Despite frequent calls for its release, the Henderson-Brooks report still remains classified.

Second Kashmir War (1965)

A second confrontation with Pakistan took place in 1965, largely over Kashmir. Pakistani President Ayub Khan launched *Operation Gibraltar* in August 1965 during which several

Pakistani paramilitary troops infiltrated into Indian-administered Kashmir and tried to spark an anti-India rebellion. Pakistani leaders believed that India, which was still recovering from the disastrous Sino-Indian War, would be unable to deal with a military thrust and rebellion.

However, the operation was a major failure since the Kashmiri people showed little support for such a rebellion and India quickly moved forces to drive the infiltrators out. Within a fortnight of the launch of the Indian counter-attack, most of the infiltrators had retreated back to Pakistan. Battered by the failure of Operation Gibraltar and expecting a major invasion by Indian forces across the border, Pakistan launched Operation Grand Slam on September 1, invading India's Chamb-Jaurian sector.

In retaliation, the India's Army launched major offensive throughout its border with Pakistan, with Lahore as its prime target. Though the Indian Army's break through of the final phases of Pakistani defense was considerably delayed due to logistical issues, the conflict was largely seen as a debacle for the Pakistani Army. Initially, the Indian Army met with considerable success in the northern sector.

After launching prolonged artillery barrages against Pakistan, India was able to capture three important mountain positions in Kashmir. By September 9, the Indian Army had made considerable in-roads into Pakistan. India had its largest haul of Pakistani tanks when the offensive of Pakistan's 1 Armoured Division was blunted at the Battle of Asal Uttar which took place on September 10 near Khemkaran. Six Pakistani Armoured Regiments took part in the battle against three Indian Armoured Regiments with inferior tanks. By the time the battle had ended, the 4th Indian Division had captured about 97 Pakistani tanks in either destroyed, or damaged, or in intact condition. This included 72 Patton tanks and 25 Chafees and Shermans. 32 of the 97 tanks, including 28 Pattons, were in running condition. In comparison, the Indians lost only 32 tanks at Khemkaran-Bhikkiwind. About fifteen of them were captured by the Pakistan Army, mostly Sherman tanks.

Pakistan's overwhelming defeat at the decisive battle of Assal Uttar hastened the end of the conflict.

At the time of ceasefire declaration, India reported casualties of about 2,000 were killed. On the other hand, it was estimated that about 3,800 Pakistani soldiers were killed in the battle, 9,000 were wounded and about 2,000 were taken as prisoners of war. About 300 Pakistani tanks were either destroyed or captured by India and an additional 150 were permanently put out of service. India lost a total of 190 tanks during the conflict and about 100 more had to undergo repair. In all, India lost about half as many tanks as Pakistan lost during the war. Given India's advantageous position at the end of the war, the decision to return back to pre-war positions, following the Tashkent Declaration, caused an outcry among the polity in New Delhi. It was widely believed that India's decision to accept the ceasefire was due to political factors, and not military, since it was facing considerable pressure from the United States and the UN to stop hostilities.

Bangladesh Liberation War (1971)

An independence movement broke out in East Pakistan which was brutally crushed by Pakistani forces. Due to large-scale atrocities against them, thousands of Bengalis took refuge in neighboring India causing a major refugee crisis there. In early 1971, India declared its full-support for the Bengali rebels, known as Mukti Bahini, and Indian agents were extensively involved in covert operations to aid them.

On November 20, 1971, Indian Army moved the 14 Punjab Battalion and 45 Cavalry into Garibpur, a strategically important town near India's border with East Pakistan, and successfully captured it. The following day, more clashes took place between Indian and Pakistani forces. Wary of India's growing involvement in the Bengali rebellion, the Pakistan Air Force (PAF) launched a pre-emptive strike on Indian military positions near its border with East Pakistan on December 3. The aerial operation, however, failed to accomplish its stated objectives and caused India to declare a full-scale war against

Pakistan the same day. By midnight, the Indian Army, accompanied by Indian Air Force, launched major military thrust into East Pakistan. The Indian Army won several battles on the eastern front including the decisive of battle of Hilli, which was the only front where the Pakistani Army was able to buildup considerable resistance. India's massive early gains was largely attributed to the speed and flexibility with which Indian armoured divisions moved across East Pakistan.

Pakistan launched a counter-attack against India on the western front. On December 4, 1971, the A company of the 23rd Battalion of India's Punjab Regiment detected and intercepted the movement of the 51st Infantry Division of the Pakistani Army near Ramgarh, Rajasthan.

The battle of Longewala ensued during which the A company, though being outnumbered, thwarted the Pakistani advance until the Indian Air Force directed its fighters to engage the Pakistani tanks. By the time the battle had ended, 34 Pakistani tanks and 50 armoured vehicles were either destroyed or abandoned. About 200 Pakistani troops were killed in action during the battle while only 2 Indian soldiers lost their lives.

Pakistan suffered another major defeat on the western front during the battle of Basantar which was fought from December 4 to 16th. By the end of the battle, about 66 Pakistani tanks were destroyed and 40 more were captured. In return, Pakistani forces were able to destroy only 11 Indian tanks. None of the numerous Pakistani offensives on the Western front materialized. By December 16, Pakistan had lost sizable territory on both eastern and western fronts.

Under the command of Lt. General J.S Aurora, the three corps of the Indian Army, who had invaded East Pakistan, entered Dhaka and forced Pakistani forces to surrender on 16 December, 1971, one day after the conclusion of the battle of Basantar. After Pakistan's Lt. General A.A.K. Niazi signed the Instrument of Surrender, India took more than 90,000 Pakistani prisoners of war, which included about 38,000 armed forces personnel and 52,000 militia and bureaucrats of West Pakistani origin. At the time of the signing of the Instrument of Surrender, 9,000 Pakistani soldiers were killed-in-action while India suffered only 2,500 battle-related deaths. In addition, Pakistan lost 200 tanks during the battle compared to India's 80.

In 1972, the Simla Agreement was signed between the two countries and tensions simmered. However, there were occasional spurts in diplomatic tensions which culminated into increased military vigilance on both sides.

Siachen Conflict (1984)

The Siachen Glacier, though a part of the Kashmir region, is not officially demarcated. As a consequence, prior to the 1980s, neither India nor Pakistan maintained permanent military presence in the region. However, Pakistan started hosting a series of mountaineering expeditions to the glacier during the 1950s. By early 1980s, the government of Pakistan was granting special expedition permits to mountaineers and United States Army maps deliberately showed Siachen as a part of Pakistan. This practice gave rise to the contemporary meaning of the term *oropolitics*.

An irked India launched Operation Meghdoot in April 1984 during which the entire Kumaon Regiment of the Indian Army was airlifted to the glacier. Pakistani forces responded quickly and clashes between the two followed. Indian Army secured the strategic Sia La and Bilafond La mountain passes and by 1985, more than 1000 sq. miles of territory, claimed by Pakistan, was under Indian control.

The Indian Army continues to control more than 2/3rd of the glacier. Pakistan made several unsuccessful attempts to regain control over Siachen. In late 1987, Pakistan mobilized about 8,000 troops and garrisoned them near Khapalu, aiming to capture Bilafond La. However, they were thrown back after engaging the Indian Army personnel guarding Bilafond. During the battle, about 23 Indian soldiers lost their lives while more than 150 Pakistani troops perished. Further unsuccessful attempts to reclaim positions were launched by Pakistan in 1990, 1995, 1996 and 1999.

India continues to maintain a strong military presence in the region despite extremely inhospitable conditions and the conflict over Siachen is regularly cited as an example of mountain warfare. The highest peak in the Siachen glacier region, Siakangri, is strategically important for India because its immense altitude and proximity to the Karakoram Highway enables the Indian forces to keep check on any Pakistani or Chinese movement in the region. Maintaining control over Siachen poses several logistical challenges for the Indian Army. Several infrastructure projects were constructed in the region, including a helipad 21,000 feet (6,400 m) above the sea level. In 2004, Indian Army was spending an estimated US$2 million a day to support its personnel stationed in the region.

4

Make in India in Defence Production: Challenges and Opportunities

Security is one of the most important matters of the state as security issues are closely linked with legitimacy of the government. Though security encompasses many dimensions such as political including territorial security, economic security, cultural security and environmental security etc; however, defending territorial integrity of the state is prime responsibility of the government as most of the armed conflicts and wars have taken place for expansion and control over territories in order to enhance the tangible and intangible resources of state. Accordingly, concerns for security of state necessitate defence preparedness by maintaining strong, adequate and effective armed forces at least to deter and counter the perceived external threats.

Defence preparedness requires acquisition of "means" for the fighting forces to match the capability of perceived adversaries in addition to will power, well trained armed forces, well planned strategies, information gathering, and soft power etc. The means include weapons, equipment and other supplies required for fighting forces during operation in theatre of war. Modern warfare is highly technology intensive, so major challenge before armed forces of any nation is acquisition of weapons and equipment with adequately high technology matching to or better than that of the perceived adversaries. Current NDA government inIndialed by Prime Minister Narendra Modi since May, 2014 has accorded highest priority to "Make inIndia" for boosting economy ofIndiaand creating employment to its young population. Moreover,Indiais heavily dependent on import to meet the defence acquisition requirements. About 70 percent of capital acquisitions for equipping armed forces are met through imports. Therefore, one of the focussed areas for "make inIndia" is defence industry that provides support to the national security in addition to creating employment. Thus "Make inIndia" programme in defence sector is highly relevant with twin objectives of creating employment as well as to bolster defence preparedness in order to strengthen security ofIndia.

Government ofIndiahas provided adequate budgetary allocations in the past for acquisition of weapons, equipment and other supplies for armed forces, but many times the same could not be fully utilized due to non availability of adequate indigenous sources of supplies. Indigenous sources of supply of these weapons, equipment and supplies have been heavily dependent on Defence Research and Development Organisation (DRDO) for design and development, and state owned production units and Defence Public Sector Undertakings (DPSU) for production; and on account of poor performance of these entities due to a host of structural, operational and cultural problems on account of exogenous as well as endogenous factors, desired level of defence acquisition could not be met. Private sector has not yet been able to make an appreciable presence in defence supplies especially in critical defence technologies. The Department of Defence Production (DDP) has long acquisition process consisting of eleven steps starting with framing of services quality requirements (SQR) at Planning Directorate of each service at lowest level to Defence Acquisition Council (DAC) at highest level, and that is very time consuming. In some cases, when delivery of weapon or equipment takes place, new sets of upgrades become necessity. Acquisition of the critical weapons and equipment through importation sinks into quagmire of corruption in many cases leading to delay or cancellation of acquisition process. Moreover, due to global political constraints wherever defence acquisitions through imports were made, in most of the cases, it was not a contemporary world class technology available. So, high priority on defence production in make inIndiacan boost development of indigenous defence industries in high end technologies that is essential for ensuring defence preparedness.

Defence production is also one of the priority areas for make inIndiawith a perspective to create additional employment as well as to makeIndiaself reliant in defence production where about 70 percent of capital acquisitions in weapon and equipment comes through import. Despite high dependency on import for capital acquisitions in weapon and equipment, state owned defence production units and DPSU are growing annually barely at an average rate varying from 2 to 5 percent in terms of value of production (VOP) on account of a number of endogenous and exogenous factors. High dependence on import and low growth rate of DPSU and state owned defence production units make sense of nurturing defence industries in private sector and bring foreign direct investment (FDI) in defence industries for self reliance in defence system. Self reliance in defence production will prepare the nation better to meet the security challenges and to deter the perceived adversaries. Total global defence export business is estimated to the tune of 1.5 trillion dollars. Therefore, it makes a good sense to give a boost to defence production in make inIndiaprogramme as there is ample opportunities to meet national requirements and vie for a share in global export potential of about 1.5 trillion dollars after meeting the national requirements.

It makes one to pause and think that how countries likeChinaandSouth Koreathat were either at par or inferior toIndiain industrial and technological development till 1970s became now exporter of defence items andIndiaremained one of the biggest importers of the defence items inAsia. Definitely, the answer lies in technology acquisitions through foreign direct investment (FDI) in civil as well as in defence technology coupled with research and development (R&D) pursued by these countries. Therefore,Indiaalso needs to boost its defence production taking lessons fromChinaandSouth Korea; and should attract FDI in defence production as well as in civil sector as many civil sector technologies find usage in defence sector also. Despite their strength and hidden potential state owned defence manufacturing units and DPSU could not do much towards development of defence technologies as it was not their main mandate. Whatever little bit they do in R&D is limited to incremental improvement in process improvement and component design that too after a rigours process of consultations and approvals. DRDO, which is responsible for development of defence technologies, is constrained by its inefficiency in developing new products and systems. Most of the DRDO projects, ranging from, gas turbine engine Kaveri, light combat aircraft Tejas to long-range surface-to-air missile systems, after all, are running years behind schedule with huge cost overruns. Even international peer group and experts also see lacklustre inIndia's development of military technology. Given below is the view of international expert published in SIPRI especially about missile development programme.

Military research and development (R&D) in India is not progressing as rapidly or as far as its leaders had hoped and observers had predicted. The obstacles preventing India from developing a more advanced military technology base are primarily technical and economic, stemming from chronic problems with project management rather than any lack of scientific resources. Indian military R&D programmes have achieved some immediate goals but have not created the anticipated technological momentum that would allow them to move from limited import substitution to indigenous innovation.

Moreover, lack of clarity and transparency in identifying the main attributes of weapon and equipment required for armed forces, delays in framing its specifications and frequently changing the specifications by procuring agencies also retarded the process of development of new weapons and equipment. Whatever little bit these state owned defence production units and DPSU could produce, it is mainly due to technologies provided by erstwhile USSR during cold war.

However, prospects of getting military technology from advance country are becoming better with changing global and regional security scenario. With changing geo-political scenario in Asia-pacific and importance attached to this region by global power and emerging global power, Indiais being considered to be a key player in maintaining the regional stability in this region. In the recent past there have been paradigm shift in out look of security architecture of Asia Pacific by key stakeholders of this region, and now the term Asia-Pacific is being replaced to Indo-Pacific in many security thinking and discourses. This has provided a new opportunity for Indiato have access to some of the key defence technologies from some of the key stake holders in this region who are well advance in military technology. An outcome of the same is reflected in commitment of USgovernment in recently concluded 10-year defence framework agreement singed on 3rd June, 2015 between Indian Defence Minister and hisUS counterpart Defence Secretary, Ash Carter where commitment has been made in providing high end military technology like Jet Engine and Aircraft Carrier design and many more.India needs to exploit such opportunities by making it defence acquisition policies more conducive to receive technology and investment in defence sector.

For acquisition of technology, two pronged strategies have to be adopted. First strategy which is relatively short term is to attract FDI in defence production as it will bring not only the contemporary or best technology but will also bring capital required and will also enhance the technical skills of work force. Government has already increased the FDI from 26 to 49 percent in defence sector, and in strategic defence technologies there is a mechanism to increase the share of FDI beyond 49 percent also. The other strategy which is long term, may focus on invigorating DRDO through structural reforms and creating R&D division parallel to DRDO in defence public sector units and state owned defence production units. R&D in defence in joint venture under Public Private Partnership (PPP) model with well defined public funding and Intellectual Property Right (IPR) sharing mechanism could also be considered so that development of indigenous defence technology could be propelled.

However, in order to boost up the make in India programme in defence sector in short term through FDI route, it needs to be realised that defence industries works in monopolistic or oligopolistic buyer's market where buyers and sellers are few, mainly the government organizations involved in external and internal security. Therefore, it needs to be ensured that sustained market exists for those investors who are investing in defence production so that reasonable returns on investment are assured to investors. Without assured market for a reasonable period of time, no investor will invest money in defence sector. This requires that a foreign investors must be given adequate economic order quantity over a reasonably long period so that with optimum investment, investing firm could meet the commitment of delivering goods and services timely in phased manner and could earn a reasonable return on their investment.

Therefore, in order to inculcate confidence among investors for sustained demand of defence products, first reform has to be made at demand side in terms of quantity and phased delivery of defence products by freezing the specifications. In long term perspective plan for acquisition, specifications needs to be frozen for a reasonable period of time keeping in mind the availability of technologies at competitive and affordable cost, strategic requirements based on capabilities of potential adversaries through intelligence gathering and incubation period of next generation weapon system development. General Service Quality Requirements (GSQR) or SQR should not be based on whims and fancies of some of the decision makers with vested interest, but it should be worthy for their operation as well as pragmatic to manufacture and should not change frequently as it may put extra burden on investors in form of acquisition of additional technology, plant and machines to meet requirements of changed specifications. Manufactures views should also be invited and examined for consideration while framing GSQR/ SQR. If a contract is won by one company, then that company should supply the item for 5 to 10 years till it recovers its return on investment or technology is phased out globally or becomes irrelevant.

Besides providing stable, predictable and assured indigenous market, government should also help the investors in accessing the selective global market through diplomatic means as this requires a lot of considerations on national security, regional stability, human right considerations etc. Government needs to put in place a mechanism to promote and support defence export involving main stakeholders such as Ministry of Defence, Ministry of External Affairs, Department of Commerce and Industry, and defence industry associations etc.

Apart from above, development of defence industry will also require adequate infrastructure facilities in form of road, power, water, port, communication etc; and ease of doing business through tax and labour reforms, hassle free land acquisition, simple environmental and other statuary clearances.

As a long term strategy to boost defence production capability of nation, research and development capability has to be strengthened. DRDO needs to ensure delivery of cutting-edge weapon technologies and systems to the armed forces in time to keep Indiaahead in the national security arena as lackadaisical attitude on this account will cost heavily to national security.

DRDO which is entrusted with the task of design and development has monopoly in R&D in defence sector to makeIndiaself reliant in defence system. However, DRDO has failed to meet the expectations of armed forces in delivering cutting edge technologies. Therefore, there should not be monopoly of DRDO in R&D in defence sector. There is a need to create competition in R&D in defence sector. All the DPSU and state owned units in defence production should be mandated to undertake the R&D activities either independently or in collaboration with DRDO, other Laboratories and academic institutions of their choice. And for this purpose government may also consider providing funds for R&D to certain credible private firms that have been supplying critical weapons and equipment to Indian armed forces for a considerable period of time on sustained basis on suitable terms and conditions that could take care of proper utilization of fund for designated project and address intellectual property right (IPR) issues. There are many dual technologies that find application in both civil and defence sectors, and development of these technologies could be funded by Technology Development Board, Government of India on priority. The first and foremost requirement will be to increase gross expenditure on research and development (GERD) to 3 percent which is currently around 1 percent. Small and medium enterprises (SME) provide a large number of employments in the country and employment generation is one of the focus areas in make inIndia. There are many credible small and medium enterprises (SME) that can also undertake design, development and production of small sub-systems of defence equipment, for which they need to be encouraged by providing certain financial and other incentives.

Therefore, if India wants to become self reliant in meeting its requirement of defence supplies in weapon and equipment and aspire to be defence exporter in near future, it needs to streamline acquisition policies and processes making it stable and easy for existing firms and new investors to meet the supply obligations over a reasonable period of time without incurring extra cost. Structural reforms in existing state owned design, development and manufacturing institutions are required to invigorate them in order to tap their full potential. Indigenous private and foreign investors needs to be roped in defence design, development and manufacturing by assuring the investors a long term supply orders and providing assistance in accessing export market so that a reasonable return on investment could be assured to investors. Collaboration and cooperation in private sector and public sector defence units may create synergy in defence production. R&D needs to be taken to private firms and SME needs to be encouraged to undertake development and production of critical sub-assemblies through various policy supports. A boost in defence production inIndiawill improve its defence preparedness, boost economy and provide employment apart from changing the technological landscape ofIndiaas it will also boost civil industries.

'FROM SMALL STEPS TO FASTER PACE, KEY TO DEVELOPING INDIA'S DEFENCE INDUSTRY'

India steps into a new era with a new government, new agenda and the opportunity to make fresh beginnings. Over the years, the Indian defence industry has been taking small steps towards becoming a modern, globally competitive defence development and production base. It is apparent that the ingredients for moving forward at a much faster pace and taking giant strides are present. All that is needed is determined action.

India is today a hub for many global defence companies for high-end development work. Indian engineers are working – both in India and abroad – on cutting-edge defence systems. The private sector has also spent long years getting their bearings in the sector and some of them have made impressive investments. India has shown remarkable capacity for absorbing technology: the Indian armed forces have earned a reputation of being users with high technical acumen and ability to extract superior standards of performance from their equipment.

Given all these, the time is ripe to act on policies that have been in the making for a while. India's drive towards indigenous defence capability requires partners with state-of-the-art technology that can be transferred to India with the support of their respective governments. More importantly, such companies should be driven by self-interest to carry out real transfer of technology and have a real interest in joint development of new generations of products.

The challenge is to build domestic capability without foregoing cutting-edge systems. The process requires Indian public and private sector defence companies to leapfrog technologies and start designing, developing and producing state-of-the-art systems in the immediate future and not through protracted development programmes.

The only way to do so in a rapid way is to make use of technology developed by companies outside India. Thus far, India has tried to tackle this challenge through strong offset provisions in procurement programmes. While offsets do meet the requirement of a return on expenditure, it has not proven to be adequate for developing an industrial base.

The end result should be the creation of a defence industrial base that will ensure that the country does not need to look externally for most of its future defence requirements. In addition, such programmes should have significant spillover of technology to nondefence sectors.

The entry of highly technologically advanced Indian private sector companies, which today design and engineer world-class products ranging from automobiles to pharmaceuticals, tells much about the inherent potential to rapidly build an indigenous defence production capability.

However, most Indian companies are unwilling to commit to large-scale investments without a contract in place. The belief is that there is not sufficient business basis for them to take the required risks and initiative. Investments in the defence sector are further slowed down by the equity ceiling of 26 per cent for FDI in defence. In the absence of the necessary capital investments in the private sector and the overburdened state of the public sector, it is apparent that the fundamental business drivers for a healthy indigenous defence industry are missing.

For companies to make meaningful investments and bring in cutting edge technology to India, a much higher FDI provision than 26 per cent is essential. In many countries, including my own, there is no limitation for FDI in the defence sector at all. As a first step, an increase of the threshold to 51 per cent is urgently called for.

A stronger status for FDI in defence will enable Indian companies to find meaningful partners who are interested in their own survival by investing and building profitable businesses in India. Saab is a trusted supplier to the Indian armed forces for over three decades and we bring to India world leading products, services and solutions ranging from military defence to civil security.

We are teaming up with Indian public and private companies and leveraging their engineering and manufacturing strengths to meet the needs of India as well as for exports of defence systems to world markets. Saab is committed to true transfer of technology and investing in the future of Indian defence industry. We are here to stay for the long haul to build an indigenous defence industry in India.

POLICY CHANGES IN DEFENCE INDUSTRY

The first set of major policy changes were promulgated by the Government to give a fillip to our stagnating and moribund defence industry. The fundamental underpinnings to the policy changes were two: firstly, bring in the private sector; and secondly, opening the door for foreign companies by permitting up to 26 percent investment, so that technology inflows are facilitated. It was perhaps rightly believed that these were the two principle measures that were required to catalyse our ailing military industrial capabilities.

While most observers welcomed the policy announcements, there was considerable scepticism over the Governments' resolve to implement them. Could a system that was wedded to the philosophy of state led industrialisation for almost fifty years, change course that easily? Unlikely! Then there was the problem of our establishments' recognised and reputed talent for conceptualising great ideas, but seldom demonstrating the capacity to execute them. However, after having out-of-habit taken recourse to castigating the Government, it would be prudent to also try and understand its compulsions and concerns. The first is that given the nature of the UPA Government, no reforms can be implemented without the Left's concurrence.

The Left's dogma is to stonewall any measure that appears to threaten the interests of the PSUs and the Ordnance Factory

Board (OFB). Thus the Left would not be inclined to acquiesce to proposals that contemplate the relaxation of state control over most core industrial sectors. Similarly, the defence PSUs and the OFB, would also not be willing to dilute their monopoly of their defence market.

Then there is the problem of the huge investments and the capacities created in all our Government owned defence industrial under-takings. Logically, it cannot be any one's case, that these assets are permitted to decay instead of putting them to optimal use. With the private sectors' case for a level playing field, the fear that over time, the Government owned defence industrial establishments would be progressively edged out of business, is genuine.

The third concern, and not easy to counter, pertains to the argument of national security. Since the private sector is not under Government control, in times of a crisis it may not respond to national requirements in the same manner that a Government owned unit would do. It is a combination of the preceding concerns that explain the Government's hesitation in letting go the control that we have witnessed since the policy changes were promulgated in May 2001. Having acknowledged the issues, it must be conceded that these are not new or unique to us. All nations have had to grapple with the same set of dilemmas, and since we are in the catch-up game, our problems ought to be easier to solve, for we have the experience of other countries to learn and benefit from.

So, while the Government at one level remained wedded to the policy of reforms, in its implementation, it dragged its feet. Consequently, the practice of doing business only with the Government owned industries did continue unchanged for three to four years, much to the frustration of the private sector. This ambivalence of the Government impacted negatively on the private sectors' attempts at collaboration with foreign companies. It should therefore be accepted that foreign partnership was, and is, vital for our industry to take off.

Indigenously we do not have the technology, nor the know-how, for state-of-the-art systems that the defence services aspire for. Since foreign defence companies were unclear of the Governments' intent, they were not prepared to enter into collaborative arrangements with the private sector. For quite a while they remained cautious, indulged in fence sitting-hedging their bets.

The air was finally cleared with the Government's announcement of the Defence Procurement Policy of 2006. The most significant features of this policy were its 'offset clauses' and the concept of RURs (Raksha Utpadan Ratnas). Of the two, it is the offset policy that has the potential to yield spectacular results in energising our defence industry.

The billions of dollars of business that this policy will bring to the Indian industry has generated unprecedented excitement among our domestic players. In excitement lies the challenge. They will have to be prepared to absorb complex technologies and engineering skills, and then manufacture components, assemble subsystems, and systems, at a cost that is competitive and sufficiently profitable. Ever since the idea of the offset policy was mooted, all foreign multi-nationals have been lobbying intensely to sabotage it. Arguments-that the policy would push up prices, that the Indian industry is incapable of absorbing high technology 'direct offsets', that monitoring mechanisms cannot be effective etc-have been in the air for a while.

The Government is considering some relaxation in the policy. The areas mentioned were the adjustment of the cost of technology transfer against offsets, banking of offsets and the acceptance of indirect offsets. Though these issues may merit consideration, it would be somewhat premature to accept policy changes even before we have begun. The pressure on foreign vendors to fulfil their offset obligations must remain undiluted. Concurrently, we must concentrate on finding satisfactory solutions to the issues being raised. Having dwelt somewhat cursorily on policy issues, an objective assessment of our present industrial capability and its growth potential would now be in order. The Defence industry cannot be viewed in isolation. It has to be a manifestation of the nation's overall industrial and technological capabilities. Often we tend to ignore this fundamental. The first place to begin this survey would be to look at the captains of our industry. There is a growing realisation that they have arrived. Globally, they are winning admiration and recognition. In the early nineties, when the first steps of liberalisation were initiated, they nurtured apprehensions about their survival. Having successfully negotiated that phase of transition in our economy, they have at the beginning of the twenty first century emerged with renewed strategic sense that has a global sweep. Witness the takeovers and the expansion plans of quite a few of our companies. Just a decade ago, who could have imagined, that the Jaguar brand car would be owned by an Indian Company? They have in the recent past displayed vision, and matched that vision with the capacity to implement.

The next requirement is of the work force. It is abundantly available in all categories; managerial, technical and in terms of working hands-our biggest asset being the young age profile of our people. Some intervention can be expected from the government in its labour policies. But being a politically sensitive issue, the Industry will have to live with this problem, till a change becomes environmentally possible. In terms of spheres in which we have advanced to global standards our range has remained somewhat limited to the automobile sector, pharmaceuticals and a few other disciplines. We have hardly any capabilities in electronics, communications, optics and in the field of aviation. Our industrial policies should focus on these voids. To become a meaningful player in the defence sector, these technologies are vital.

Our biggest strength is software services. Infosys, Wipro and TCS are globally among the best. In addition, there are a host of second tier companies, clocking rapid growth, while doing both domestic and international business. Unfortunately, this strength has not been effectively harnessed to give the requisite impetus to our defence industry. Particularly, because the new generation of weapon systems and related support systems, are all heavily dependent on extremely sophisticated software, the cost of which may be as high as 30-40 percent of the total value of the platform. Electronics we know takes up another 30-40 percent.

The Left and a few other groups have consistently opposed the opening up of the defence industry to the private sector. They have repeatedly been claiming that the public sector units can produce all that our armed forces need. A brief look at their track record will establish that such confidence in the state owned establishments is quite misplaced.

We have 39 Ordnance Factories, 8 Defence PSUs and 50 Defence Research Laboratories, ie. close to 100 establishments, all well equipped, extravagantly staffed, with some excellent scientists and managers, and yet no creditworthy achievements to show. And what equipment do they produce which is to the satisfaction of our Armed Forces?

It would be difficult to list any, other than the ALH from HAL, which has the potential to be a good product. The DRDO might want to take credit for the Agni (1 and 2) and the Prithvi. These are good systems but lose a fair amount of their sheen since they come twenty to thirty years after similar systems were inducted in China.

Our process of reforms in the management of the Government controlled defence research and production establishments, have regrettably floundered. Many studies have been done, yet-to all intent and purposes-the drift continues. Over the last three to four years the Government has been pushing for public private partnership. The idea being that such association would bring about the desired efficiencies in the public sector. But the problem is that such forced marriages do not really work. Driven by expediency, some private companies, may consider coming to an under-standing with PSUs for the short term, but such arrangements are not likely to be conducive to the real growth of the defence industry.

The policy of opening up of the defence industry to the private sector was successful in attracting quite a few industrial houses-large, medium and small, to enter the fray. Even prior to the formal opening of the defence sector, some had indirectly been in the business by manufacturing components, subsystems and systems-for integration by the defence PSUs.

Besides, our nuclear and space programmes had involved the private industry. Such companies have executed sophisticated design and engineering jobs that include special metals and alloys, and therefore have acquired the confidence to take on the development and manufacture of defence systems. L&T, Tatas, Mahindras, Godrej Boyce, Bharat Forge and more recently Punj Lloyd, are some of the major industrial houses that have staked their claim for defence contracts. Following them, are a large number of second and third tier companies covering a wide range of technologies.

The basic handicap of all these companies at the time the policy change was announced in 2001 was their lack of domain knowledge. They did not know weapon systems, or what force multipliers were, or how the procurement procedures worked. They also did not know how the global arms market operated. They were equally unaware of the equipment profile of our armed forces and their future requirement.

Even though these companies inducted service officers whose advice was available, lack of personal knowledge of the business inhibited executives from pursuing projects that entailed taking investment decisions. Increased involvement in the defence sector; and interaction with the defence services, the procurement arm of the Ministry of Defence, and the big multinational defence companies, over the last five to six years; has impacted positively on the confidence levels of company executives.

The role of defence service officers in galvanising the industry merits special attention. Other than these officers, not many in India, have any idea of modern warfare, military organisations, weapon systems, munitions and the support systems. Such domain knowledge within the industry is imperative. All over the world companies engaged in the business of military hardware extensively employ service officers to develop products and promote business. Not only this, even governments in order to support domestic industries, lend serving officers and men to participate in trials or make presentations. We may recall some of the service-industry seminars held in Delhi in the recent past which had serving officers endorsing products.

Unfortunately, the environment that we have nurtured in India discourages our retired/retiring officers from being employed. If employed they cannot be optimally used because of the establishments' attitude towards them. Who benefits? Only the foreign companies and maybe our adversaries! This must change. By encouraging the absorption of service officers by the defence industry, the nation will reap multiple benefits. Firstly, the users would have access to informed inputs on developments, which would contribute to better decisions on choice of systems and the formulation of specifications. Rather the industry would gain from the expertise of these officers in an area which they have much to learn about. Secondly, to some extent, the problem of rehabilitation of officers who retire at relatively younger ages would get addressed. It is important that the Government revisits this issue.

The central issue facing the defence industry is access to contemporary technology, its absorption and assimilation, and then the use of domestic research and development to graduate to next generation systems. South Africa, Israel, China, South Korea, Brazil, and even Singapore, have learnt to successfully navigate this cycle. There is no reason why we cannot emulate their example. In our case, so far, technology transfers have taken place only to the OFB and the defence PSUs. Their experience should not become the only basis for drawing conclusions on this subject. The appetite for growth of the private sector, and its new found confidence, would undoubtedly yield different results.

A survey of the global defence market will reveal that we are currently the biggest importers of defence systems. The US and China do spend more but they mostly buy domestic. The figures of our projected purchases are being regularly quoted in thousands of crores. They do give us sufficient strength to extract terms that could be used to considerable advantage.

Look at the pending procurements: some 200 helicopters, 126 advanced fighters, approximately 800-1000 artillery guns, and half a dozen submarines. Each of these would run into billions of dollars. The conclusion is obvious-buy sensibly. With these purchases in the pipeline, if we did not get all the technologies we need, we will have only ourselves to blame. Procurement terms must state our purchase imperatives unambiguously. As a matter of fact we could consider modifying our procedures when acquiring big ticket items. Take the case of advanced fighters. All contenders have proven comparable systems. The differences essentially stem from design philosophies and the source of subsystems and systems that have been selected for integration.

The gaps in features are so narrow that quite often the choice can be a matter of individual predilection. The same arguments can be applied to the helicopters we want or the submarines. Selection could therefore be based on the totality of the package a vendor offers and not just the L-1 criteria after qualifying. To what extent and in what manner is technology being offered? What are the long term buy back agreements? What kind of investments is the vendor making in India? For such high value transactions we must extract much more than what we have done hither to. We need to therefore delve deeper into the manner in which we pursue major acquisitions. There could also be a case for some coordination with say the Civil Aviation Ministry taking into account the carriers that Air India would be planning to induct. An important caveat at this point would be in order: under no circumstances should the views of the concerned service headquarter not be the ultimate deciding factor.

While charting the strategy for the development of our domestic defence industry we must identify technologies that require special attention; technologies where our capabilities merit quantum upgradation. It can be assumed that the DRDO, the services headquarters, and also the CII, would have undertaken studies on this subject. Our acquisition plans must look at integrating the road map that we should have drawn for technology inflows and digestion. Electronics, optics, communications and avionics, are generally the areas that we should be focusing on. We have for a few decades depended exclusively on Bharat Electronics for all our communication requirements as also all our electro-optical products.

Today Bharat Electronics may be a profit making company but has little to offer in terms of future technologies or next generation products. The same story applies to HAL, notwithstanding the successful development of the ALH, which should have been offered at least ten years earlier. There is therefore a strong case to encourage private sector companies to enter these fields. The logic that since the Government has made investments in creating capabilities, all orders must be confined to these companies has proven over time to be counterproductive.

A change in approach is long overdue. India urgently needs an HAL/BE in the private sector. The Government must encourage and support their emergence. The subject of exports has also been grossly neglected. There may be a Joint Secretary in the Department of Defence Production responsible for promoting exports, but he can do little under the present dispensation. Pakistan's Ordnance Factories have consistently exported more than us. No defence industry can expect to sustain itself purely on the basis of sales in the domestic market.

Our private sector, unlike our Government owned establishments, have understood this. But they need much more support. The Government and the industry have to work together in a closely coordinated manner. Witness the way in which over the past few months the Heads of Governments of Germany, UK and France have brought with them the captains of their defence industries to India.

The agenda requires no amplification. Here again we must push to get our act together If India's defence industry is today on the threshold of transformation, considerable credit must be given to the role played by the CII. FICCI has also contributed, but only marginally. We may recall the first Army-Industry Partnership Seminar conducted in the mid nineties under the aegis of the CII. Many of us sceptics murmured-'what's the point?' But CII persevered. It continued with its efforts to nudge the industry and simultaneously influence our policy makers. It has also been actively persuading the big global players to look at teaming with the Indian industry. The results though slow, in the coming times would soon be there for us to witness. Having reached thus far, the CII must not take its foot off the pedal. Much more still needs to be done. Before concluding, some of the suggestions made are listed below:

- Protection to the PSUs and the OFB from domestic players must be progressively withdrawn.
- A major overhaul of the functioning control, organisation and functioning of the OFB and the defence PSUs has been long overdue. Can we not figure out a way to move forward on this issue?
- Pressures to dilute the 'offset clause' of the DPP must be resisted. What we should be focusing on is the mechanisms for monitoring post contract implementation.
- Encourage the absorption of service officers in the defence industry. The rules of interaction with industry representatives must change. The MOD and the services headquarters should be more accessible to domestic industry. Currently doors for foreigners open up much more easily.
- Put in special efforts to promote and assist the growth of the private sector in the areas of aviation, communications, electronics and sensors (optics). There should be a comprehensive action plan for the acquisition of key technologies. The Government and the industry should work in concert on this issue.
- Re-examine our procurement policies and strategies for major purchases. Given the nature of the global market we can perhaps extract much more from our big deals.
- The growth of our defence industry can only be sustained if its business model takes into account the imperative of exports for sustenance.

- The laudable role played by the CII merits recognition. Both the Government and the industry should continue to encourage the CII to step up its activities to accelerate reforms and change.

Our vision for India in the next two decades would be flawed if it did not envisage a sizeable, vibrant and sophisticated defence industry for us that is globally competitive and has the capacity to research and develop new state of the art cutting edge technologies. Our industry has acquired a new found confidence. All it needs is direction and support form the Government. The launch of the Nano within four years of it being conceived has been inspiring. We hope the global awe it has attracted is repeated time and again. We want Nano clones now coming out of India's defence industry stable. With increasing outsourcing opportunities, the Indian aerospace and defence industry is emerging as a key participant in the Asia Pacific aerospace and defence market. Apart from India's perceived viability as an outsourcing hub for aerospace and defence products, the overwhelming involvement of the Government in areas of supply and demand cements its advantage in the industry.

The Government's pro-active soliciting of international cooperation has seen production moving to India, generating more opportunities for the country. Export competitiveness has been given priority, hence, there has been an increased thrust towards reduced import dependency. The Indian economy is one the fastest growing in the world, reflecting the successful reform process initiated in 1991.

The Indian Government has gradually opened its key sectors to foreign participation and foreign investment in the Indian aerospace and defence industry which currently has a 26 percent cap.

Meanwhile, since two-thirds of the Indian population depends on agricultural income, reforms in this area are widely considered necessary to aid economic growth. Development of the agriculture sector, trade, as well as capital liberalisation, and improvement in investments, are some vital areas being focused upon by the current Government. The *Frost & Sullivan* Country Industry Forecast service for the Indian aerospace and defence industry uses a macroeconomic perspective to provide a focused analysis of the industry.

This service covers an array of issues pertaining to the industry including political stances, trade policies, industry regulations, as well as their overall impact. Besides enabling decision makers to assess the impact of non-market forces, this analysis also helps in identifying new opportunities in the industry. In addition, it provides a strong base for preparing business contingency plans.

CHALLENGES OF INDIGENISATION FOR AVIATION INDUSTRY

It would be appropriate to introduce on the working conditions that the airborne items are subjected during service application. This forms the basis of stringent airworthiness requirements and quality control checks before acceptance of spares in service. A few conditions that pose challenges to the development agencies are :-

(a) Aviation Grade Material and Design : The primary challenge is the material selection and structural design, as it involves characterisation of long-term responses of materials and structures to complex and cyclic environmental conditions. Aviation grade materials are required to have minimum scatter property. The simulated service testing to characterise aging is not foolproof due to the inability to reproduce complex service conditions in the laboratory. Important aspects of the environmental conditions encountered in-service cannot be accurately simulated.

(b) Operating Conditions and Stresses :Among the variables that must be considered for the high-speed aircraft applications are operating temperatures, loads, ambient environmental conditions, moisture and fluid exposures, radiation, maintenance, and ground handling. These environments are influenced by changing loads, temperature, humidity, radiation, and other effects that are interactive and cannot be consistently recreated and controlled.

The typical mission of an aircraft involves variations in stress and temperature during flight. The modern day aircraft experience temperature variations due to the effect of aerodynamic heating at supersonic speeds. The skin temperature drops initially as the aircraft climbs due to exposure to decreasing ambient air temperatures. As the speed increases the temperature begins to increase, the skin temperature is in the range of 120°C to 150°C in the speed range of Mach1 to Mach 2.4. Differences in temperature throughout the structure cause different parts of the structure to expand by different amounts, giving rise to thermal stresses, which are added to the other imposed stresses. Once per flight, there is stress variation due to cabin pressurisation and de-pressurisation, as well as stresses that occur during take-off and landing. In addition, there are stresses due to maneuvering and gusts.

The exposure to extremes in ambient temperature ranging from about 60°C to-30°C, moisture from extreme humidity to desert conditions, and radiation, especially ultra-violet can cause degradation of coatings and structural materials or accelerate the damaging effects of flight exposure conditions.

(c) Operating Environment and Corrosion : Corrosion damage to aircraft fuselages is an example of atmospheric corrosion. Aircraft operating in marine environment deserve special mention in this context. The risk and cost of corrosion damage are particularly high in aging aircraft. Corrosion manifests in many different forms. Concentration cell corrosion, or crevice corrosion, is the most common type found in airplanes, occurring whenever water is trapped between two surfaces, such as under loose paint, within a delaminated bond-line, or in an unsealed joint. It can quickly develop into pitting or exfoliation corrosion, depending on the alloy, form, and temper of the material being attacked.

(d) Electromagnetic Interference :Electromagnetic interference is an undesirable disturbance that affects an electrical circuit due to electromagnetic radiation emitted from an external source. The disturbance may interrupt, obstruct, or otherwise degrade or limit the effective performance of the circuit. Aircraft control systems are located entirely within the aircraft and are shielded from absolutely any signals not coming from one of their own devices. They are based entirely on electrical signals conducted through wires, as are most computers. Navigation avionics, on the other hand, must have some designed sensitivity to environmental radio signals in order to perform their function.

(e) Reengineering :Indigenous designs and developments pose greater challenges, particularly in the field of aviation where the know-how is not available from the developed countries due to political and strategic considerations. It is an engineering process of discovering the technological principles of a device, object or system through analysis of its structure, function and operation. It involves considering a mechanical device, electronic component, or software program in isolation and analysing its workings in detail, usually to try to make a new device or program that does the same thing without copying anything from the original.

(f) High Reliability Requirement : The nature of task to be accomplished by an aircraft or missile system leaves no scope for laxity in the quality and reliability of the component. Malfunctioning of even a small component can lead to loss of hundred of crores and human life.

(g) Service Life Average life of an aircraft or weapon system is 20 to 25 years. It is desirable that the component sees through the expected life of system.

INDIA'S DEFENCE POLICY CHALLENGES IN THE 21ST CENTURY

The first macro problem that must be resolved, if India is to rise as a great power, is achieving higher rates of economic growth. The reason for that is simple. A competent military costs money and modern defence capabilities, which are sophisticated and effective, are priced in numbers that boggle the imagination. For a country like India, which has to deal not simply with questions of defence but also questions of development simultaneously, high economic growth becomes the only solution especially in those situations when India cannot choose between the objectives of defence and development. When one begins to think of the revolution in military affairs — the kind of capabilities today that characterize the military forces of the great powers — it is simply impossible for India to acquire such capabilities without sustaining economic growth of at least 7 to 9 per cent per annum consistently.

China is a good example. A country that has experienced close to double-digit growth for more than twenty years since 1978, still finds it hard to develop the kinds of sophisticated military capabilities it seeks to acquire across the board.

Therefore, one must be prepared for the fact that even if the Indian economy were to grow between 7 and 9 per cent consistently for the next twenty years, the best India would be able to do in the area of cutting edge defence technology is to acquire niche capabilities. But those niche capabilities may be enough for the specific strategic circumstances that it faces. The second macro problem that India needs to engage and satisfy is the development of an appropriate national vision and appropriate institutions designed to manage the acquisition of great power capabilities.

What substantive goals, defined in terms of national interest, does India really seek to service? The answer to this question cannot be defined in terms of platitudes like a "just world order." That is a useful phrase for a political campaign. It is a terrible criterion for defence planning and force structuring. The other aspect of this question of defining India's goals and creating the appropriate institutions pertains to the issue of whether India will be able to achieve the right balance between state control and societal autonomy. It is very important to realize that successful states in the modern era have been those that have maintained this balance in the most creative way possible. 77The third macro challenge that I would highlight for your consideration is whether India is capable of exploiting the existing structure of the international system to its advantage. In this context, I think India should get rid of the notion of a multipolar world order as a practical outcome in the relevant future. Pursuing chimerical goals like multipolarity does not make for good policy. The international system, for all practical purposes, is going to remain a unipolar system for at least the next half century. By all indicators, if you define power in terms of comprehensive national strength, it is unlikely that the United States will face serious peer competitors for at least another fifty years.

Consequently, the challenge for India becomes, can it develop a viable strategic partnership with the United States that serves both mutual interests and India's own unilateral interests? Can India develop a relationship with the United States that helps it enhance and magnify its own power?

This is not to suggest that the United States is the only power in the international system. Clearly not — there are many others. This is also not to suggest that India's goals ought to consist solely of developing a relationship with the United States, or that India somehow is constrained solely to develop a relationship with the United States and no other. Not true. India has the flexibility to maneuver within the interstices of the international system. But at the end of the day, there is one eight hundred pound gorilla that has to be engaged. And that is the United States.

That gorilla is not going to go away. That gorilla has already put its nose for the first time in modern history, into the physical environment of the subcontinent. And it is in India's national interest, and important for its capacity to generate and magnify its power, to develop a productive and a collaborative relationship with the United States that enhances the interests of the two countries. First, India has to deal with the challenge of neutering internal security threats without undermining its capacity for effective external defence. This is harder to do than is sometimes imagined. It is unfortunate that the principal security threat that India is going to have to deal with on a day-to-day basis is the threat to internal security. There is no running away from this problem. Historically, India dealt with this challenge by essentially throwing manpower at the threat instead of technology. And the reason it did this was simply because it enjoyed a surfeit of manpower and a deficit of technology.

There were two consequences to this strategy. One was that its approach to preserving internal defence was probably not as effective as it could be, because technology could provide that valuable supplement which was not available to India. The second consequence was that preserving internal security became extremely expensive and has now come at the cost of being able to acquire the new technologies required to raise a modern military force. It is a myth that India's manpower is cheap. Maintaining the size and kind of forces that India does, if maintained over the secular period, will undercut its ability to acquire the kind of RMA capabilities that wins modern wars. And this is going to require India to make very painful choices — painful choices about reducing its manpower strength and changing the inter-service budgetary balances, choices that it cannot make today because of the gravity, importance, and burdens of its internal security commitments.

The next micro issue is the need to preserve effective external defence, now in a nuclear shadowed environment. This brings us face to face with the vexed question of whether India has the capacity to successfully prosecute a limited war. Most commentary so far has focused on the issue of limited war as an example of Indian recklessness. People have chastised that limited war in fact represents a solution to India's external security problems. My take on the issue is somewhat different. I believe that limited war should be viewed not as a product of the proclivities of the state, but rather as a predicament resulting from a specific set of structural circumstances.

The transparent presence of nuclear weapons in the subcontinent for the first time makes unlimited wars untenable as a matter of state policy. This is not simply India's choice — it actually represents a dilemma of the nuclear age. And it is a challenge that faces India both with respect to Pakistan and with respect to China. In both cases, unlimited war is not feasible. There is also no guarantee that war is obsolete. And therefore the challenge of limited war confronts India squarely, both with respect to its northern and its western borders.

What does limited war mean for Indian defence policy? It means that India is now confronted with the task of being required to hit hard and effectively enough to punish an adversary, but not hit so hard or so effectively as to cause inadvertent escalation. This in turn leads to questions like "how do you avoid escalation?" Most commentaries have focused on this aspect of the problem. But there is another aspect to the problem, which has largely escaped attention. Because it is going to demand of India a new style of war fighting that New Delhi traditionally has been uncomfortable with and which historically it has been relatively incapable of. It is a style of war fighting that puts a premium on achieving very speedy decision on the battlefield and then terminating offensive action either before the international community intervenes or before the conflict degenerates into unavoidable attrition. Getting the Indian military to successfully prosecute a fast paced war that generates quick decisions is something that we have not seen in fifty years of India's independence. It is also the kind of war that traditionally the United States was not very good at. We preferred wars that allowed us plenty of time to mobilize, plenty of time to deploy, and then plenty of time to be able to grind down the adversary at our convenience. If India is to be able to prosecute the opposite kind of war, as the United States is now proficient at — fast, decisive, and yet limited — it is going to require an investment in new technologies and new operating skills apart from new doctrines and new concepts of operation.

Third, if India is to become a great power of the sort that it seeks to become, it also has to become a net provider of regional security, both in the sub-continental and in the extra sub-continental arenas. This is easier said than done; yet at one level it is the quintessential part of the definition of a great power. After all, what is the meaning of having great power capabilities if at the end of the day you cannot extend net security to others? And yet any Indian attempt to provide the kind of regional security that I am talking of, even in the sub-continental arena, is fraught with hazards because it risks deepening intra-regional rivalries and it risks deepening the suspicions India's weaker neighbours have of its capabilities and its intentions. Finally, will India develop the organizational structures that are required to maintain and operate these capabilities if it seeks to provide the kind of regional security that is to be expected of a great power?

The fourth micro problem pertains to whether India can acquire an effective nuclear deterrent without breaking the bank. My view is that nuclear weapons are important for India's security in some limited sense, but it is also essential to remember that they are actually relatively obsolescent technologies. Nuclear weapons are now over fifty years old and they are generally unusable as instruments of international politics.

DEFENCE PRODUCTION AND SUPPLY

The Defence Production Department created in 1962 and the Department of Defence Supply set up in 1965 were merged in 1984 to constitute the Department of Defence Production and Supplies. Presently, 39 Ordnance factories and eight Defence Public Sector Undertakings (DPSUs) come under this department. The Directorate of Quality Assurance, Air Technical Development and Production (Air), Standardisation, and Exhibition Organisation also form part of this Department.

The Ordnance Factories produce more than 1,500 items of arms, ammunition, equipment and components. Most of these products constitute relatively low to medium technology items. Twenty per cent of the output goes to non-defence customers. Due to the very high cost of production, delivery delays and suspect quality, it has not been possible to meet export targets and, sometimes, even orders given by the Services. Ordnance factories as well as DPSUs need to shed the manufacture of low technology items to the private sector and focus on hi-tech products. They should also be in a position to take up substantial product improvement themselves and not be dependent on DRDO.

Defence Planning Tools

In recent years, defence economics and management techniques have made an important contribution to defence planning. A number of techniques such as Operational Research and Systems Analysis (ORSA), Planning Programming and Budgeting System have been developed to make the planning process more systematic and to maximise the benefits obtained from the given amount of resources. Systems Analysis can assist in developing rational procedures for procurement of new weapons systems. Systems performance at design stage can be evaluated through computer simulation. Planners all over the world are using computerised war-gaming techniques and structure analysis. Prospects exist for a more enlightened approach that can bring together military officers, historians, technologists and quantitative analysts.

In many countries, there is a growing interest in analytical realism, operational relevance and integrated defence planning. In India the Services are far behind in introducing these aids in our defence planning system. The planning directorates in Service Headquarters do not even have data banks which can provide relevant information on a specified subject. Most of the planners have high combat and command qualifications but little clue of the modern techniques. There is an urgent need to introduce modern planning aids into our planning system. Defence planners should also learn the basic principles and techniques of economic analysis and not leave it to their 'Finance' colleagues.

Management of Defence Budget

A major lacuna in defence planning and implementation has been lack of financial commitment for the Plan period. Financially, the defence plans are treated more as annual plans rather than composite five years plan. There is a rush to spend the annual capital budget by the end of the financial year since the amount not spent has to be surrendered. In FY 2004-05, the previous government had proposed to institute a non-lapsable Defence Modernisation Fund of Rs 25,000 crore. This was a long awaited reform in the defence-finance mechanism as budgeted capital expenditure worth thousands of crores was surrendered year after year. However, the new government, being of the view that there are no provisions in the budgetary rules and regulations to carry forward unspent funds for three years, has done away with this reform.

It needs to be pointed out that a similar procedure was being followed in the 1930s and 1940s. The provisions invoked at that time need to be studied carefully and could be used as a precedent. Action should be taken expeditiously to revive the Defence Modernization Fund. Otherwise, funds earmarked for capital expenditure on an annual basis will continue to lapse, leading to lack of systematic defence preparedness.

In the Revenue Budget, there is a need to include incentives to save and reduce annual maintenance expenditure without adversely affecting operational efficiency. It is also necessary to exploit the increasing domestic industrial capability to support the existing infrastructure and thus reduce maintenance costs and enhance the quality of maintenance.

Human Resources Management

The development of human resources must keep pace with the modernisation of the armed forces so that new, state-of-the-art equipment can be optimally exploited by well trained and motivated soldiers, sailors and airmen. The age profile of military personnel, particularly in the Army, and the age of commanders at battalion and brigade levels needs to be looked into. Currently, a soldier has to serve for 15 to 17 years to earn his pension. When he retires, besides the lifelong pension that has to be paid, a trained individual is lost to the nation. Similarly, while there is a shortage of approximately 14,000 officers, most officers retire in rank of Lieutenant Colonel or Colonel at the age of 52-54 years when they still have years of productive life ahead though they are no longer fit for active combat. Innovative measures need to be adopted to reduce the effects of the current national loss on this account. The best method would be to institute a procedure of 'lateral induction" under which both officers and personnel below officer rank can be transferred to central police and paramilitary forces(CPMFs). The colour (active) service of jawans should be reduced to 7-10 years with no pension liability after which the volunteers are transferred to the BSF, CRPF, ITBP, CISF and other such forces. Similarly, the Shipping Corporation of India, National Port Trust and other such maritime organisations can fruitfully employ Naval personnel. Ex-servicemen will be expected to serve in these organisations till superannuation, after which they would be entitled to pension. This will improve the age profile of the Services, provide trained manpower to the CPMFs, ensure productive long-term employment for a large number of trained men till superannuation, and also reduce the pension bill of the Central Government.

The Army should increase the recruitment of Short Service Officers to make up its shortfall. Induction of these officers to the CPMFs after five years of service will improve junior leadership and effectiveness of these forces in internal security and counter insurgency operations.

Recommendations

- Given the fluid strategic environment and the rapid advances in defence technology, there is a need for judicious allocation of the limited budgetary resources. Long lead times are required for creating futuristic

Forces, hence the need to make long-term defence planning mandatory. Greater synergy between defence and development plans is required.

- The lack of a cohesive national security strategy and defence policy has resulted in inadequate political direction regarding politico-military objectives. The Government should prepare a clear national security strategy, defence policy, and review it every 4-5 years.
- In view of the time taken to create the capabilities necessary for facing future threats and challenges, it is essential for the Defence Services to evolve 10 to 15-year perspective plans with the required budgetary support.
- The Chiefs of Staff Committee has not been successful in preparing comprehensive 'integrated defence plans' due to emphasis on single Service planning and constant competition among the Services for a bigger share of resources. The civilian bureaucrats in the MoD do not have the professional expertise to decide on inter-Service priorities. Hence, the early appointment of Chief of Defence Staff (CDS) is essential as he will be the cornerstone for integrated defence and operational planning.
- A non-lapsable Defence Modernisation Fund must be expeditiously created to ensure that allocations are optimally utilised and funds earmarked for capital acquisitions are not allowed to lapse.
- The Revenue Budget of the Services needs to be better managed. Annual maintenance expenditure can be curtailed by greater exploitation of the available public and private sector industrial infrastructure capability and offering incentives to the Services to save.
- To ensure smooth progress towards self-reliance in defence technology, the Government must undertake a periodic performance audit of the DRDO plans and projects. The review should reinforce efforts in areas of success and weed out unproductive projects.

- Ordnance Factories should produce only hi-tech products and shed the production of low-tech items to the private sector.
- Integrated Defence Staff and the Services' perspective planners should acquire expertise in operational research and systems analysis, as also financial planning, for evolving complex integrated defence plans.
- In order to improve the age profile of the Services and simultaneously reduce the pension bill of the Central Government, personnel below officer rank should be transferred to central police and paramilitary forces (CPMFs) after active service of 7-10 years.
- The Army should increase recruitment of Short Service Officers to make up its shortfall. Induction of these officers to the CPMFs after five years of service will improve junior leadership and effectiveness of these forces in internal security and counter insurgency operations.

Defence planning has been neglected for long in India. This has led to ad-hocism in decision-making and adversely affected the modernisation plans of the Services. The key issues needing immediate attention include the need for formal prior approval for five-year defence Plans, better management of the defence revenue and capital acquisition budgets, streamlining of the defence procurement process and better human resources management. The Government of India should appoint a group of eminent experts to study the present defence planning process, identify the lacunae and grey areas in the process and recommend structural and procedural changes. The aim should be to streamline defence planning, harmonize it with national development plans, and make the process more responsive in order to deal effectively with the rapidly changing geo-strategic and regional security environment.

CHALLENGES IN DEFENCE PLANNING

Defence planning is essentially a subset of overall national level planning in the political, economic and social spheres and has to be evolved in the context of global and proximate factors affecting the nation.. It has also to take into account the philosophy and ethos animating the national psyche; in other words the historical and cultural forces which have shaped the collective memory and outlook of the people over the centuries. The Cold War, was a classic example of the factors stated above. There were fundamental philosophical differences between the adversaries – the western bloc, advocating the virtues of free enterprise and its own interpretations of democracy, and the Soviet bloc, equally strongly asserting the merits of the socialist system as the only one genuinely meeting democratic aspirations and assuring social equality and economic well-being of the people as a whole, rather than for a few. Fifty years of the Cold War could not conclude the capitalism-socialism debate, though, in the end, it did push the socialist forces into, perhaps temporary, retreat. This was because the struggle was really for power and domination. "The evil empire" of Ronald Reagan's description may have withered away, but the necessity for the US to target the so called "rogue states" has not disappeared.

Many examples can be found of philosophical differences leading to stand-offs, usually with the USA as one of the parties. The USA-Cuba divide is a long-standing one. USA-Venezuela stand-off is just developing and resonating in other Latin American countries. Sometimes the differences are couched in the language of anticipated threats, such as in US-North Korea, or US-Iran relations. The true reasons and underlying causes are buried in verbiage and obfuscation. A more serious rift has developed over the selective and poorly conceptualised US war on terrorism, launched for spurious reasons in Iraq, when the real source of terror was elsewhere and far more complex. Differing religious beliefs and rigidities are often cited as causes but do not sufficiently explain conflicts within the same religion, as between Protestants and Catholics in Northern Ireland or the Shias and Sunnis in Iraq and elsewhere.

Planning for the security and defence of a vast country like India with its particular geographic location, historical experiences and associations, social, ethnic, religious and cultural diversity, political and economic structure and a large, relatively poor, democratically governed population, is a complex and challenging task. It is rendered more so in the context of the national and international situation in the last sixty years or so, embracing post-World War II de-colonisation, partition, the creation of Pakistan and later Bangladesh, conflicts with Pakistan and China, the Cold War and its aftermath, the disintegration of the Soviet Union, the re-definition of NATO's role, and of most recent and decisive significance, the September 11, 2001 terror attack on the United States mainland. This last factor is significant because it resulted in a major re-orientation in US foreign policy.

Strategic Overview

Planning for defence pre-supposes identification of threats and contingencies. Until about five years ago, the strategic situation for India was difficult but relatively clear. Pakistan was a definite threat, conventional, clandestine and nuclear. China was a strategically reducing threat, though its international power, influence and economy were growing. Uncertainties in Bangladesh and Nepal required us to be vigilant for fall-out effects. There were problems in the north-east of insurgent groups exploiting the ethnic ties and jungles in Myanmar, and the destabilising spill-over effects of the activities of the Liberation Tigers for Tamil Eelam(LTTE) in Sri Lanka. The presence in our proximate waters, of non-littoral naval forces in substantial numbers, such as those of the US, which has been traditionally supportive of Pakistan, had to be taken cognisance of.

Also the fact that warfare at sea, because of its distinctive characteristics of rapidity of concentration and dispersal of forces, mobility, flexibility and speed of execution, requires a different, longer term approach to threat assessment. Strategically the global situation is now evolving in a manner less inimical to India's interests than in the preceding fifty years. Yet the end of the Cold War did not see any easing of pressures on India. On the contrary, economic sanctions and technology denials were increased so as to coerce India to conform to norms of international behaviour prescribed by dominant world powers, led by the US and the European Union on the one hand and China on the other. The reason was the desire of the P-5, the five permanent members of the UN Security Council, who are also the N-5, the self-certified nuclear powers, to preserve their monopoly power status in the face of India's challenge through the nuclear tests of 1998. Yet, the re-evaluation of foreign policies by leading powers set off by the September 11, 2001 terrorist attack on the USA, has initiated processes that are, by and large, beneficial to India. An indication of this is the US declaration of seeing India as a strategic partner for the 21st century, and its efforts to legislate exceptions to its domestic laws to allow supply of nuclear materials for peaceful civilian use to India by the cartel operated by the Nuclear Suppliers Group (NSG).

Nearer home, the pathological hostility of the Pakistanis establishment towards India is rooted in its quest for a national identity, which no novel interpretations, distortions or reinventions of sub-continental history seem able to provide. It will be a long time before there can be normal relations with Pakistan because they are influenced more by the internal contradictions and dynamics of the Pakistani state rather than considerations of mutual benefits through good relations. Since the Pakistan army is the self-appointed guardian of the undefined "ideology of Pakistan", normalcy will come when the Army decides it should be so; or the cost-benefit equation alters.

With China, there is perceptible progress on resolving disputes and fostering economic and cultural relations. As for Nepal, Bangladesh, Myanmar and Sri Lanka, there is no significant positive change, and because of shared borders, internal problems in those countries will continue to spill over into India. Instability in Afghanistan remains a cause of concern, especially because of Pakistan's dubious role, and this will have its impact on the pursuit of India's energy and strategic interests in Central Asia.

Non-littoral naval forces in significant numbers are still present in the Indian Ocean, but there is no coercive or inimical intent as in the past. Indeed, the Indian Navy holds regular friendly exercises with them on a routine basis. China's long term plans for a naval presence in the region have to be taken note of. There are ample signs of Chinese maritime interest, starting from building and operating communications facilities in Myanmar to financing and building Pakistan's Gwadar Port on the Makran coast, collaboration in building warships for the Pakistan navy at Karachi shipyard, as well as port building in Sri Lanka. On the western rim of the Indian Ocean, China is vigorously pursuing options in Africa, underlined by the meeting of 49 heads of state/government in Beijing in early November this year.

National Objectives in the Long Term

Planning for defence has to be in the framework of national objectives over a period of decades ahead, even if these are not publicly articulated. USA does not hesitate to state its intention to remain the dominant global technological, space and military power for the foreseeable future and tailors strategic policies accordingly. China has, by its actions, investments and developments over the years, demonstrated that it intends to be at least the equal of the USA, though with "Chinese characteristics". Pakistan makes no secret of its intention to be "different" from India, and to compete with and undermine India at every opportunity.

India too has shown in various ways that it intends to be in the forefront of nations in every sphere: economic, technological, industrial and human development. What about military capability? Does it wish to have only a capacity to ward off aggression by land and sea? Or does it aspire to play a larger role in the region? If it emerges as the world's third or fourth largest economy in a few years, would a commensurate military role follow? Or are national objectives to be largely achieved by a combination of diplomacy and economic policies? If it aspires for a permanent seat in the UN Security Council, is it prepared for the increased diplomatic and military responsibilities attached? Many of these seemingly philosophical issues require to be debated to facilitate meaningful defence planning for the future.

ORGANISATION FOR DEFENCE PLANNING

Planning for defence involves almost all aspects of government, not only because of the extreme seriousness of the undertaking, but also because a long duration war will require marshalling the total resources of the nation. It can never be presumed that hostilities will always be of short duration, as there is a tendency to do so in the context of India-Pakistan conflicts. Many instances in history illustrate this, for example the US misadventure in Iraq. The US-led coalition forces were injected on the assumption of a quick victory, a warm welcome by Iraqi citizenry and a glorious return home for Christmas. They are still there nearly three years later, as also in Afghanistan, with no indications of an early resolution of the conflicts. Madeleine Albright, the former US Secretary of State has this to say about the US Iraq expedition: "We have damaged our reputation very badly. Iraq may turn out to be the greatest disaster in American foreign policy, which by its very nature means that it is worse than Vietnam.

In this context, it is worth recalling the words attributed to Fredrick the Great: "No war is accidental or unintended. The only thing unintended is the bloodiness and duration of the conflict. Defeat too is unintended".

No rational planning can be done on basis of a worst-case scenario. Apart from being illogical, it is unaffordable, and therefore unachievable. Rather, realistic defence planning requires a thorough and detailed analysis and evaluation of the security environment, threat perceptions, technological assessments, etc. and should result in an integrated defence plan. Such a plan should be linked to national capacity in the civil sector and integrate utilisation of resources such as road transport, civil aviation and technical manpower in a pre-determined manner for war.

British Example Through almost four hundred years of wars and colonial expansion and contraction, the British learnt to restructure their fleets and armies as the situation demanded and finances allowed.

This was not done at the cost of contingency planning and military effectiveness, as the rapid mobilisation at the time of the Falklands war in 1982 showed. A major defence costs study, *Front Line First* was initiated in 1994, whereby the entire UK defence organisation was to be reorganised to effect economies, especially at headquarters, with maximum integration of civil and military staff at all levels, enhanced delegation of financial powers and simplification of procedures.

Some of the conclusions of the Study could apply equally to Indian defence organisations:

The Ministry of Defence Head Office and other headquarters at all levels were seen as being too large, too top heavy and too bureaucratic. The process of delegating responsibility to individual budgetholders was generally seen as the key to maximising efficiency. There were too many minor rules and regulations that were rigidly applied, and stood in the way of maximising value for money.

There was a need for greater cost consciousnessso that costs could be linked more explicitly to output. Rationalisation of command, training and support structures on a joint Service basis could increase operational effectiveness as well as offer savings. (Huge differences in the size of the three services and the sub-continental geographic spread would make this impractical in India).

Changes were necessary in the culture of the Department, in simplification of working practices and in placing more weight on personal responsibility and accountability. The possible savings envisaged according to the study were:

- Equipment and Logistics-51 per cent.
- Estate and Support Infrastructure – 14 per cent.
- Organisation and Management – 16 per cent.
- Personnel and Training – 19 per cent.

The reduction in Head Office personnel was to be drastic indeed, from 12,700 in 1990, to 5,200 in 1995 and finally to 3,750 by 1998.

The report contains other interesting observations that have relevance for us:

- There is no single body below the Ministerial level with authority and responsibility for the full range of the Department's policy activity and management. (One may ask whether this is feasible or even desirable).
- Align single Service Chief of Staff's responsibility as professional head, with financial responsibility and accountability.

The MoD in UK is a unique *integrated* organisation in the government, as it is both a Department of State, as well as the headquarters of the Armed Forces as a whole. The Study states: "The importance of preserving clear lines of functional responsibility to Ministers for the different aspects of the business remains. We do not believe that this requires parallel, separate, military or civilian hierarchies. It was encouraging that the study found little evidence of this in the existing structure".

United States Experience

Whereas the UK defence organisation has evolved over a considerable period in a measured way, the Defence structure in the United States in its present form is largely a post-World War II creation. Due to the preponderant role of the US armed forces during and after the war ("*military policy was foreign policy*"), its emergence as a SuperPower with a global reach, the requirements of major wars (Korea and Vietnam), the Cold War, numerous smaller military involvements, and because of the possibility of nuclear war, the US defence organisation has become extraordinarily large and complex.

A further impetus for change and streamlining of the US, UK and other European defence organisations, was the creation of the North Atlantic Treaty Organisation(NATO) and the Warsaw Pact and the half-century long nuclear stand-off between the Western and the Soviet blocs. These changes were brought about by stark necessity and were *politically driven*, often in the teeth of opposition and even sabotage by the civil and military establishments. The fear of a pre-emptive nuclear attack without warning drove the adversaries to demonstrate an organisational capability to retaliate instantaneously and overwhelmingly, and thus hope to deter the attack altogether.

Major organisational changes in the USA, such as the creation of a Joint Chiefs of Staff Committee (JCSC), and a national security set-up were initiated during President Truman's time in 1947. The last major reorganisation was in 1986 under the Goldwater-Nichols Act of 1986.

Changes in UK followed, notably under Prime Minister Margaret Thatcher. It should be remembered that fear of nuclear war was very real in the minds of national leaderships and military planners during the Cold War. Extremely complex and high cost weapon systems were developed and money had to be found by curtailing duplication and waste in the armed forces and in the civilian and military bureaucracies.

Apart from operational considerations, the creation of the Joint Chiefs of Staff (JCS) in the USA and the CDS in the UK were felt to be necessary for budgetary reasons, to clarify lines of control and responsibility, and to facilitate legislative supervision. All democracies require that armed forces be firmly under civil direction and control, but there is also nagging fear that somehow they manage to evade legislative oversight. In mature democracies, these concerns are not necessarily about relative power, but about better financial management of the requirements of the state, and the apportioning of the budgetary pie. The aim is also to forestall military inspired adventures. Sometimes, however, it is the civilian political authority that goads the military into action, as the USA did in Iraq, despite sound advice to the contrary.

Delays, Cost Overruns and Failures

Despite the more evolved and refined systems of defence management in advanced countries, delays, cost overruns and plain failures of major weapons systems are not infrequent. Here is what the US Government Accountability Office has to say about the Pentagon's failure "to deliver high quality products in a timely and cost-efficient fashion", asserting that future national security is at risk as a result It is "not unusual to see cost increases that add up to tens or hundreds of millions of dollars, schedule delays that add up to years and large and expensive programmes frequently re-baselined or even scrapped after years of failing to achieve promised capability". The GAO also criticised the lack of accountability in the Department of Defence, and that the Pentagon "has never clearly specified who is accountable for what, invested responsibility for execution in any single individual, or even required programme leaders to stay until the job is done."

The UK experience is much the same as far as major defence projects are concerned. For example, according to the National Audit Office major projects report, the current cost estimates for the three latest Astute class nuclear attack submarines (SSNs) has risen from UK Pounds 2.6 billion to UK Pounds 3.5 billion. The project has barely survived "cost overruns and schedule delays, arising from a combination of poor project management, an immature computer-aided design (CAD) tool and a haemorrhaging of skills and experience in the submarine industry".

Planning for a future submarine nuclear deterrent platform is also not very optimistic. Assuming the UK government takes a decision in 2006, the submarine is not likely to be delivered before 2024, which according to the UK Director General Nuclear and Controller of the Navy, Rear Admiral Andy Mathews, "sounds a long way off, but is actually quite a tight timescale for something like this". If this is the fate of defence planning in mature and experienced countries such as in the UK and the USA, is it any surprise that our planning too is beset with inadequacies?

5

Make in India: Challenges Before Defence Manufacturing

There is a distinctive buzz about Prime Minister Modi's new campaign for "Make in India". The thrust is to increase share of manufacturing from the current level of 15 per cent of Gross Domestic Product (GDP) to 25 per cent and create additional employment opportunity of ten million per year. This has led a few cynics to observe that, "There is a lot of sizzle but where is the steak?" Columnists such as Swaminathan Iyer are of the view that "Make in India" is only an outcome and not a policy while Governor of RBI Raghuram Rajan is of the view that the government is putting too much of thrust on export-led growth and should give primacy to "Make for India". Discerning writers such as Debasis Basu however, feel that what is germane to the debate is the "cost of doing business" in India.

The defence services account for nearly Rs 2.29 lakh crore of the Central Government Budget... Defence manufacturing came out of the stranglehold of Public Sector Undertakings-Ordnance Factories (PSU-OF) monopoly with major liberalisation in 2001 with 100 per cent private sector participation and the recently announced 49 per cent in Foreign Direct Investment. Policy footprints such as the Defence Procurement Policy (DPP) 2013 have created a level playing field for the private sector. The Defence Production Policy 2011 aims at higher self reliance in critical technology and the Offsets Policy 2012 which seeks to leverage our big arms' acquisition to bring in state-of-art technology, and long term partnership with Original Equipment Manufacturers (OEMs). The Self Reliance Index of our defence acquisition, however, remains at a wobbly 30 per cent despite spasmodic policy posturing to improve indigenisation.

Defence industry is a subset of a nation's concern to ramp up manufacturing capability. The capability of our defence industry in terms of value addition, self reliance in critical technology and policy initiatives so far and their impact needs to examined and a possible synergy between "Make in India" policy and defence industry capability needs to be brought about.

DEFENCE MANUFACTURING AND CHALLENGES IN SELF RELIANCE

The defence services account for nearly Rs 2.29 lakh crore of the Central Government Budget which is nearly 2.5 per cent of the GDP and 13 per cent of the Central Government expenditure. The trend of allocation to revenue and capital acquisition schemes is given below.

It would be worth to note that while the increase in the revenue allocation roughly matches with the wholesale price escalation, the capital acquisition budget has witnessed significant growth of around 20 per cent per year, far outstripping the overall trend of increase in defence expenditure. Capital Acquisition constitutes nearly 40 per cent of the defence budget of which the value of production of the Defence PSUs and the OFs account for the following:

It would be seen from the above that while the average yearly increase in Value of Production (VOP) of Defence PSUs is around five per cent per year, in case of the OFs it is only two per cent. It would be interesting to note that the value addition of different defence PSUs varies between 23 per cent and 57 per cent; it is very high, about 85 per cent, for OFB.

PSUs such as HAL and MDL show a poor level of value addition as they are largely system integrators while Midhani and BDL have contributed handsomely to indigenisation. The higher indigenisation in case of OFBs is largely attributable to the low end technology.

Historically, India has been availing of technology through licence agreements from Russia and a smattering of Western countries. The exceptions are some of the missile systems, small arms and their ammunition and tanks where technology has been indigenously developed by the Defence Research and Development Organisation (DRDO). The Light Combat Aircraft (LCA) Tejas with Final Operational Clearance (FOC) will hopefully be a major "Make in India" platform. It must be mentioned that indigenisation has effected a substantial reduction in cost of the systems due to India's labour arbitrage, good facilities and fairly well-trained labour force. The following table brings out the cost savings of a few major products through the Transfer of Technology (ToT) route.

Self-Reliance Trends

Self-reliance trends in defence acquisition present a dismal picture. A committee under Dr APJ Abdul Kalam, the then Scientific Advisor to the Raksha Mantri, had recommended that India should ramp up this quotient from 30 per cent (1995) to 70 per cent by (2005). The following table, however, brings out how the Self Reliance Index has remained sticky at around 30 per cent.

The principal reason for this state of affairs is our poor design capability in critical technologies, inadequate investment in R&D and our inability to manufacture major sub-systems and components. The Transfer of Technology route has provided India with the know-how without providing the clue for know why. It is due to this that even for an upgrade of the systems, defence PSUs are critically dependent on the original licensors. A case in point is the SU-30 upgrade where the Russians often hold HAL to ransom. The following table brings out the gaps in critical technology of different systems.

From the table above, it would be seen that the major deficiency in terms of capability is in the areas of propulsion, weapons and sensors. Some of the critical technologies where progress made by the DRDO has been abysmally poor are Focal Plane Array (FPA), Active Electronically Scanned Array (AESA) Radar and Stealth Technology. India is presently engaged in the design and production collaboration with Russia for a Fifth Generation Fighter Aircraft (FGFA), that will have stealth features.

India is presently engaged in the design and production collaboration with Russia for a Fifth Generation Fighter Aircraft.

PROCUREMENT, PRODUCTION AND OFFSETS POLICY IN RETROSPECT AND THEIR IMPACT

The Defence Procurement Policy 2013 envisages higher preference to Buy (India), Buy and Make (India), and Make options over the earlier thrust towards Buy (Global) or the import option. It ostensibly looks at creating a better level playing field between the Public and Private sector with greater impetus towards indigenisation. A major departure from the previous policy is allowing the private Indian industry to avail of ToT which was earlier the exclusive domain of DPSUs/OFs. The policy also encourages Joint Venture with OEMs. Prime Minister Modi's "Make in India" campaign has added another category to Defence Acquisition though it would include cases coming under the panoply of 'Buy and Make' and 'Make' where technology is indigenously developed.

The Offset Policy guidelines (2012) have for the first time allowed ToT through the JV or through non-equity route. It has also allowed multiplier for critical technology areas such as FPAs, Nano Technology-based sensor, fiber laser technology and THZ technologies.

The Defence Production Policy (2011) aimed at achieving substantive self-reliance in design, development and production of critical sub-systems by forming consortia, JVs by involving academia and R&D institutions. It also promised to set up a defence technology fund to support public, private sector as well as academic and scientific institutions for pursuing high-end research. The impact of all such policies on FDI inflow, export, augmentation and long term partnership has been quite disappointing for reasons enumerated below. Value addition in the global value chain for India was only one per cent in 2009 as against nine per cent in China and Germany...

FDI Policy

The OEMs for setting up business in India in partnership with public/private players want to have a major say in the management of manufacturing. While the announcement to scale up the FDI limit from 26 per cent to 49 per cent in the last budget has been a step in the right direction, it is unlikely to enthuse reputed global manufacturing houses to set up manufacturing bases and bring in front-end technology though some Joint Venture intents have been evinced for companies like the Tatas. On the other hand, countries such as China and South Korea have become major manufacturing hubs in aeronautics and ship building technology by being very liberal in their FDI policy and providing high modicum of 'Ease of Doing' business compared to India.

Besides the FDI policy, inadequate investment in R&D and lip service to technology funding by making a token allocation of Rs100 crore to Defence Technology Fund in the last budget is adequate commentary on our lack of seriousness in the area of Research and Development. The allocation to DRDO remains sticky – around six per cent of defence expenditure though successive parliamentary committees have recommended a minimum allocation of ten per cent. Private sector giants such as the Tata, L&T and Mahindra and Mahindra invest less than one per cent of their turnover in R&D unlike in countries such as France where corporate organisations invest more than ten per cent in R&D. It would also be interesting to note that the overall allocation to R&D is significantly lower (0.85 per cent) in India compared to advanced countries which spend in the range of 2.2 per cent to 3.5 per cent. The following table would bring out the trend.

Manufacturing

Manufacturing accounts for 14 to 16 per cent of the GDP with 85 per cent of employment in unorganised sector, with a 'missing middle'. This is unlike manufacturing hubs in Korea, China, Germany and Japan where 50 per cent of the firms are large with the benefit of economy of scale and 20 per cent are SEMs. Value addition in the global value chain for India was only one per cent in 2009 as against nine per cent in China and Germany. National Manufacturing Zone (NMZ) 2011 policy is limping big time in the absence of Centre – State synergy, tardy land acquisition and long drawn environmental clearances. Subir Gokran has rightly observed that increase in Incremental Capital Output Ratio (ICOR) from 3.1 per cent (2005-2006) to 5.9 per cent (2012-2013) is largely attributable to supply constraints such as power-coal imbalance and inordinate project delays.

Export Promotion

The following table provides a trend analysis of exports by Defence PSUs and Ordnance Factories since 2008 – 2009. Of the PSUs/OFB, HAL & BEL account for 66 per cent of exports. Export as share of Value of Sales (VOS) has remained around three per cent for HAL and around three to four per cent for BEL thereby showing the policies so far have not impacted on their export performance.

Almost 50 per cent of China's GDP growth is attributable to total factor productivity growth... Raghuram Rajan sounds a note of caution regarding the obsession for export-led growth by heavily subsidising inputs at the cost of fostering domestic demand. His call for "Make for India" to supplement "Make in India" is an extremely welcome alternative.

Impact of Offset Contracts

After promulgation of this policy in 2005, 24 contracts have been signed for $4.8 billion. However, discerning analysts observe that the expected benefit in terms of FDI inflow, high end technology, increased export and outsourcing have not taken place. The C&AG, in its performance audit of Fleet Tanker Contract (2010), has brought out how the full benefit of offsets provision has not been availed of from the OEM. Further, the C&AG's comprehensive report of 2012 on offsets contracts severely castigates the inept contractual arrangement that underlies such offset arrangements and additional cost implication.

Manufacturing, "Make In India" Policy and Defence Manufacturing

Since liberalisation in the 1990s, the sectoral share of the primary, secondary and tertiary segments shows a tectonic shift wafting through the corridors. The share of Agriculture in the GDP shows a significant reduction while the share of Industry has remained stagnant with the Service sector showing the way as the sunshine sector.

The following table brings out the trends in the compositional shift. A disaggregation of the Secondary sector shows that the share of manufacturing sector has increased from around 15 per cent to 25 per cent. The experience of manufacturing giants like Germany, South Korea and China reveal that manufacturing accounts for 30 per cent of their GDP.

The defence industry, be it public sector or private, has to be part of the national manufacturing policy mosaic... Therefore, the thrust of the government to encourage "Make in India" option by facilitating the enabling environment to manufacture, improving ease of doing business, encouraging creation of national manufacturing zones in tandem with the states and investing one trillion dollar through the PPP route in the infrastructural sector make eminent sense. Professor Basu rightly observes out that the success of the "Make in India" policy will critically hinge on the cost of doing business in India.

Two critical factors for this would be the quality of human resources and cost of capital. India's education system is presently mired in a mess and needs millions of skilled workers coming out of the ITIs with quality training. While access to education at the primary level through the Right to Education has improved access significantly, the quality deficit, both in the primary segment and higher education is palpable. While the private sector has contributed handsomely to the growth of technical and management education, the quality of education and lack of research impact on the employability of students adversely despite the global opportunity.

As regards the Cost of Capital, the following table would bring out the disturbing trend of exorbitant Costs of Capital in India compared to the developed countries. What is interesting also to note that most of the BRIC countries are bedeviled by high Cost of Capital and unacceptable levels of inflation accentuating their "Misery Index".

Importance of Total Factor Productivity

Professor Solow, a Nobel Laureate, in his seminal paper had brought out the importance of factor productivity. His equation Q=A * K" Lâ where Q is the production function, A is the level of technology and scale, K & L are factors of production " & â are factor efficiency has demonstrated how US has become the premier technological hegemon after World War II. A case in point is the phenomenal growth in China from 1979 as would be evident from the following table. Almost 50 per cent of China's GDP growth is attributable to total factor productivity growth.

Lessons for India's Defence Industry

The defence industry in India cannot be impervious to these trends. It has to be sensitive to skill requirements in order to absorb high technology which comes as part of ToT. One of the predominant reasons for Japan's phenomenal growth since the 1950s has been their highly skilled labour force which could absorb front-end technology from the US quickly and adopt it to harness commercial success through dual use technology. Japan's success in electronics and automobile is testimony to this.

The DRDO remains mired in inordinate delay, huge cost overruns and deficient in critical technology areas like 'seekers' and 'stealth'... In India, on the other hand, the ToT experience reveals that the technology absorption has been inordinately slow leading to continued dependence for our foreign collaborators well beyond the originally contracted period. Experience of HAL in terms of production of the MiG series of aircraft and SU-30 and for MDL for producing Scorpene submarines are grim reminders of our poor high skill absorbing capability.

Conclusion

India is witnessing a significant stickiness in its manufacturing sector which is bedeviled by the huge presence of small scale and informal sector that are bereft of requisite skill levels and economy of scale. Their access to capital is also seriously impeded. However, the manufacturing sector provides a wonderful opportunity for India to be part of the global supply chain and generate high levels of employment opportunity to absorb around ten million young Indians who will come in to the market in search of employment every year. They also need to be properly skilled and trained and networked with their global peers.

The defence industry, be it public sector or private, has to be part of the national manufacturing policy mosaic. Unfortunately, the defence sector often chooses to distance itself in its interface with other civilian sectors. There is opportunity aplenty in areas such as aerospace and ship building where there is considerable civilian and military market. Lack of design capability to manufacture critical subsystems remains a major handicap. The DRDO remains mired in inordinate delay, huge cost overruns and deficient in critical technology areas like 'seekers' and 'stealth'.

Tokenism like Rs. 100 crore allocation towards Technology Acquisition Fund or lip service to FDI policy by increasing to 49 per cent are not the way forward. Public Private Partnership, Joint Venture with foreign OEMs and design houses will require bolder policies such as FDI ceiling higher than 50 per cent and the political will to mentor and hold together the different stakeholders who are often at cross purposes. The new Prime Minister has set his foot in the right place. The Ministry of Defence, however, has to match his steps, shed its ghetto mentality and strive for better synergy with other manufacturing sectors to make "Make in India" the mantra for the days ahead.

FIVE REASONS WHY DEFENCE PRODUCTION IN INDIA WILL TAKE OFF

Since assuming office, the National Democratic Alliance (NDA) government has been stressing that defence manufacturing is a crucial pillar to revitalise the manufacturing sector and put India on the road to self-reliance in defence products. The Make in India initiative is over 18 months old and despite promises from a significant number of foreign original equipment manufacturers (OEMs) nothing seems to have happened at the ground level.

This begs the question whether the sector would actually deliver or whether it would be reduced to an obscure mediocre project. The answer to the question is yes, the sector will deliver. Here are five reasons:

Establishment of a new procurement regime: The industry has been waiting for the new defence procurement procedures (DPP) for over a year. While, the delay may be perceived to be due to the typical bureaucratic hurdles, which are faced by any set of new regulations, in this case, it has largely been due to constant suggestions being taken from stakeholders to remove past hurdles. A few glimpses of simplification can be seen based on the amendments introduced in DPP 2013 where relaxations have been made to appointment of offset partners to reduce lead times.

Another example has been the constructive feedback taken from the empowered committee to outline the issues and its suggested remedial steps. In the past era, a committee recommendations would have been reduced to an academic endeavour with little in way of implementation, however, the government has been quick to act on a few of the suggestions which means that it's listening to the industry and stakeholders.

Push to domestic industry: The present DPP provides a few categories exclusively to cater to the Indian industry, these are Buy (Indian), Buy & Make (India) and Make. All these categories have faced individual challenges and have not been as successful as expected. To streamline the capability of the domestic industry, the concept of strategic partners is being introduced. This would mean that an identified Indian company would be vested the development, implementation and maintenance of a particular platform (helicopters, weapons, aircraft, etc).

There are two distinct advantages which would result from this: firstly, it would ensure a more comprehensive skill building and knowledge transfer for these platforms in India and secondly, the domestic industry would not be required to compete amongst themselves. Early signs of this can be seen with Bharat Forge and Tata Group joining hands along with General Dynamics for the Future Infantry Combat Vehicle project. A related but critical advantage of this initiative would be that foreign OEMs would deal directly with private enterprises instead of long negotiations with the government.

Simplification of offset regime: After the initial failed experiments with offsets, the government is devising new ways to keep OEMs invested. For example an OEM has been given the option to select the offset partner till the time the offsets need to be completed and filed. The approach is not as cavalier as it may seem, since the government has increased the penalties for non-compliance in direct proportion to the flexibility exercised. This is one of the key areas where the government has shown that it is willing to get out of the way of businesses to achieve the end goal. However, the true test of success in the offset regime will only be witnessed when the new DPP is announced and analysed in entirety.

Increasing involvement of states: India's federal regime is one of the most defining characteristics of our democracy. It has done wonders in some spheres and has been a debilitating handicap for some. A few states such as Andhra Pradesh, Telangana, Karnataka and Maharashtra have shown a clear indication to attract the defence manufacturing industry by welcoming companies and putting in place clear policies for the industry.

The resistance faced by industries at the state levels and the inability of the lower bureaucratic levels to appreciate or understand business requirements have seen several projects stalled and caught in bureaucratic quagmire.

The efforts introduced by the above mentioned states have also seen rewards since Andhra Pradesh, Telangana and Karnataka are evolving as India's aerospace hub.

Maturity in Indian industry: The domestic industry has matured significantly in the last few years. Companies such as Bharat Forge and Tata have shown that Indian companies can work seamlessly with the global industry and can deliver on the most exacting standards.

Tatas are servicing Lockheed, Sikorsky, Airbus and Boeing who are in the very upper echelons of the industry. Bharat Forge has tied up with Rolls-Royce, Elbit, Saab, Rafael on a variety of programmes and is investing equally or more than the foreign partners—a sign of the industry willing to shed its inhibitions and reservations on past concerns of being sidelined by the foreign OEMs.

The Indian industry has also shown its ability to innovate and there are many categories of products where the domestic industry has significantly worked and developed improved designs from existing equipment.

There are several other reasons where the commitment from the government can be seen. The facilitating role of department of industrial policy and promotion, frequent Defence Acquisition Council (DAC) approvals to projects all indicate a thriving and robust engine being created to make defence manufacturing the bedrock of Indian industry a question of "when" and not "if".

Despite the several encouraging steps mentioned above, there is a lot of ground to cover and a large part of it can be achieved if the opposition realizes that the roadblocks to key legislation such as goods and services tax, land acquisition, etc.

compromise national interests and not just political interest. However, despite the challenges, the defence manufacturing industry in India is the beginning of an optimistic tale.

THE CHALLENGES TO INDIA'S DEFENCE MODERNISATION

Taking into account the changing nature of threats in the emerging geopolitical scenario, India has to focus on building capacity for continuous modernisation of the Armed Forces. The policy priority for the Indian defence establishment should be to ensure that it maximises its indigenous production while also ensuring the availability of quality defence equipment.

The developments in India's immediate neighbourhood over the past decade have led India to take a close look at her foreign and security policies. There is a widely-sensed need for the rapid modernisation of the Indian Armed Forces, which is being reflected in some of the key initiatives that have been taken up by the Indian government so far, such as 'Make in India', so as to address the complex security challenges that emanate from its hostile neighbourhood.

However, the pace of modernisation of the Indian Armed Forces over the years has been rather slow and, technologically, they are not where they should have been. Indigenous development of modern defence hardware continues to remain a concern, and Indian policy aspiration for defence self-sufficiency remains largely elusive. The aim of the research is to highlight how the Indian Armed Forces are responding to the emerging security scenario in the region and beyond, and to address issues in defence policy-making, progress with defence modernisation and military effectiveness.

The Indian defence industry suffers from major policy, structural, and cultural challenges that beset a military-industrial complex that continues to struggle in terms of delivering modern defence hardware that could have added to the greater Indian defence indigenisation and production. Experts see a number of systemic flaws in the Indian defence establishment and civil-military relations, which present major challenges for India's military modernisation aspirations. As India's defence requirements are likely to increase in the foreseeable future because of the dynamic security environment, indigenous development of modern defence hardware and technology is likely to remain a top priority.

As India is an aspiring great power (and it is believed that great powers have great arms industries), its ability to acquire autarky and self-sufficiency, in terms of the development of advanced defence hardware and technology, to fulfil the requirements of its Armed Forces would be crucial so as to address its national security concerns. The study here shall highlight the impediments to India's defence modernisation and its likely implications for India's national security.

India's National Security Concerns And Defence Preparedness

India today faces the most complex threats and challenges that range from nuclear to sub-conventional spectrum of conflict. Issues such as the unresolved territorial disputes with China and Pakistan, the insurgency in Jammu and Kashmir (J&K) and the North-Eastern states, the growing menace of left-wing extremism and the rising threat of urban terrorism has further exacerbated India's security environment.

In the regional security milieu, it has clearly emerged that China poses the most potent military threat to India—given the advantages it has over India in nuclear, missile and military hardware. Moreover, the China-Pakistan nexus and increased strategic engagements between the two have increased the probability that India might face a two-front war in the future.

Therefore, the need for augmenting defence capabilities, i.e., land, air and sea capabilities, is being largely reflected in the Indian policy towards defence modernisation today (initiatives such as 'Make in India') to meet the challenges that emanate from both traditional and non-traditional threats that pose severe threats to India's national security.

India's defence industry, however, has failed to manage India's defence requirements as of today. India is one of the largest arms importers in the world as the indigenous production of technology is one area where India continues to struggle. India's defence preparedness, therefore, remains a question as some of the most crucial requirements in various services of the Armed Forces have not been fulfilled because of severe deficiencies in the defence industry.

India's land forces lack sophisticated weapons and armoury, the navy's submarine fleet has dwindled down to 40 percent of the minimum requirements and the fighter squadrons are at the level of 60 percent of the mandatory need which, indeed, is a cause for concern considering the slow pace of India's defence modernisation.

Therefore, when taking into account the changing nature of threats in the emerging geopolitical scenario (also considering the changing nature of warfare with the rise of non-state actors), India has to focus on building capacity for continuous modernisation of the Armed Forces while directing it towards achieving the desired capability which will, in turn, depend on the analysis of threats.

Articulating India's Defence Needs And Requirements

India's defence requirements are likely to be influenced especially by external factors such as the threats that emanate from two of its primary adversaries, i.e., Pakistan and China. Though Pakistan will continue to remain an immediate threat, China will be the major concern as China is more likely to be a medium-term threat for India, according to some observers. Therefore, India's defence requirements are likely to be based on capabilities that cater to the larger threat, which would take adequate care of the threat from its more traditional adversary, Pakistan.

As India is much more superior in conventional and strategic capabilities when compared to Pakistan, articulation of India's defence requirements is likely to be influenced by the growing offensive capabilities of China that have been demonstrated over the years, which has created huge debates among the members of the strategic and the academic community on the need for pro-active decision making in terms of streamlining defence acquisition and procurement processes, while also focusing on indigenisation, thereby leading to the augmentation of India's overall war deterrence.

Therefore, there is a growing understanding within India's security establishment that Indian defence modernisation and capacity building should focus on China. The need of the hour is to change the "understanding" into "urgency" in order to build a comprehensive national capability to counter any threat that arises from China or the collusive threat of China and Pakistan.

Given India's current deficiencies in the Armed Forces, there is an imperative for India to focus on the development of advanced and sophisticated weapons system for various platforms of combat, i.e., land, sea, and air, and ensure necessary integration within the services of the Armed Forces as well as intelligence organisations to ensure an effective and a viable response to the threats that emanate in the immediate regional security environment.

There is a need to make a thorough assessment of the security threats and accordingly articulate the needs of the services of the Armed Forces and take necessary steps to procure advanced weapons system that, in turn, will augment India's national power.

Issues In India's Defence Modernisation

India faces a whole range of complex challenges in its defence modernisation aspirations, which are aimed at containing the threats that it perceives to be having severe implications for its national security. Looking into the current capacities of India's defence industry, it is not hard to say that many observers remain dismissive of the same and have proposed a number of reforms aimed at bolstering India's defence production capabilities, thereby achieving self-reliance in building such capabilities and streamlining India's defence procurement procedures for lesser procedural delays in acquiring advanced weapons system.

As India is one of the largest importers of arms in the world, its over-dependency over other countries for sophisticated weapons system for the services of the Armed Forces is likely to affect negatively India's aspirations of becoming a great power. It is widely believed that great powers are supposed to have a great arms industries. The challenges that India's defence industry today faces in terms of producing and procuring advanced weapons system to fulfil the requirements of the services of the Armed Forces are immense and need critical examination. The issues that India faces today are hereby discussed one by one.

Self-Reliance And Enduring Challenges

India's defence industrial policy during the initial years of its independence was guided by the phrase 'self-sufficiency'. This was subsequently modified to 'self-reliance' in defence production, and now it has long been a fundamental goal of indigenous armaments production in India. However, India's heavy dependence on arms imports has been a matter of concern for parliamentarians, oversight agencies, policy makers and defence analysts.

India's inability to meet its own defence needs through indigenous production (The two flagship programs Main Battle Tank Arjun and Light Combat Aircraft Tejas are examples where the Indian defence research organisations have gone through several production delays and cost-overruns.) is drawing wider concerns over the challenges that the Indian defence industry has been going through in terms of being efficient, productive and more capable in research and development (R&D) of advanced weapons system and defence technology. The targets that have been set over the years have not been achieved, and that raises questions about the ability of India's defence industry to produce weapons system and defence technology to meet the requirements of the services of the Armed Forces.

There is an urgent need for the government to focus on the indigenous production of defence hardware and technology by carefully articulating long-term strategic plans to augment India's military power. As India is a rising power with a huge economic base, India has to look beyond the buyer-seller relationship that had almost become a feature of its defence industrial policy, and should instead develop means to produce advanced weapons system and defence technology indigenously.

The policy priority for the Indian defence establishment should be to ensure that India maximises its indigenous production so that the quantitative requirements of the Armed Forces are met while also ensuring quality in the variety of defence equipment and items that should be made available to meet the ever-increasing demand of the services of the Armed Forces with rapid changes in technology. The need of the hour is to increase the budget allocation for defence R&D and utilise the manpower in its defence laboratories to promote research for advances in defence equipment, hardware, and technology. These practical steps would ensure that India meets the demands of the time, and is in continued possession of cutting-edge defence technology as a result of indigenous production by its defence industry.

Decision-Making and National Security Strategy

While looking into India's present defence status, there has been a long ongoing debate on what are the impediments to India's defence modernisation pace, which, in turn, has been severely affecting India's ability to enhance its defence capabilities. As threats to India's national security are both traditional and non-traditional, effective defence preparedness is the key to secure its national interests, which would depend on the ability to produce and procure advanced, sophisticated weapons and high-tech technological devices in order to ensure that the services of the Armed Forces and their requirements are fulfilled, which would enhance India's war capabilities, naturally augmenting its military power.

The decision-making in India in national security and strategic matters have been however projected to be slow and complex because of the hierarchical structure of the decision-making process, which affects India's ability to produce and procure weapons on time, which, in turn, affects India's defence preparedness. Today, the services of the Armed Forces are suffering from a severe lack of necessary war-fighting capabilities, which has severe implications for India's national security considering the actual requirements.

India's aspirations of becoming self-reliant in indigenous defence production and also acquiring advanced weapons system faster would, however, depend on the effectiveness of the decision-making at the apex-level while taking into consideration India's national security interests. Some observers have questioned the efficacy of the established process of decision-making in defence acquisition or during times of crises, which is managed by the Cabinet Committee on Security (CCS).

The lack of military inputs in decision-making is considered to be the most significant lacuna. It is also observed that the national security strategy of India suffers from flaws such as the absence of a National Security Doctrine and the absence of long-term defence planning. Moreover, the need for a Chief of Defence Staff (CDS), a supposedly single point of advice to the CCS on military affairs and defence acquisitions, has been long felt.

There are an increasing number of opinions on the need for key structural reforms in India's higher defence management and the national security decision-making process, which shall in the long run help improve India's defence R&D, self-reliance in defence production and civil-military relations.

Acquisition And Offset Strategy

To expand India's defence industrial base, India has long relied on its offset policy to engage in transactions with foreign suppliers and promote transfer of technology, thereby leading to indigenous defence production. First introduced in 2005, the offset policy has gone through several revisions in the Defence Procurement Policy (DPP) that have been released over the years (the latest one came out in March 2016). The transactions with foreign suppliers are aimed at enhancing the economic, technological, and the industrial capabilities of India. India, as it is well known, has long relied on licensed production with overseas defence contractors. And as now offset is mandatory, India is likely to benefit from a transfer of technology with the rise in the number of offset agreements as a result of India's increasing defence acquisition budget.

The increase in defence spending has become possible not just because of the tensions in the immediate regional security environment but also because of its rapid economic growth over the years that has given it a solid economic base. This should play a major role in increasing India's defence offset appetite, which would give it the necessary financial resources to promote indigenous defence production.

However, India's defence offset policy suffers from major challenges that require attention. India's offset policy requires foreign vendors to engage with local defence companies through co-development, co-production, joint ventures, maintenance, and upgrades, but full mergers and acquisitions are not allowed. Therefore, foreign companies are hesitant to invest in a defence industry without having full stakes in the defence production.

Foreign Direct Investment (FDI) in the defence sector is capped at 49 percent, which again is a sore point for many foreign firms, as they believe that investments involve huge financial risks, and therefore, FDI cap in defence should be raised to 74 percent or even 100 percent.

Secondly, the expectation that a foreign vendor will engage in 'complete' transfer of technology to the Indian pattern of the system's subsystems, modules, assemblies, and specific parts or components is too much to ask, given the commitments the offset policy of India demands.

Thirdly, India's offset policy is based on an inflexible doctrine of indigenisation, and India's offset policy should be made compatible with the economic dynamism of the global defence industry.

And finally, other issues in the offset policy should be addressed, such as the policy's obligatory nature, objectives that need broadening, and most importantly, the inherent complexities, which need reduction.

Under the current offset policy, India under 'Buy (Global)' would purchase from the foreign or Indian seller, and under 'Buy and Make with Transfer of Technology' would acquire defence hardware from foreign sellers, which would be followed by co-development and joint-production. The estimated cost of acquisition proposal should be Rs 300 crore or more, 'compensation' or offset for the cost of acquisition under the 'Buy (Global)' category would be 30 percent, and foreign exchange component under 'Buy and Make with Transfer of Technology' would be 30 percent.

Foreign firms from major defence hardware exporting countries find such conditions difficult to fulfil as there are literally no incentives, and because of a lack of proper monitoring mechanism and issues related to intellectual property rights.

The Ministry of Defence (MOD) released an incomplete version of DPP 2016 on 28 March 2016, which saw the introduction of a new category titled 'Buy (Indian Designed, Developed, and Manufactured)' or Buy (IDDM) for the first time since its inception in 2002. That means the Indian government has recognised the need for encouraging scientific talent in India and has placed importance on "indigenous design", development, and manufacture. However, critics would argue that it is too early to judge or predict the efficacy of the document as it misses many critical issues and does little to address problems that beset decision-making in the MoD.

What India Needs

Each of the services of the Indian Armed Forces today needs urgent modernisation to face the complex security challenges that emanate in an increasingly unstable neighbourhood and a complex strategic regional security environment. The Indian Army, which is one of the largest standing forces in the world, possesses weapons and equipment that are bordering on obsolescence and need to be replaced. The next step should be to acquire network-centric capabilities to optimise the Army's full potential in defensive and offensive operations.

The critical capabilities that are needed to be enhanced (as Lieutenant General JP Singh noted in an interview with Centre for Land and Warfare Studies, New Delhi) are "battlefield transparency, battlefield management systems, night-fighting capability, enhanced firepower, including terminally guided munitions, integrated manoeuvre capability to include self-propelled artillery, quick reaction surface-to-air missiles, the latest assault engineer equipment, tactical control systems, integral combat aviation support, and network centricity."

Also, urgent steps should be taken to enhance the operational capabilities of Army aviation, engineers, signal communications, reconnaissance, surveillance, and target acquisition branches in order to improve the Army's overall combat potential so that it can face aggression of any magnitude.

India needs to take urgent steps towards extensive naval modernisation so as to secure its security interests in the Indian Ocean Region and beyond. India should look to augment its naval power by acquiring capabilities for maritime domain awareness in the area of responsibility, including space-based surveillance, maritime reconnaissance, airborne early warning and control (AEW&C), and unmanned aerial vehicles (UAVs).

The Indian Navy should be equipped with modern capabilities in fields of tactical aviation, anti-submarine warfare (ASW), anti-air/anti-missile, land-attack, mine counter-measures, and electronic warfare. It is equally important to make sure that Indian Navy is integrated by the networking of ships, submarines, and airborne platforms via satellites. In the end, the government should commit to self-reliance and indigenisation, with the objective of harnessing national strengths in ship-building, engineering, electronics, and information technology (IT).

The Indian naval modernisation, though much delayed, has begun to pick up steam as seen from the recent developments where deals worth thousands of crore have been made to expand India's naval fleet and India's naval dominance capabilities.

The Indian Air Force (IAF) is a full-spectrum force equipped with very capable platforms and trained manpower, but the numbers are inadequate for intense and lengthy operations. India must take urgent steps to maintain an edge over the adversary through technology and force employment.

The IAF is at the forefront of technology, but India should push towards self-reliance, as it has to develop its own technology and defence industrial base. India's track record in R&D, however, has been dismal, and it is continuing to face a number of challenges in terms of meeting the quantitative requirements to defend the Indian skies. As per one of the recent reports, the IAF has only 32 squadrons of fighters, the lowest in a decade, while it needs at least 42 squadrons to protect its western and northern borders from Pakistan and China. Also, as aircraft such as MiG-21s and MiG-27s in the IAF are old and ageing (which date back to the Soviet era), India is likely to lose another 14 squadrons by 2019-2020.

Commercial negotiations with France on the deal over Rafale fighter jets are far from over, and India has yet to start the production of its first indigenously built aircraft Tejas (the project is more than 30 years old). India has to focus urgently on air dominance and control of the air by building capacity to indigenously produce future capabilities for the design and development of aircraft, heavy attack helicopters, and other combat and surveillance-related capabilities for further projection of air power.

From India's point of view, the most crucial component that has to be implemented for better integration of the services of the Armed Forces is a robust and an efficient Command, Control, Computers, Communication, Intelligence, Surveillance, and Reconnaissance (C4ISR) system. An integrated Indian C4ISR system will be central to augmenting India's overall defence capability.

With better integration of the services of the Armed Forces, it is also essential that there is integration between the Armed Forces, defence and intelligence agencies, and other government and private organisations as well. This would provide a joint force that would protect the country from traditional as well as asymmetric threats while providing flexibility, analysis, interpretation, and efficiency. This would also give advantages such as information assurance, control and disruption of information, data processing and management, quicker decision-making, and larger system integration.

A strong political will and an enabling framework for the involvement of players from different sectors (such as private sector or academia) for indigenous production of such capabilities would be essential, which is turning out to be a key national security imperative.

Conclusion

Threats from China and Pakistan leave India with no other option but to augment its defence capabilities to secure its national security interests. India's pace of defence modernisation, however, has been slow because of a number of inherent holes in the system, such as the lack of a National Security Strategy doctrine, or a long-term strategic defence plan, which are impediments in terms of evolving a clear-cut strategy to meet the defence requirements of the Armed Forces by making a thorough analysis of the security challenges in the immediate regional security environment.

Moreover, India's inability to produce advanced, sophisticated weapons systems and advanced defence technologies indigenously has severely affected its aspirations of becoming self-reliant in defence production, thereby remaining heavily dependent on foreign sellers for defence purchases, which in a way or other, do expose India's vulnerabilities. Adversaries may seek advantage in case they happen to know India's vulnerabilities, which in turn would have severe implications for India's national security. Therefore, the policy priority for the Indian civil and defence establishment should be to take necessary decisions to ensure that India's defence requirements are met as soon as possible through indigenous production. India's indigenous defence production capabilities have, however, not grown because of a number of challenges.

There is a lack of the greater political will that has severely affected decision-making in terms of acquiring weapons on time as per the needs of the Armed Forces. The Indian defence industry suffers because of under-utilisation of human resources that has negatively affected India's defence R&D base. Because of the unfriendly defence industrial procurement system, it has resulted in few co-development and co-production ventures with foreign firms.

The lack of a conducive financial framework for the local industry to do business in the defence sector, especially for the private sector, has also negatively impacted private participation in the defence sector. Therefore, the urgent focus for the Indian government should be to encourage private individuals and entities in India that could contribute in indigenous defence production. This would mean that India would achieve its goal of self-reliance only if it allows more private players in India to participate in the defence sector, and the true potential of the Indian minds are utilised.

Also, initiating or implementing further defence reforms, such as streamlining procurement and offset policy and introducing newer positions and staffs for better policy coordination, would be essential if India wants to reduce the qualitative and quantitative gaps between its defence industrial base with that of the other major powers.

MAKING MAKE IN INDIA A REALITY IN DEFENCE AND AEROSPACE SECTOR

India, an aspiring world power, has long harboured the goal of possessing a technologically-advanced, self-sufficient arms industry. While its economic power has expanded, and its technological prowess in certain areas — such as information technologies — has grown, it has not been able to create a world-class globally-competitive defence industry. Consequently, India is still saddled with a bloated, non-competitive, non-responsive military, capable of producing only technologically inferior military equipments, and that too never on time and mostly exceeding their original cost estimates.

The result is that India still imports 70% of its defence requirements and the armed forces continue to grapple with the outdated, vintage and obsolete weapon platforms — submarines, fighter aircraft (MiG-21) and helicopters (Cheetah, Chetak, MI-8 and Seaking). A two-million-strong military (the third largest in the world), which has fought four wars since the country's independence and continues to confront an unstable security situation in its neighbourhood, certainly deserves better.

Traditionally, Indian armaments production has been entirely embedded within a government-run military industrial complex — eight Defence Public Sector Undertakings (DPSUs), 41 Ordinance factories and the powerful Defence Research and Development Organisation (DRDO). The Indian Government has for long been aware of the deficiencies affecting the defence industrial base and has pursued a number of initiatives to reform and revitalise the defence sector, including allowing the recent entry of the private sector. Barring a few modest reforms, the vast bulk of defence and aerospace manufacturing still remains in the hands of the State. It is, therefore, surprising that a nation, which stunned the world by putting a satellite in Mars orbit in its very first attempt, is dependent on the western world and Russia for 70% of its military hardware.

Make in India - a reality check

The new government's 'Make In India' policy and increase in the Foreign Direct Investment (FDI) cap in the revised defence FDI policy (from 26% to 49%), announced with a lot of fanfare during the Aero India show in February this year, was seen as a major step to revitalise the defence industry and awaken it from its long slumber. This government action was expected to infuse refreshingly new attitudinal change in India's policy-making processes, foster a trust between the government and the industry, and usher in major reforms to improve India's standing in World Bank rankings.

Accordingly, a number of committees under retired bureaucrats were set up by the government to review the problems being faced, and recommend suitable solutions to improve the business environment in India. However, despite the prime minister's personal thrust toward the 'Make in India' mantra, very little has changed on the ground. This is evident from the fact that even though the government has increased the FDI in the defence sector to 49%, there are almost no takers so far. According to the latest figures tabled in the Parliament in March 2015, in the last seven months, only six proposals worth USD15.3 million have been received. Out of these six proposals, only two are for FDI of 49%. So, why are things not working out? Let's find out...

Despite various committees being appointed, no marked changes are visible on the ground — be it the negative fiscal environment (including taxation), the lack of critical infrastructure (roads, ports and power), antiquated labour laws, or corruption continuing to loom large. Manufacturing requires a significant edifice of infrastructural support, which is currently absent in India. There is a lack of regulatory framework, especially in the general aviation sector, which has a huge growth potential. Reforms require ongoing consultations with the industry, and presently, there is no positive movement on this.

Regardless of all the tall talk of tax reforms in the defence and aerospace industries, they continue to be taxed as before. It should be noted that the high rate of service tax has placed India's Maintenance, Repair and Overhaul (MRO) industry at a disadvantage vis-à-vis the MROs in Gulf countries and South East Asia.

The biggest challenge in 'Make in India' policy framework is the existing antiquated Research & Development infrastructure with severely constrained design capability and limited support, both scientifically and financially. The issue that needs to be addressed is whether the government and the DRDO are following the right approach and strategy for R&D and technological development. What India needs is a research and development institution like the Defence Advanced Research Projects Agency (DARPA) in the US.

One of the key reasons behind this sorry state of affairs is the complete side-lining of the Indian private sector by DRDO and DPSUs in design, production and maintenance. Public sector monopolies breed complacency, arrogance and incompetency. Continued reliance on licensed production by many state-owned enterprises, especially the Hindustan Aeronautics Limited (HAL) has compromised the domestic competence and capability to develop a product from scratch.

Further, decision-making in defence procurement is bureaucratic, as compared to the space and nuclear sectors where the respective commissions report straight to the prime minister.

Global Original equipment manufacturers (OEMs) have developed sensitive and strategic technologies, especially in the aviation sector, related to engines, navigation, surveillance, avionics and state-of-the-art weapon systems over several decades, investing billions of dollars. It is a fallacy that these can be handed over to India without a majority control. The range of emerging technologies is so complex that even the US has 100% subsidiaries of foreign defence OEMs, like Airbus, BAE, Saab, Rolls Royce, etc. Competing with them improves the standard of US defence companies and prevents complacency.

The way forward

What India needs is a single FDI slab of 74% in defence with clear norms and a level-playing field. Forty-nine percent is of no use and 100% may be too one-sided. The Indian obsession with 'ownership and control' needs to be curtailed. Higher FDI limit will also expose certain global OEMs that are not keen to invest in India, and are using 49% FDI as a 'convenient' excuse to stay out.

The Indian private sector needs to be co-opted as partners and not vendors by DPSUs. Certain non-performing labs and plants of DRDO and DPSUs respectively need to be privatised. R&D funds for defence need to be allocated to the best Indian organisations and universities.

The 'Make in India' programme in defence will have to be facilitated by way of bold reforms in policy, procedures and our approach towards global investors. There is an urgent need to facilitate removal of other manufacturing roadblocks, like land, power, transportation infrastructure, taxation and multifarious government clearances. The idea of technology transfer through either licence production or offsets is misunderstood by the decision makers.

Making this the principal strategy and cornerstone of defence technology development and self-reliance in the country is like chasing a mirage. All it does is, perhaps, short-circuit or kick-start a process. But it can never lead to realising the national strategy of indigenous capability and self-reliance. Nothing can substitute strategic research and development and it can be achieved only by involving the entire knowledge sector of the economy. The private sector in India today is in an embryonic stage when it comes to the matters of defence technology. Setting up manufacturing facilities, and fabricating buy-back components using outdated technologies as a part of the offset policy, may perhaps be a good start in their learning cycle. However, major efforts have to be made to hop step this learning curve and mature fast.

One sure way to do this is to develop technologies in-house, both designing as well as manufacturing, so as to catch up. India has to deliberately enter the age of innovation in which research and development becomes an integral component of science, technology and engineering development, an element totally disregarded by the Indian industries so far and unthinkable in the aerospace sector. HAL has singularly survived on licence production and shown improved bottom lines on captive production without any investment in strategic research and development.

National Aerospace Laboratories (NAL) could be made a centre for excellence in aerospace, with capabilities in developing analytical tools, simulation tools, simulator platforms, and a centre of flight research with a fully-capable experimental flight laboratory with their own experimental helicopters and aircraft.

This is indeed a task that requires an honest effort, planning and sincere implementation. If it remains simply a vision, as is typical of the Indian bureaucracy, and stagnates with time, then all this would be hallucination; a dream in futility. There is a need to incorporate mechanisms for formal public consultations with the Indian defence. industry, both private and public, on proposed changes before their adoption by the Defence Procurement Board (DPB) and the Defence Acquisition Council (DAC). Under the US public procurement system (both defence and non-defence), initial drafts of proposed regulatory changes are mandatorily published with a standard 30-day notice period and the final regulations necessarily indicate how certain public suggestions have been incorporated therein, or why certain stakeholder suggestions have not been accepted in the final rules. This ensures transparency. In contrast, the suggestions on defence acquisition reforms made by the Naresh Chandra Committee and the Rabindra Gupta Committee have remained unavailable to Indian industry stakeholders, virtually ignoring the latter's potential for contributing meaningfully to the reforms process.

The next set of Defence Procurement Procedure (DPP) reforms could therefore focus on improved information-sharing protocols between the MoD and the Indian industry, perhaps along the lines of the US system where security-vetted key management personnel from its domestic industry routinely enter into in-depth, wide-ranging discussions on planned capabilities with the DoD's acquisition wing — right from the planning stage of the acquisition process. In contrast, DPP's present system of industry meetings facilitated by Headquarters Integrated Defence Staff (HQIDS) is rather ad-hoc, with unilateral presentations by industry associations based on 'hearsay' information on user requirements. Improved dialogue and consultations could eventually help MoD in more ways than one. Hopefully, the DPP 2015 will address these issues.

It is time that a level-playing field is provided to the Indian defence industry for being able to showcase its capabilities and manufacturing plans to users in the defence establishment in a much more structured and formal manner than is possible at present. Even though the MoD does interact with the Indian defence industry in a number of small and ad-hoc ways, the challenge going forward — for the 'Make in India' mantra to become an all-pervasive reality in defence acquisitions — will be to multiply manifold the onset, frequency, range and depth of its industry engagements.

Many Indian companies, especially the new entrants into defence, are yet to understand the finer details of the Long Term Integrated Perspective Plan (LTIPP) and its public version the Technology Perspective Technology Roadmap (TPCR). The MoD needs to make this process more interactive; this would benefit the end users as well as industry. The MoD's procurement procedures are still very cumbersome and time consuming; these need to have clarity and the procurement cycle shortened.

While the modernisation of the military requires substantial budgetary outlays, in reality, the gap between the requirement of funds projected by MoD and the actual budgetary allocation has been widening over the years. This trend is likely to continue, as is clearly evident in the defence budget for 2015-2016. But of greater concern is the fact that the MoD surrendered a total of Rs 28,000 crores between 2001- 02 and 2010-11 under the capital head. This was mainly due to stalled projects amidst allegations of wrong doing, lack of indigenisation and complexity of procedures. However, grave the situation, the way out of the morass has to be found to ensure the acquisition of operationally-critical weapon systems, including guns, helicopters, submarines, aircraft and ammunitions that form the core of a nation's defence capability.

Conclusion

The entry of the private sector into defence sector is a game changer. This revered holy cow no longer remains the preserve of the State. The challenges to the Indian defence industry are likely to increase over the next few years as the country embarks on the massive modernisation of its military. The private industry can play a very crucial and positive role to help overcome these challenges. While the government has displayed the necessary political will for indigenisation and establishment of an advanced manufacturing base in the country, the challenge lies in its comprehensive implementation — an enabling policy framework, focus and commitment, including addressing the fiscal and taxation issues, which currently impact negatively on the private industry. In this context, the prime minister's directive to the secretary-level officers to take decisions and implement policies without fear is very reassuring.

This will provide them protection against the 3Cs — the Central Bureau of Investigation (CBI), Central Vigilance Commission (CVC) and the Comptroller and Auditor General of India (CAG). With the government committed to carry out reforms in defence sector, we are likely to witness a greater participation of the domestic industry (both private and public) in the design and production of defence equipment. The government and the defence industry need to work together on the model of 3Cs — compete, co-operate and collaborate to ensure that 'Make in India' becomes a reality.

The good news is that the revised DPP 2015 will be out in two months with the basic thrust on 'Make in India.' It will be useful to envision how India's DPP could be retrofitted with this new vision by incorporating a culture of dialogue and consultations into the defence acquisition process itself, as a necessary prerequisite for building enhanced confidence and trust in MoD's procurement systems in the longer-run

6

The Unfinished Defence Reform Agenda and Make in India Manufacturing

At Aero India 2015, when Prime Minister Narendra Modi emphatically said the defence industry was at the heart of the 'Make in India' programme, he conveyed his government's intent to reform an archaic arms production base whose inefficiency has earned India the dubious distinction of being the world's largest arms importer. To be sure, the government has taken a host of measures to incentivise local arms production.

These measures include a simplified and streamlined industrial licensing process, improvements to the taxation system, a set of export promotion measures, a liberalised defence foreign direct investment (FDI) policy and comprehensively revised defence procurement procedures. Are these measures sufficient to change the fortunes of the Indian arms industry, enable the country to not meet its own defence needs but also export to others?

The conclusive answer to the above question is 'no'. The reasons are two-fold. The first and foremost is the lack of reform in state-owned entities engaged in research and development (R&D) and production. Comprising 40-odd ordnance factories, nine defence public sector undertakings, and over 50 dedicated research labs and establishments under the umbrella of the Defence Research and Development

Organization (DRDO), these government-owned/controlled entities have an overwhelming share of India's defence industrial base.

At the same time, they are also hugely inefficient and are directly responsible for India's poor self-reliance index. Measured by any parameter, be it innovation, timely execution, labour productivity, foreign exchange earnings, and customer satisfaction, they paint a dismal picture.

Given the poor performance of the ordnance factories, defence public sector undertakings and the DRDO, one would have expected some meaningful reforms under the guidance of the 'Make in India' programme, which is now running into its third year. However, to the dismay of many, the government has been extremely slow on this crucial front, with the only piece of reform being a plan to privatize BEML (formerly Bharat Earth Movers Ltd), one of the public sector units that function under the defence ministry. Even though it is late, one would hope that the BEML model of privatization is applied to other government-owned production agencies to bring about a marked improvement in their functioning. For the DRDO, which has a complete monopoly over defence R&D, a crucial piece of reform is needed to make the organization accountable for all the projects it is involved in.

Second, the 'Make in India' programme is yet to create a conducive climate for the private sector to contribute in a meaningful manner. The biggest challenge for the private sector is the step-motherly attitude of the government. Despite numerous policy announcements, the private sector is still treated as a poor cousin of the public sector.

When it comes to big-ticket procurement contracts, it is the public sector which gets preferential treatment. The apathy towards the private sector is also seen in the extremely slow decision making process of the defence ministry. It is an irony that for all the hue and cry about 'Make in India', the private sector is yet to bag a big defence contract. It is high time the government took some bold decisions to create a thriving defence industrial base.

STREAMLINING DEFENCE PROCUREMENTS

The defence reforms were carried out in 2001 to evolve integrated and joint structures for higher defence organization in order to face the emerging threats and consequently achieve the desired levels of modernization. These reforms have achieved some degree of maturity and have been periodically updated. Formation of HQ Integrated Defence Staff has been instrumental for a joint approach towards building military capability. Streamlining defence procurement procedures, involving private sector in defence-production, spurring research and development, taking long term perspective in defence planning and budgeting, up-gradation of quality of personnel in the armed forces and rationalization of manpower were among many of the key reforms recommended by the Group of Ministers Report of 2001. However; these need to be implemented fully, as lack of a central policy planning staff and absence of Chief of Defence Staff greatly inhibit integrated effort in defence modernization. A few instances of malpractices in defence purchases should not derail the entire procurement programme; instead the guilty should be given suitable punishment and the planned inductions continued. Today the entire decision making apparatus appears paralyzed once a scandal in the defence purchase is reported and the Capital budget for procurements remains unspent, adversely affecting the defence capability.

Technology Induction

At the present juncture, our armed forces are in transition from industrial age forces to knowledge age forces with a portion being equipped with the state-of-the art weapons. While the Army is more manpower intensive, the Navy and the Air Force are more technology intensive forces and are much better on the equipment profile. Availability of state-of-the art technology is dependent on international relations and strategic partnerships between us and the major militaries. A collaborative approach between the users, DRDO, the industry and foreign vendors is the only way ahead. We must transform our buyer-seller relationship to joint-ventures. Transfer of technology being undertaken at the HAL aircraft manufacturing factory and some of the other joint ventures with countries like Israel, Russia and France for various weapon systems is the right step from the earlier days of licensed production system. Defence Public Sector Units and DRDO must adopt time bound processes and adopt bold management practices and scrap the process if it does not conform to a reasonable time-frame, rather than seeking frequent time extension, as shelf-life of equipment is becoming shorter by the day due to obsolescence.

Precision Guided Munitions (PGMs)

Precision engagement is considered one of the most important aspects of the ongoing modernisation. And this is one of the niche capabilities which are being strengthened in our armed forces. The benefits of PGMs are well known. Precision weapons are a far more efficient substitute for heavy mass retaliation. They enable concentration of effects from geographically widely dispersed forces, contribute to reduced logistics tail, and help in reducing collateral damage. Therefore, increasing the accuracy and range of our missiles, and acquiring and developing a family of PGMs should receive greater attention in our armed forces.

However, long ranges of weapon platforms are of no use unless they are complemented by matching surveillance, target acquisition, battle damage assessment and weapon guidance capabilities. Therefore, besides ground based and air borne early warning systems, space based assets assume importance for imparting force-multiplication effects to air and surface forces. In addition, space is another area which is being used basically for communications and navigations and we are in the process of increasing our capabilities in this area too. Aerospace capabilities have a long gestation period. It is necessary to carry out cost-effective replacements and selective upgradation of existing systems. All platforms including transport support aircraft and helicopters with residual life must be upgraded, along with the weapon systems.

Surveillance and Night Vision Devices

With the change of battlefield scenario, Indian Army is now equipping itself with latest state of the art technology and looking for night vision equipment between 3000-5000 meters range. This would give a tactical advantage for our forces which would enhance their night fighting skills and improve surveillance and reconnaissance capabilities greatly, but the numbers are large and would take time for induction. Army feels that the night vision equipment will enhance combat potential to facilitate operations over 24 hours cycle. As a part of its modernization and upgrading weaponry, Indian Army has planned to equip all its battalions with night vision equipments but the progress is painfully slow. We need to push these on fast-track procurement procedure by intervention at the highest level.

'MBT-Arjun' Tank Production

The inordinate delay in the production of the ARJUN Tank and its design faults is a major cause of worry. Indian Defence Minister has admitted that frequent design modification and assembling format have also caused additional delay in its induction. His assurance that necessary steps have been taken to ensure the timely availability of all critical aggregates, is still far from the reality. The Ministry of Defence in regular intervals comes out with promising statements only to justify the public-sector defence undertakings and to secure uninterrupted financial grants. Meanwhile, we continue to import the Russian T-90 and T-72 tanks, which are far superior but involve huge expenditure on imports from foreign sources.

Modernisation of Field Artillery (155mm guns)

As part of the field artillery modernization programme, Army is looking to purchase artillery guns since mid-80s as well as increase domestic manufacture of field guns. Artillery modernization programme has been held hostage to various scandals and pressures and the Army is even considering buying older models of 130 mm guns as a desperate measure. Despite the Army repeatedly requesting for induction of 155 mm guns, due to irregularities in the procurement process and the unscrupulous role of middlemen and agents, this has not seen the light of day. It needs to be realized that even after giving the go-ahead, it takes at least five years for the equipment to reach the Army units since these products are not available off-the-shelf and the numbers to be inducted are large. This is a matter of serious concern and the operational readiness of the Army is jeopardized by continued inaction of the Government.

Building Maritime Capability

India's peninsular configuration invests her with an opportunity to project maritime power in the Indian Ocean. This enables her to protect its Sea-Lanes as also to interdict hostile shipping, which traverse through the Indian Ocean. The rationale for an extensive PLA Navy build-up, development of Gwadar port in Pakistan, surveillance outposts on Myanmar islands, and beefing of ports in Sri Lanka and Bangladesh by the Chinese, suggest an intention to use these during forays of the PLA Navy into the Indian ocean. India, therefore, needs to enhance its naval build –up and expedite induction of the planned aircraft-carrier, the Scorpene submarines and the Maritime surveillance aircraft. Whereas, India can meet some of the challenges independently, others require rallying together Indian Ocean region Navies.

BALLISTIC AND CRUISE MISSILE PROLIFERATION

In the nuclear delivery front, both India and Pakistan have a series of ballistic and cruise missiles in addition to ground attack aircrafts. The maximum range among India's operational ballistic missiles is 2000 km achieved by Agni-2. India's Agni ballistic missiles are indigenously developed by its own missile defence industry known as *IGMDP*. The maximum range among Pakistan's missiles is by *Hatf V Gauri* which is reported to do over 2200 kms. Pakistan's Hatf missiles are based on North Korean *No-Dong* series of IRBMs. Both Pakistan's *Hatf* and

India's *Agni* ballistic missiles are nuclear capable. India has also developed a supersonic cruise missile *BrahMos* which is by far the fastest cruise missile at Mach 2.6 and maximum range of 290 km. It is reported to be nuclear capable but it is not confirmed yet. On the Pakistan side, its *Babur* cruise missile has a reported range of 700 km and a maximum speed of 880 km/h (Mach 0.7). As with India *BrahMos*, *Babur* is also reported to be nuclear capable but there is no confirmation yet.

The Final Verdict

Both Pakistan and India are almost evenly matched head to head in nuclear and missile fronts, however India has strategic and technological superiority over the conventional forces of Pakistan. Indian Navy is larger in fleet and personnel size with a more varied range of ships including an aircraft carrier while Pakistan's Navy is smaller and has no aircraft carriers. Indian's IAF is equipped with highly capable fighters like 4.5th generation *Su-30*s and 4th gen *Mirage 2000*s which are technologically superior to Pakistan PAF's *F-16*s and *Mirage III*s. Additionally Indian pilots are better trained and more capable in air combat than Pakistani forces as was demonstrated by its various wars with Pakistan or joint exercises with US and UK. In the area of conventional ground forces both the Indian as well as Pakistani Army is well equipped and highly trained to survive in extremities of topography and climate in combat conditions, like wars in the high Himalayas.

If a purely conventional war were to take place between both these countries, India would most likely overpower Pakistan owing to its superior military technology and infrastructure, larger manpower, more territorial area and a strategic advantage in its sea and air forces. It must also be noted that a war between these two countries will matter more than India's conventional superiority as both these nations are nuclear powers on an equal deadlock. India has maintained a 'no first use' nuclear policy in the lines of a similar policy by China while Pakistan does not have any such policy, considering their only hope against India is in nuclear deterrance. It would be risky for India at the present scenario to go into any aggressive war against Pakistan as the repercussions would be serious a nuclear devastation for both countries.

Unfortunately India and Pakistan had adversarial relations since sixty years. After the Mumbai carnage Pakistan is under threat of pre-emptive strikes. Fourth Indo-Pakistan war could be triggered by another terrorist attack anywhere in India. This is a dangerous scenario. India and Pakistan have fought three wars, and war drums for the fourth war are getting louder.

It is in order therefore to comprehend Indian military capabilities, and Pakistan's ability to defend itself. Defense capability is an interplay of economic and military potential. Indian economy is booming, and its GDP growth is in double digits. The global recession has impacted Indian economy, but its defense capability remains intact. Military power and capabilities are sustained by economic and industrial potential. Geography, demography, population, oil resources and reserves, industrial capability including defense production, dollar reserves, self reliance, education, quality of manpower and leadership have a bearing on military power. Seven lakh Indian troops are tied down in Jammu and Kashmir. India has over one hundred billion dollar reserves. The West, Israel and Russia are India's weapon suppliers.

Indian Army has eighteen Corps with 34 Divisions including four Rapid Action Divisions, which would spear head ground offensives. Pakistan Army has ten Corps and twenty five divisions. Indian Army has eighteen Infantry, ten Mountain, three Armoured, and two Artillery Divisions. Besides it has five Infantry, one parachute, thirteen Air Defense, and four Engineering Brigades, designated as independent formations. In addition there are two Air Defense Groups, and fourteen Army Aviation Helicopter units. This is a sizeable force, capable of launching major offensives from several fronts.

The decentralized command structure will be an advantage, as compared to Pakistan's centralized Army command organization. Pakistan Army has an active force of 620,000 well trained personnel, with 528000 reservists, and 150000 para-military troops. Pakistan armed forces are seventh largest in the world. Pakistan Army's doctrine of "Offensive Defense", evolved by General Mirza Aslam Beg was put to test in 1989 in Exercise Zarb-e Momin.

The doctrine is to launch a sizeable offensive into enemy territory, rather than wait for enemy strikes or attacks. In case of Indian land offensive Pakistan Army and Air Force will respond with land and air offensives to gain and hold enemy territory. Before embarking on further offensive, gains shall be consolidated. In 1990 the Central Corps of Reserves was created to fight in the desert sectors , where enemy land offensives are expected. These dual capable formations trained for offensive and holding actions are fully mechanized.

Pakistan Army has ten Corps including the newly formed Strategic Corps. The Army has twenty six divisions (eight less than India). Two more divisions were raised as Corps reserves for V and XXXI Corps. Pakistan Army has two armoured divisions, and ten independent armoured brigades. Presently one hundred thousand troops are stationed on the Pak Afghan border to fight terror. Special Service Group-SSG comprises two airborne Brigades i.e. six battalions.

Pakistan Army has 360 helicopters, over two thousand heavy guns, and 3000 APC's. Its main anti-tank weapons are Tow, Tow Mk II, Bakter Shiken and FGM 148 ATGM. The Army Air Defence Command has S.A- 7 Grail, General Dynamics FIM-92 Stinger, GD FIM Red Eye, and ANZA Mk-I, Mk-II, Mk-III and HQ 2 B surface ti air missiles. Radar controlled Oerlikon is the standard Ack Ack weapon system.

The ballistic missile inventory of the Army is substantial. It comprises Ghauri III and Shaheen III IRB'S; medium range Ghauri I and II and Shaheen II, and short range Hatf I- B, Abdali, Ghaznavi, Shaheen I and M -11 missiles. All the ballistic missiles can carry nuclear war heads. Nuclear and conventional weapon capable Babur Cruise missile is the new addition to Pakistan's strategic weapon inventory. Number of ballistic missiles and war heads are almost the same as India has. So there is a parity in nuclear weapons, which is a deterrent. Indian armor is of Russian origin. Out of 2295 Indian Army's Main Battle tanks, 2235 are of Russian origin. The main battle tanks are; 310 T-90-S Bishsma's (300 are on order), 1925 T-72M Ajeya's.. The T-90 and the T-72 have 125 mm smooth barrel guns. T-72 though old is the backbone of Indian Armor Corp's. 268 Ajeya's have been upgraded with Israeli Elbit thermal imaging systems. 1000 T-72 MBT's are awaiting up-gradation.

There have been several instances of T-72's gun barrel bursting. 124 Indian made Arjun (heavy 56 ton) MBT are on order. Sixty Arjun's are in operational service. Arjun's engine overheating problem has not been solved. Arjun has a 120 mm gun, but is unfit or desert operations. Pakistan Army is equally strong in armor, capable of giving a fitting response to any Indian military adventure.

Main Battle tanks Al-Khalid and Al-Zarrar are the backbone of Pakistan's armor Corp's. Both are Pakistan made. Pakistan's tank armory comprises :five hundred Al-Khalid MBT's; 320 Al-Zarrar type 85 II MBT's, 500 Al-Zarrar MBT's; 450 79II AP (Chinese type 81 upgrade, and 570 T-80 UD MBT of Ukranian make. In addition Pakistan has 880 Type 59, which were procured from China in 1970.This makes a total of three thousand six hundred and twenty tanks.

All Pakistani MBT's except T-59's have 125 mm smooth barrel guns. Indian armor offensives in Kashmir, Punjab, and Sind would be effectively challenged by Pakistani armor and mechanized formations, depending on PAF's ability to keep the skies over the battle areas clear of Indian Air Force. India's modern air defense system has Israeli Arrow anti-missile missiles, and 90,000 surface to air missiles-SAM's. India has one hundred nuclear armed ballistic missiles (Agni-1 and Agni II), and Brahmos the new supersonic cruise missile. Indian Army is well trained, equipped and highly professional, and so is Pakistan Army. Air power is likely to play a key, if not a decisive role in any future major or minor India-Pakistan armed conflict. The aim of Indian pre-emptive strikes will be maximum destruction by surprise air attacks, combined with shock commando action. A possibe scenario is; intensive bombing of the target to be followed by attacks by armed helicopters and ground assault by heliborne Commandoes. An overview of Indian Air Force and Pakistan Air Force will help comprehension of IAF's offensive capabilities, and defensive capabilities of Pakistan Air Force.

Indian Air Force has 3000 aircraft including training, transport, helicopters and 800-1000 combat air craft, which operate from sixty air bases, including Farkhor airbase in Tajikistan.. Six hundred IAF's strike and air defense fighters are expected to be operational. Pakistan Air Force has 630 aircraft, which include 530 combat aircraft, with 400 operational at any time. In 1996 India signed an agreement with Russia for the purchase of 90 Su 30 Mk-1 multi-role fighter-bombers. In 2004 a multi-billion licence was signed for building additional 140. 240 Su30-Mk-1's were ordered, 120 are already in service. With a maximum speed of Mach 2.3 and range of 8000 Km with refueling and ability to carry tons of conventional munitions and nuclear weapons, it is a lethal and menacing weapon system for the strike and interception role.

Other IAF's advanced strike and combat aircraft are: 51 Mirage-2000 (of Kargil fame), 60 Mig-29's (for air defense), 250 old Mig-21's (110 have been refurbished with Israeli help), 47 Jaguars and 70 Mig-27's for ground attack. 220 LCA Teja's under manufacture at HAL Bangalore will start entering service in 2010... IAF's fighter pilots are well trained and have out shone American pilots during joint exercises.

Pakistan Air Force has 200 rebuilt Mirage- 3's (for night air defense) and Mirage-5's for the strike role. They can carry nuclear weapons. They have been upgraded with new weapon systems, radars, and avionics. Additionally the PAF has 42 F-16's, 150 F-7's including 55 latest F-7 PG's. Manufacture of 150 JF 17 Thunder fighters (jointly designed) is underway at Pakistan Aeronautical Complex Kamra. The JF -17 Thunder is a 4th generation fly by wire multi-role fighter aircraft. Eight are already in PAF service. An order has been placed with China for the purchase of 36 JF-10, a Mach 2.3 -5th generation multi-role fighter, comparable in performance to the Su-30 Mk-1 with the Indian Air Force. PAF is on Red Alert, and is maintaining full vigil to intercept and destroy IAF intruders.

During the recent air space violation, the IAF intruders were in the sights of PAF's F-16's, but were allowed to escape unscathed to avoid a major diplomatic crisis. PAF pilots and technicians are well trained, high professionals, who will be able to prove their mettle in the future battle with India. A comparison of Indian Navy and Pakistan Navy reveals that Pakistan Navy could inflict substantial damage to the Indian Navy. Indian Navy has 16 submarines; Pakistan Navy has ten, some are brand new. Indian Navy has 27 war ships, Pakistan Navy has ten. Indian Aircraft Carrier Veerat, will be a menace, and must be sunk by submarine or air attacks, if it attempts to block Pakistan's sea lanes or ports. It is hoped that better sense prevails and India desists from invading and attacking Pakistan. If it does, the consequences will be horrible for both the countries.

Manpower and Ground Forces

India has the second largest manpower in its military globally - at 3,773,300 personell (2005), next only to China. Pakistan has a much smaller manpower of 1,449,000 personell which is proportionally higher than India in terms of their population ratios. Pakistan's ground forces are equipped with American or Chinese weapons like FIM 92 Stinger SAMs, BGM-71 TOW anti-tank missiles, T-82 tanks and other equipments. Indian ground forces are equipped mostly by home-made or Soviet technologies like IR guided 9K35 Strela-10 SAMs, 3rd Gen IR guided Nag anti-tank missiles, UAVs and a large inventory of tanks and support vehicles. In terms of numbers and equipments, both Indian and Pakistani ground forces are on an closely equal footing.

Comparison of Air Forces

As of 2006, Indian Air Force (IAF) has over 170,000 personnel and 3,382 aircrafts of which 1,330 are combat aircrafts operating off 61 airbases - making it the fourth largest air force in the world. India's strike fighters consist of Russian and French aircrafts like Mikoyan MiG-29, Dassault Mirage 2000, Sukhoi Su-30 - the last one developed under dual licensing by HAL, India's aerospace industry in Bangalore.

In addition to these, India's air force owns ground attack aircrafts, reconnaissance aircrafts, UAVs and support helicopters - a majority of them either of Soviet or French origin. Pakistan Air Force (PAF) has about 530 combat aircrafts and over 65,000 active personnel, operating out of 9 airbases. Its strike fighters consist of US, Chinese and French fighters like F-16 Fighting Falcon, JF-17 Thunder and Dassault Mirage ROSE-III. It also has transport aircrafts like Lockheed Martin C-130 and Airbus A310, however there are no UAVs or reconnaissance aircrafts in the Pakistani Air Force.

Naval and Sea Based Forces

After the overwhelming losses in the 1971 war against India, Pakistan rapidly increased the size of its naval fleet which doubled in the 1980s after a massive 3.2 billion dollar military and economic aid by US President Ronald Reagan. At present, Pakistan's navy owns over 45 vessels , most of them of US or European origin which include submarines, destroyers, frigates, patrol and mine warfare boats. It operates from its sole naval port in Karachi and naval facilities in UK, USA and France. It had recently been involved in various humanitarian operations during the 2005 Tsunami in South East Asia. Indian Navy on the other hand, is a three dimensional naval force consisting of missile-capable warships, an aircraft carrier, mine sweepers and a host of marine aircrafts; most of its warships indigenously built in its own dockyards. The navy operates from its major naval bases in Visakhapatnam, Mumbai, Goa and the Andaman Islands. Indian Navy has significant capabilities of being a true blue water Navy and is experienced both in war and peacekeeping operations in the Indian Ocean.

The Nuclear Club

India tested a nuclear bomb in 1974 using materials from Canada and technical help from Soviet Union. However the embargo in heavy water export from Canada after the test stalled India's nuclear ambitions till 1998, when it shocked the world by conducting five nuclear detonations termed as Shakti tests.

The highest yield was by a 48 kiloton staged fusion device, which India claimed was a thermonuclear bomb but seismic data on the tests proved otherwise. In the same year 1998, Pakistan conducted a series of six nuclear detonations in a test termed as Chagai.

The highest yield was reported to be about 25 kiloton from a two stage boosted device. At present Pakistan's nuclear stockpile is slated to be around 30-40 warheads while India possesses 70-100 warheads. The nuclearisation of India and Pakistan became a turning point in the history of conflicts between these two countries with high tensions but no war, not very much unlike the US vs USSR Cold War.

Ballistic and Cruise Missile Proliferation

In the nuclear delivery front, both India and Pakistan have a series of ballistic and cruise missiles in addition to ground attack aircrafts. The maximum range among India's operational ballistic missiles is 2000 km achieved by Agni-2. India's Agni ballistic missiles are indigenously developed by its own missile defence industry known as IGMDP.

The maximum range among Pakistan's missiles is by Hatf V Gauri which is reported to do over 2200 kms. Pakistan's Hatf missiles are based on North Korean No-Dong series of IRBMs. Both Pakistan's Hatf and India's Agni ballistic missiles are nuclear capable.

India has also developed a supersonic cruise missile BrahMos which is by far the fastest cruise missile at Mach 2.6 and maximum range of 290 km. It is reported to be nuclear capable but it is not confirmed yet. On the Pakistan side, its Babur cruise missile has a reported range of 700 km and a maximum speed of 880 km/h (Mach 0.7). As with India BrahMos, Babur is also reported to be nuclear capable but there is no confirmation yet.

The Final Verdict

Both Pakistan and India are almost evenly matched head to head in nuclear and missile fronts, however India has strategic and technological superiority over the conventional forces of Pakistan. Indian Navy is larger in fleet and personnel size with a more varied range of ships including an aircraft carrier while Pakistan's Navy is smaller and has no aircraft carriers. Indian's IAF is equipped with highly capable fighters like 4.5th generation Su-30s and 4th gen Mirage 2000s which are technologically superior to Pakistan PAF's F-16s and Mirage IIIs. Additionally Indian pilots are better trained and more capable in air combat than Pakistani forces as was demonstrated by its various wars with Pakistan or joint exercises with US and UK. In the area of conventional ground forces both the Indian as well as Pakistani Army is well equipped and highly trained to survive in extremities of topography and climate in combat conditions, like wars in the high Himalayas.

If a purely conventional war were to take place between both these countries, India would most likely overpower Pakistan owing to its superior military technology and infrastructure, larger manpower, more territorial area and a strategic advantage in its sea and air forces. It must also be noted that a war between these two countries will matter more than India's conventional superiority as both these nations are nuclear powers on an equal deadlock. India has maintained a 'no first use' nuclear policy on the lines of a similar policy by China while Pakistan does not have any such policy, considering their only hope against India is in nuclear deterrence. It would be risky for India at the present scenario to go into any aggressive war against Pakistan as the repercussions would be serious a nuclear devastation for both countries.

India's numerical and technical superiority in a conventional war is beyond question - therefore Pakistan's low nuclear threshold and maintenance of the first-use option.

However, in a surgical kind of strike being talked about in Indian and Pakistani circles, over Muridke or Muzaffarabad , cruise missiles are likely to be used. The Pakistani and Indian capability is evenly matched in these except for India's supersonic cruise missile with a speed of Mach 2.6 which is an obvious advantage in this kind of a strike, but it only has a range of 290 kms - enough to reach Muridke if launched from East Punjab but not much more. Pakistan's answer is the Babur cruise missile with a range of 700 km and a speed of Mach 0.7 - sub-sonic but pretty fast.

UAV's was the other Indian advantage which has recently been matched by Pakistan. With the evenly matched air, missile and nuclear capability, a surgical strike doesn't seem to be the best option. If India is to win, it will have to be a full-scale conventional war with both sides avoiding breaching the other's nuclear threshold.

ASSESSMENT OF MOVES TOWARDS PRIVATISATION

As a result of the above, increase private sector participation in defence production is increasingly being pursued: according to the latest reports more than 300 companies have already registered their interest in participating in the defence sector. Thus far, the following areas appear to have borne the greatest fruit.

IT and Communications. According to the MTCL India's capabilities in areas such as super-computing and software development are very strong indeed. With this in mind, it is understandable that a number of senior military figures have recently made clear their desire to upgrade the Armed Force's communication and IT capabilities through private sector involvement. Speaking during an August 2000 CII seminar, for instance, General V.P Malik observed that: "the private sector, which had not previously participated in defence production, had expanded in size and reach and now has the capability to produce non-lethal items such as communications and IT related' products He also stated that: 'the army would be requiring radios of all types, ATM switches, optical fibre cable, satellite systems, power sources of all types and micro and macro cellular systems' and that the Army was looking at buying these technologies off the shelf from private companies.

Service Contracts and Outsourcing: There is a growing interest in outsourcing to the private sector within the military The IAF, for example, is exploring the possibility of privatising its base-repair depots, accounts, and areas of administrative work. According to the Chief of the Air Staff, Air Chief Marshall A.Y. Tipinis, there is also scope to involve the private sector in the maintenance and operation of fighter aircraft, air-launched guided missiles and ground to air missiles as well as support equipment such as radars, communications networks, and specialist vehicles. Outsourcing is also an option for the PSUs; indeed they are increasingly shedding the production of low technology items to the private sector. For example, both Bharat Electronics and Garden Reach Shipbuilders have developed a network of small-scale industries and ancillary units around them. Likewise, the ordnance factories have been sourcing various raw materials and small parts from a range of indigenous industries. Some effort has also been made to involve the private sector in the production of middle level technologies: for example, at one stage Kirloskars was involved in the development of an indigenous engine for the Arjun tank.

Foreign Participation. There is mounting evidence to suggest that the country's eight PSU's will be allowed to enter into 'strategic alliances' and partnerships with foreign defence manufacturers. On 12 October, for example, George Fernandes, stated that 'India provides an excellent opportunity for the developed and developing world to source cost-effective goods and services from our defence production industry' He also talked of the 'opportunities that India offers for joint-ventures, technology transfers, and co-production facilities for export to other markets'. Currently the amount of foreign investment in the Indian defence sector is small. But a number of foreign manufacturers have already taken him up on the offer. During the visit of the Russian President Vladimir Putin to India this October, for example, the two sides signed a new military and technical co-operation agreement to establish joint ventures for the production of a variety of armaments and military hardware and establishing joint sales and marketing structures for the products. The Russian government is also thought to be considering investing a share of proceeds of its recent sales to India for creating after-care and upgrading facilities in the country. Looking to the future it is possible that Russian companies will invite their Indian (and Chinese) counterparts to participate in the development of next generation weapons systems. Russia is not the only country assessing this option. Somewhere in the region of 20 partnership agreements covering a range of cooperative arrangements, including co-production of aircraft equipment, joint development of communications equipment, and co-operation in software and electronic design, are believed to have been signed between British companies and the eight PSUs. Similar discussion have also been held with France, Poland and others. Every effort is also being made to ensure that these partnerships are not limited to the public sector.

Research and Development: There is some reason to believe that private companies will be encouraged to participate in defence R&D. Participation in this area received a significant boost following the May 1998 nuclear tests, when the imposition of sanctions on India prompted the Defence Research and Development Agency (DRDO) to open up eight labs in non-strategic areas to private participation. In addition to this, the DRDO now claims to have 'various levels of partnership' with 250 industries.

Defence Exports: In a related development, the government is now actively assessing the possibility of increasing exports of defence related equipment. Traditionally, modern India has eschewed the option of selling arms abroad, and relatively speaking its defence exports are minimal, although a defence exports cell was established in 1973. In recent years, however, the country has held a number of defence export shows in co-operation with the CII, while Indian PSUs have participated in defence shows abroad. Currently, the main products exported are from the country's ordnance factories and include small arms ammunition, explosives, rockets, spares for rifles and guns, clothing items, parachutes, aeronautical stores, communications equipment, and components and sub-systems. India's main export markets are Asia and Africa although some equipment has gone to Europe. Old export markets are also being expanded and new ones being sought out: following a visit to Vietnam in March 2000 by George Fernandes, for example, both countries, who signed a Protocol on Defence Co-operation in 1994, initialled a new agreement to enhance defence cooperation in areas of training. Algeria is also considering buying defence equipment from India, including spares for its MiG combat aircraft, and helicopters, vehicles, night vision devices and communications equipment. India's hope is probably that it will be able to use the revenue from sales to reduce its own unit purchase costs as well as provide an extra flow of money into defence R&D.

Future Prospects

Despite these positive signs, at this stage there are still a number of factors inhibiting increased private sector (and possibly even foreign) involvement in defence production.

The main stumbling block is that in order to increase private sector involvement the Indian government would have to scrap the 1948 and 1956 Industrial Policy Resolutions. This is unlikely at this stage because many of the country's bureaucrats and politicians fear that such a decision will lead to mass lay-offs and possibly social turbulence. (Incidentally, these same individuals are also against the privatisation of India's other PSUs). As is traditionally the case, pressure against change is also likely to come from both the management and the workforce from within the sector. In short, the momentum and support for the economic reform programme in India has yet to gather the momentum necessary to allow fully fledged private participation and competition in defence production. Private participation in the sensitive areas of defence R&D is likely to be limited due to concerns about security. Substantial foreign participation in the form of joint ventures particularly with Western companies, meanwhile, is likely to be limited by concerns about security and the reliability of Western suppliers in meeting their obligations. (By way of an example, the fact that a number of Indian Navy SeaKing helicopters have been stranded in Britain because they contain American parts, which the country is restricted from selling to India as part of the sanctions imposed following the May 1998 nuclear tests, is believed to one of the reasons why the deal to sell the BAE SYSTEMS Hawk has been further delayed) Organisational problems within the MOD are also likely to hinder any advantages to be gained by through the greater involvement of the private sector. The isolation of defence production from defence R&D, for example, is seen by many in India as inhibiting sensible planning and management of India's defence programmes.

Despite all the problems and challenges of the past decade India is unlikely to abandon the dream of establishing its own defence industry. Paradoxically, however, it is becoming increasingly apparent to all concerned that the only way that the country will be able to fulfil (even partly) its ambition of designing and manufacturing its own top-end defence equipment will be to dismantle the system of public ownership on which it is based. As the process of globalisation and consolidation in the defence industry continues to gather pace and the price of designing, developing and producing modern defence equipment increases rapidly, India's aspirations would also be greatly helped if it could rapidly involve foreign companies in the process of defence production.

Five to Ten Year Forecast

In the near term (5-10 years) the evidence collected in the paper suggests that this is unlikely to happen. Rather, the development of a hybrid model in which the core of PSUs and the DRDO will be maintained, while private sector participation will be sought in non-sensitive/peripheral areas such as IT and communications will probably dominate. This process will be complemented by an increased effort both to seek partnerships with largely Russian put possibly some European defence companies. However, if past efforts to establish joint ventures with Indian companies in both the civil and defence sector are anything to go by the scope of these will be limited. India's attempts to increase its defence exports profile partly as a way to fund its indigenous R&D programme will also be limited to the sale of low and middle level technologies to cash-strapped and politically isolated regimes, such as Algeria and Vietnam. The perceived need to modernise its armed forces quickly, which has taken root in the wake of the Kargil crisis and the impending obsolescence of many of its existing platform, however, means that India will continue to look abroad to full-fill the majority of its top-end defence needs. This will be reflected in the division of resources within the defence budget, which is also likely to continue to grow over this period.

Ten to Twenty Year Forecast

Potentially, India's long term prospects (10-20) years are better. There is a good chance, for example, that by 2010 the Indian government will have made real advances down the path of economic reform and that the climate for private sector participation and perhaps even the privatisation of the PSUs will be more favourable. Crucial to India's success, however, will be its ability to bring together its civil and military R&D capabilities, not only in non-military/dual use areas, but across a broad spectrum. India could also use its strength in IT to strengthen its partnerships with foreign defence manufacturers and secure maintenance, upgrading and possibly production facilities in return. Parallel to this, and bearing in mind the fact that future defence platforms, such as the JSF, are unlikely to be single country ventures, there are also added advantages to be gained from India linking itself into those foreign companies associated closely with this process; indeed it may even be able to contribute in certain key areas. If this happens, although it is unlikely that India will be able to produce 70 per cent of its requirements domestically, it will certainly be able to source more from domestic producers, and more crucially will benefit from its access to technology, and participation in R&D programmes. (It is possible that India will be able to reduce its total reliance on imports to 50 per cent, although it is still unlikely to be able to produce whole systems indigenously).

Final Assessment

Naturally, this rather rosy outlook depends on India's willingness to accept not only the advantages of privatisation, but more importantly the direction in which defence industries today are going.

Arguably, the room for companies focused solely on their home markets and expecting to provide their militaries with state of the art defence equipment, not only in the developed world but also in the West, is shrinking rapidly, due to the rising cost and sophistication of the systems involved.

Put another way, participation in regional or global defence programmes will become the norm. India, with its growing strength in the new economy, has the chance this time not to miss the boat, although there is always a danger that misplaced nationalism and an unclear understanding of developments will prevent it from making the most of the opportunity.

INDIA'S DEFENCE INDUSTRY IN THE 21ST CENTURY

Major Policy Initiatives

India's defence industry entered a new phase of self-reliance on the eve of the 21st century. Since the mid-1990s, several initiatives have been undertaken by the government to effect changes in the defence industry. Soon after the liberalisation of the economy was announced in 1990/91, the defence industry started realising the importance of civil-military interaction in the industrial sector. The private industries in India, which were thus far debarred from entering into defence production and whose role in the defence sector was limited to supplying spare parts and other minor contributions, started demanding a share in defence production.

In 1994, the then Defence Minister founded six Task Forces on major areas of defence modernisation, of which reforms in defence industry was an important part. This was carried out by the government in consultation with institutions like the

Confederation of Indian Industries (CII). The CII, on its part was instrumental in bringing out a series of proposals in the broad field of private participation in the defence sector and armed forces–industry cooperation. Soon after this, the government initiated a programme called 'Army-Industry Partnership', under the auspices of CII which highlighted the importance of cooperative arrangements between the armed forces, defence industry and the government. After India's nuclear tests, various sanctions were imposed on India, of which sanctions related to the import of military and dual-use goods and technologies were considered the most important.

Sanctions were imposed on more than 150 items, which affected the progress of many defence products. However, the impact of sanctions on military technology was taken up as a another phase of challenge for the defence scientists as they had faced similar sanctions after the test in 1974. At that time they had faced more difficulties as the defence industry was not in a position to withstand such severe cuts which had resulted in delays in many major programmes. This time around, the defence industry had made significant progress to be able to withstand sanctions. After the Kargil conflict in mid-1999, the government started looking into security gaps and founded a committee under Mr K. Subrahmanyam. He brought out a major report on this conflict, which is known as the 'Kargil Committee Report'. This report, among other recommendations, highlighted the importance of reforms in higher defence management and reforms in institutional processes in the security sector.

The Government also founded a Group of Ministers' committee to look into major aspects of the overall security management of the country. The committee submitted its report to the government, which is known as GoM Report on 'Reforming the National Security System. This report highlighted the importance of self-reliance in India's defence industry and recommended several steps to introduce institutional changes into the system. Coupled with changes at institutional and organisational levels, India's defence industry entered an entirely new era after the Government announced a major change in policy by outlining codes of conduct for and inviting private participation in the defence industry. This is seen as by far the most important policy shift in the defence-industrial sector in the last fifty years. By doing so, the Government, through an official notification No. 5(37)/2001-FCI, allowed private sector participation up to 100 percent and permitted foreign direct investment (FDI) up to 26 percent. This decision has been hailed by both the private industry and the government-owned defence industry. Institutions like CII and FICCI, which represent interests and views of the private sector, have been instrumental in influencing such a marked change in policies. According to Mr Sushanto Sen, the Director General of CII, such a policy change is certainly going to benefit both the defence industry and the private sector.

In tune with the stated objectives of India's defence industry to achieve a higher degree of self-reliance and a desire to make its flagship units globally competitive, thus entering into competitive defence markets, the Government has also introduced some institutional changes that are expected to smoothen operations both at structural and organisational levels. Earlier, procurement procedures were considered cumbersome, and there were overlaps in organisational responsibilities of respective organs responsible for procurement. Under the new system, the Services Headquarters were integrated into the Ministry of Defence to provide closer interaction. The procurement structure is now a three-tier structure with the recent establishment of the Defence Acquisition Council (DAC) at the apex. Its primary role will be to accord in-principle-approval of long-term perspective plans (15-20 years), acceptance of necessity for the capital acquisition plan (5 years), identify 'Make', 'Buy' and 'Make and Buy' projects and monitor progress of the three Boards under it – the Defence Procurement Board, Defence Production Board and the Defence R&D Board. The Defence Procurement Board under the Defence Secretary will have the primary role of capital procurements and coordination. The Defence Production Board will be headed by the Secretary

Defence Production and Supplies and will oversee all activities related to indigenous manufacture, progress in 'make' projects and will provide support to DAC. The Defence R&D Board will be headed by the Secretary Defence R&D and will oversee progress, monitor and report on all R&D proposals in consultation with the user service and production board. Other measures at institutional level include direct linkages between the armed forces and the Ministry of Defence through integrated headquarters, which include respective perspective planning branches. In sum, organisational and institutional changes brought about recently seem to complement policy changes.

Problems and Prospects: An Assessment

India's quest for self-reliance has produced mixed results. Some of the lessons that India has learnt in the past fifty years are worth noting here. First, a combination of factors have led to the indigenous design and development component of self-reliance slowing down to almost zero for over a quarter of a century after 1962. This has led not only to a huge technology gap but also contributed to severe difficulties in technology assimilation in the industrial sector. However, since the mid-1980s, activities toward achieving a greater degree of self-reliance have taken up momentum. The technology gap also widened the scope for acquisition of production technology rather than design technology from foreign sources. This in turn has created a license production regime at the cost of indigenous production. During the 1990s, the activities to encourage joint ventures and co-production in the defence-industrial sector is largely seen as a step to reduce license regime and boost indigenous industrial capabilities. How far this will achieve desired results are yet to be seen as such activities are only of recent origin and they need lead time to prove themselves.

For example, the market for Brahmos missiles is estimated to be large, but it depends on how much is it likely to penetrate the cruise missile market at a global level. Success of this kind will not only validate India's defence-industrial capabilities to meet domestic demands but also increase its confidence in many ways.

Second, private participation in the defence-industrial sector has started after a long delay. This is attributable to several factors, ranging from the socialist and protective nature of the defence sector to fears of what is called 'security diffusion'.

The latter especially relates to a fear of below-expectation performance by the private sector as it is hardly specialised to meet strict high military standards, hence compromising security standards. This kind of fear has been criticised by many who argue that private participation is essential in the defence sector which is primarily technology driven and capital intensive.

The recent opening up of the defence sector for private participation has generated a lot of interest in the country. Institutions like CII caution that while such initiatives are always welcome, the government should come out with a clear 'road-map' for the private sector participants in defence so as to enable them to prepare themselves for the new reality.

Fears regarding the ability of the private sector to match expectations of the country in the highly demanding and technology-dominated industrial sector are countered by industrialists like Atul Kirloskar (Chairman of Committee on National Defence, CII), who claim to have absolute faith in their abilities. Many also claim that given a chance, the secondary role of the private sector can be turned into a primary one in a short period of time. Some of the leading industrialists even claim that they have or intend to possess capabilities to produce complete weapons systems.

Several companies like Mahindras and Mahindras (M&M), the Tata Group, Kirloskar Brothers, Larsen and Toubro (L&T), and many others have already jumped into the fray to obtain orders from the defence industry. Since 2002, the Government has received more than ten applications from the private sector to manufacture weapons systems. It has recently awarded five licenses to L&T and M&M to produce military vehicles and some weapons systems. Third, the government has emphasised measures to enhance the defence industry to cope with future challenges. Such measures are carried out by both OFs and DPSUs, apart from respective branches of the Government and the armed forces. Digitalisation, strict quality control, performance-related benefits, professional management systems, allowing the private sector to carry out R&D activities in the government-owned laboratories, are some of the measures which have come up in recent years and are likely to impinge the defence-industrial landscape.

A simplification of production and procurement rules promise better buyer-seller relations. There were some protests coming from employees' unions of OFs and DPSUs against privatisation. The Government has assured these unions that employees' interests will be borne in mind but that it will give priority to performance.

In one instance, the Defence Minister is reported to have appealed to the workers in one DPSU to not to worry about possible relocations due to privatisation and assured them to take effective steps to safeguard their interests. It seems that rationalisation of the defence industry is on the cards which might bring some unrest in the form of reduction of employment in the defence-industrial sector. There are even rumours that some of the units, especially from the ordnance sector might be closed down. The private sector participants are, however, optimistic. They argue that their factories can effectively be converted into profit making civilian units. In several rounds of interviews with senior officers and industry analysts by the author, it seems that some of the industrial units may come under close scrutiny. Conversion to civilian production in their cases is not ruled out. In brief, significant rationalisation, diversification and closer private participation are coming and are likely to influence India's defence industry in many ways.

NEVER MIND 'MAKE IN INDIA' - HERE'S WHAT INDIA'S DEFENCE SECTOR NEEDS

Speaking at an interactive session organised by the Confederation of Indian Industry at Bengaluru in February this year, Defence Minister Manohar Parrikar said we need 'implementation and action' and not 'little-little' changes in policy.

Implementation

While that is true in a general way, one policy that requires not just implementation and action but also more than 'little-little' changes is the 'Make' procedure, a curious mix of policy and procedure.

Introduced in 2006, it was intended to provide an opportunity to Indian industry to undertake research, design and development of high-technology complex systems, with government funding up to 80 per cent of the cost of prototype development and assured purchase order for the predefined quantity of the equipment so developed.

Sadly, not a single project has taken off under this category so far. The question, then, is what past experience shows, and what needs to be done now.

In 2011, the MoD came out with a Defence Production Policy whose objective was to achieve 'substantive self-reliance' through indigenization.

The next year, the MoD promulgated a new look 'offset' policy which requires foreign companies to plough back at least 30 per cent of the contract value into the Indian defence sector, if the contract is for Rs 300 crore or more, through one of several permissible modes, including transfer of technology or equipment to the Indian Offset Partners.

The hierarchical ordering of the modes of procurement that requires preference to be given to procurement from indigenous sources either by way of outright purchase or by involving the Indian industry in the manufacturing of defence equipment, was the highlight of the revised Defence Procurement Procedure (DPP) of 2013.

The latest in a series of steps taken by the MoD was raising of the FDI cap in defence production last year from 26 to 49 per cent, with removal of the condition that 51 per cent of the stake in the investee company should be in the hands of a single Indian individual or company.

These measures were expected to revolutionise indigenous defence production, but that has not happened. Ironically, this is the period when India was on its way to becoming the largest importer of arms.

Initiative

The call given by the PM to 'come, make in India' and the subsequent 'Make-in-India' blitzkrieg by the governmental agencies have raised new questions about defence production without addressing the old ones.

The question now being asked is: how does the current 'Make-in-India' initiative fit with the make procedure? While 'Make-in-India' is apparently all about inviting the foreign companies to use India's soil for manufacturing defence equipment, the make procedure is designed to promote the Indian industry to take the lead in the matter of defence procurement and production.

The information put out on the 'Make-in-India' website mostly pre-dates the PM's call and fails to address this question. There is no doubt that both foreign companies and Indian industry will have to play a role in India's quest to become a manufacturing hub.

The defence public sector in India, the ordnance factories and the defence research and development organization cannot be written off as the MoD's non-performing assets. It would be naive to argue – as some people do - that their role needs to be drastically curtailed to give the private sector an opportunity to speed up indigenization.

Clarity

Clearly, what is needed is a policy that brings clarity regarding the role each of these players is expected to take in strengthening the defence manufacturing sector in India and how these roles will be synergised. It should also address the question of transfer of technology, co-production and co-development. Such a policy will work only if it is backed by an procedural framework. The DPP 2013 will need to be reconceptualised to bring it in sync with the new policy.

In particular, the make procedure will need to be re-oriented to accommodate the spirit of 'Make-in-India'. A foreign company wanting to enter the Indian defence production sector must know how to go about it; DPP 2013 does not answer this question.

But with its 142nd ranking in the global index of ease-of-doing business India cannot expect to attract foreign companies or even fire up Indian industry, which has its own list of woes relating to taxation, deemed export status for the defence industry, industrial licensing, and the like.

All these issues need to be addressed. Disjointed measures, such as raising of the FDI limit to 49 per cent, have very limited impact when taken in isolation. Lastly, greater professionalism is required in handling several activities, such as formulation of the qualitative requirements (specifications) which have derailed several procurement programmes in the past. This entails difficult structural reforms.

The MoD could signal its intention of bringing about a change by setting up a forum where the representatives of the industry – both Indian and foreign – could regularly meet ministry officials for discussions. Pragmatic and implementable solutions will arise only from such interactions.

7

Indian Indigenisation in Defence Manufacturing in Making India

India is at the cusp of metamorphosing from a top regional player to one with global clout. As India's geo-political and economic ambitions grow, it needs to develop robust indigenous manufacturing capabilities and ecosystem to secure its ambition for self-reliance in the Aerospace and Defence industry.

Currently, the country allocates about 1.8 percent of its GDP to defence spending and imports about 70 percent of defence equipment. Owing to the dynamic security environment, India's defence requirements are likely to increase in the foreseeable future making indigenous development of modern defence hardware and technology a top priority for the government.

Glass half full: A Sea of Opportunity

The fact that India ranks amongst the top 10 countries in the world in terms of its military expenditure, makes it one of the most attractive markets for defence. With the government's agenda to reduce import dependence in defence by 35-40 percent it is actively promoting indigenous defence manufacturing with initiatives like Make in India and policy reforms including allowing 100 percent Foreign Direct Investment (FDI). Even the recently launched Defence Procurement Policy (DPP) is seen as a game changer to ensure faster pace in procurement, especially through newly introduced categories under indigenously designed, developed and manufactured (IDDM) provisions. Following the Central government's footsteps and recognising the huge potential from the defence sector, several states are also offering incentives and concessions in the form of aerospace clusters or Special Economic Zones (SEZs) for developing an ecosystem where all core and ancillary activities related to defence manufacturing can co-exist.

With the Defence Minister's intention of procuring about US$10 billion worth of defence products per year in the next 5 to 10 years, and the government undertaking several initiatives and reforms, there is a sea of opportunity available for all stakeholders in the sector. For example OEMs as well as SMEs in the defence manufacturing sector are focussing on moving from a buyer-seller to a co-developer and co-manufacturer relationship. They have not only come together and formed strategic partnerships to support the development of a sustainable supplier base for the defence sector, but have also moulded themselves quickly to foster a culture of innovation and R&D. So far, they have demonstrated a huge amount of potential and capability to deliver on this promise.

Glass half empty: necessary steps to hasten indigenisation

India offers tremendous opportunities in engineering services, supply chain sourcing and associated maintenance, repair and overhaul-related activities, however to achieve self-reliance we need to create a robust ecosystem that can address the capacity and capability requirements for the industry. While the government is taking numerous measures to bolster defence manufacturing, the pace of modernisation must be balanced with both short and long term initiatives. Here are some necessary steps that must be adopted to enable long term indigenisation:

a) Partnering for success: We believe that co-development and co-manufacturing is the way forward to achieve the vision of turning India into a global high value manufacturing destination not just for the home market but also for export. India harbours an immense amount of potential that can be tapped into by way of key strategic partnerships that add value across the entire length and breadth of R&D, manufacturing and supply chain. Foreign OEM's have already started leveraging these benefits, and are encouraging Indian industry to adopt best practices for global quality standards in their manufacturing processes to lead to the creation of a gold standard supply chain and defence manufacturing ecosystem in India.

b) A skilled talent pool: As per government estimates, a reduction in 20-25 percent in defence related imports could directly create an additional 100,000 to 120,000 highly skilled jobs in India. To be ready for the opportunities of the future, the industry needs to build and train talent to address the growing needs of the market. In addition, the academia and industry needs to forge partnerships to encourage research and technological advancements and create a talent pool that is industry ready.

c) Robust supply chain: A strong supply chain is critical for a defence manufacturer looking to optimize costs. Gradually, a handful of Indian SMEs are playing a key role in the global supply chain of OEMs. With the government's offset policies, procurement policies and regulatory incentives spurring the growth of a domestic defence industry, the SMEs need to play a more active role in developing a robust supply chain.

d) Infrastructure development: Lack of adequate infrastructure drives India's logistics costs upwards thus reducing the country's cost competitiveness and efficiency. While the government is investing in this area the pace of development needs to pick up considerably and public-private participation can go a long way in hastening this process.

Road ahead

India is uniquely positioned to create a vibrant defence manufacturing ecosystem that can help us achieve self-reliance. With defence remaining within the government's high priority focus area, I am confident that the country will soon emerge as a preferred destination for the co-development and co-creation of an indigenous and self-sufficient defence manufacturing ecosystem.

LOCAL DEFENCE MANUFACTURING IS THE HEART OF MAKE IN INDIA: MODI

Prime minister says strong Indian defence industry will boost country's security, add 200,000 skilled personnel in 10 years. With 60% of India's defence requirements met through imports, local defence production is the heart of Make In India programme, Prime Minister Narendra Modi said at the inauguration of Aero India 2015 in Bengaluru.

"We have the reputation of the largest importer of defence equipment.... We too need to increase our defence preparedness. We need to modernize our defence forces," Modi said. He said that a strong Indian defence industry will make India more secure. It will have room for the public sector, private sector and foreign firms.

Make in India—the theme of Aero India 2015, derived from the government's larger campaign of the same name—aims to transform the country into a manufacturing powerhouse and advocates boosting of exports, and incentivize import substitution. The 10th international edition of the aerospace and aviation exhibition, which opened on Wednesday, runs till 22 February. Inaugurating the air show on Wednesday, Modi said India will need about 200,000 skilled people in the defence and aerospace industry in 10 years. "There are studies showing even a 20-25% reduction in imports could directly add up to 120,000 highly skilled jobs," he said.

Modi said foreign companies can use India as an export hub and as part of a supply chain. The prime minister said India must bridge the gap between prototype and production. He said India needs to improve the acquisition and approval process and India will ensure that its technology does not fall into the wrong hands. The government, he said, is introducing a technology development fund and export policy has been made simple, clear and predictable. He also said the government will ensure the tax system does not discriminate against domestic manufacturing in comparison to imports. India's goal is to provide a level-playing field for Indian and foreign firms. The government is introducing significant reforms to defence offset policies to enable high value exports, he added.

India's defence offset policy mandates that foreign contractors source components and systems from local vendors for at least 30% of the value of government orders above Rs.300 crore. "Offset is a crucial instrument. I want India's offsets policy not as a means to export low-end products but to acquire state-of-art technology and skills," the prime minister said.

Modi said that India needs to increase defence preparedness as it has huge requirements to manage internal security. He said the air show is not a trade fair of defence equipment but a platform to showcase India's defence manufacturing sector. "More than 250 Indian firms and foreign firms are here. This is the largest ever air show." The air show will also include sectors such as defence manufacturing and airport infrastructure besides aerospace, defence and civil aviation. There are around 72 military and civil aircraft on display at the show.

Among the foreign military aircraft on display are the F-15C Eagle, Lockheed F-16C, Boeing KC-135 Stratotanker, Boeing C-17 A Globemaster III, Boeing P-8A Poseidon, Rafale Dassault and EMB-145 I.

Foreign civil aircraft include Pilatus PC-12 NG, Dassault Falcon 2000, Phenom 100E, Boeing B75, A75, Viking, Catwalk, WASP, RRJ 95, EMB 505, Bell 407 GX Helicopter, King Air 350 ER, 19-seater Turbo Prop AI Industry, Zlin Z-50 LX, Oma Sud Sky Car, Dassault Falcon 7X and Dornier 228-New Gen. "If we could raise the percentage of domestic procurement from 40% to 70% in the next five years, we would double the output in our defence industry. Imagine the impact in terms of jobs created directly and in the related manufacturing and services sector," Modi said.

He said that the government is reforming defence procurement policies and procedures. "There would be a clear preference for equipment manufactured in India. Our procurement procedures will ensure simplicity, accountability and speedy decision-making," he said. The government has raised the permitted level of foreign direct investment in the defence sector to 49%. "This can go higher, if the project brings state-of-the-art technology. We have permitted investments up to 24% by foreign institutional investments. And there is no longer a need to have a single Indian investor with at least a 51% stake," Modi said.

Industrial licensing requirements have been eliminated for a number of items. Where it is needed, the process has been simplified, he said. India is expecting a total defence budget allocation to be $620 billion between financial year 2014 and 2022 of which 50% would be on capital expenditure.

The annual opportunity for Indian companies—both public sector undertakings and private companies—is expected to reach $41 billion in size by financial year 2022 and $168 billion of cumulative opportunity between fiscal 2014 and 2022, driven by domestic and external demand. This is according to a report released by the lobby group Federation of Indian Chambers of Commerce and Industry (Ficci) and financial services company Centrum Capital Ltd early February 2015. The report noted that the domestic defence sector spends have seen continuous underspending vis-à-vis budgets, due to procedural delays.

Majority of the spending were for maintenance and salaries of the forces rather than for buying new equipment. In the aerospace value chain, there is significant movement and capability creation being seen at sub-system levels in aerostructures, avionics, and actuation and control, said Rahul Gangal, partner, aerospace and defence, Roland Berger Strategy Consultants, when asked about new capabilities added by the government in defence manufacturing.

"In the areas of engines and related components, India as a supply base is still nascent and development will take time. In the areas identified, there is capability that is evolving at multiple levels and across multiple technical and process competencies," Gangal said. India is forecast to spend $250 billion over the next decade to upgrade its military, which still largely relies on Russian equipment it bought from the 1960s to the 1980s, and catch up with strategic rivals like China.

INDIGENIZATION PUSH IN DEFENCE MANUFACTURING A FORCE MULTIPLIER

India is the world's largest importer of defence equipment, with 60% of its requirements met from outside the country. This, in itself, translates into a great business opportunity for those building domestic capabilities in defence. It is the reason why Prime Minister Narendra Modi wants local defence production to be at the heart of the government's Make in India campaign that seeks to promote manufacturing and attract foreign investment.

Speaking at the inauguration of Aero India 2015 in Bengaluru, Modi said: "We have a reputation as the largest importer of defence equipment in the world. That may be music to the ears of some of you here. But, this is one area where we would not like to be No. 1... "Our defence industry in the private sector is still small. But, it already employs thousands of people. This is despite the fact that nearly 60% of our defence equipment continues to be imported. And, we are spending tens of billions of dollars on acquisitions from abroad.

"There are studies that show that even a 20-25% reduction in imports could directly create an additional 100,000 to 120,000 highly skilled jobs in India. If we could raise the percentage of domestic procurement from 40% to 70% in the next five years, we would double the output in our defence industry.

"Imagine the impact in terms of jobs created directly and in the related manufacturing and services sector! Think of the spin-off benefits on other sectors in terms of advanced materials and technologies! "That is why we are focusing on developing

India's defence industry with a sense of mission. This is why it is at the heart of our Make in India programme."

A new defence procurement policy or DPP that accords priority to indigenously made defence products and boosts the Make in India initiative will be effective from 1 April, defence minister Manohar Parrikar said on 21 March. It will contain measures to promote indigenization and self-reliance in defence and also contain measures to ensure probity, accountability and transparency in defence procurements, the minister had said earlier in the month.

"If Make in India goes on at the same speed, growth will be in double digits, definitely more than the current 7-8%," he said. The government has no plans to make the indigenization clause in the DPP mandatory, but it will be given preference in defence acquisitions, he added.

The minister said defence acquisition spending can come down by 25% if the system is clean, without compromising on quality. He also said that skill development will be included in the offset clause in future to boost technology transfer. The government has increased the level of foreign direct investment (FDI) in the defence sector to 49%.

MAKE IN INDIA EFFECT

The idea of Make in India is now more than 18 months old. Launched on 25 September 2014, it was Modi's brainchild to make India the world's next manufacturing destination and attract FDI. Twenty-five sectors were identified—from automobiles to aviation, pharmaceuticals to tourism and wellness. In the past year-and-a-half, Make in India has become a clarion call for domestic companies and multinationals to look at increasing their investments in the country.

Since its launch, the government has taken several steps to make it easier for companies to do business in the country. And FDI has been allowed in sectors besides defence. FDI itself has received a dramatic boost since the launch of the initiative, according to the latest Economic Survey. Between October

2014 and June 2015, there was an almost 40% increase in FDI inflows.

Under the Make in India programme, the government has awarded 56 defence manufacturing permits to private sector entities in the past one year, compared with 47 granted in the preceding three years. According to the ministry of defence, the value of procurement of defence items by the armed forces from Indian sources in 2014-15 was Rs.49,531 crore, down 9.96% from Rs.55,014 crore during 2013-14.

As part of Make in India, the government proposes to encourage the manufacture of defence equipment in the country through various policy initiatives including giving preference to 'Buy (Indian)', 'Buy and Make (Indian)' and 'Make' categories of capital acquisition over 'Buy and Make (Global)' or 'Buy (Global)' categories in the DPP.

The centre has also liberalized the industrial licensing regime for Indian manufacturers and most of the components/ parts/sub-systems have been taken out of the list of defence products requiring industrial licences.

This has reduced entry barriers for new entrants in this sector, particularly small and medium enterprises. Moreover, the initial validity of an industrial licence has been increased from three years to 15 years with a provision to further extend it by three years on a case-by-case basis.

Offset implementation has been made flexible by allowing change of Indian offset partners (IOPs) and offset components even in signed contracts. Foreign original equipment manufacturers are now not required to indicate the details of IOPs and products at the time of signing of contracts. Services as an avenue for discharge of offsets have been reinstated. Offsets, currently, are a provision in the DPP that require any foreign company securing an order worth more than Rs.300 crore from India to source components worth 30% of the value of the order from India.

The Defence Acquisition Council (DAC) has also revised the so-called defence offset clause, which will now be applied to contracts of more than Rs.2,000 crore instead of the current Rs.300 crore, thereby removing a hurdle to foreign firms eyeing the Indian market.

This rule will be applicable once the new DPP comes into effect. The offsets opportunity is expected to be worth $15 billion within the next 10-15 years, assuming that several proposed purchases are completed on time, according to consultancy firm KPMG.

Parrikar said India has signed $5 billion worth of defence offset contracts while $10 billion of additional contracts are in the pipeline. He also said that better quality products will get weightage while calculating the price in special procurement cases.

Experts expect that the new DPP will boost Make in India. "India's oldest friend, Russia, agreed to take the initiative under the Make in India umbrella—perceived as a vote of confidence in India's economy—in two key strategic sectors: nuclear and defence. It is the first-ever project for a major defence platform under the Make in India mission," said Bharat Mandot, co-founder and chief executive officer at management consultancy StelCore Management Services Pvt. Ltd.

"India has relaxed its offset policy, exempting foreign firms from obligations like declaration of Indian offset partners' name, amount of FDI and value of equipment. Thus under the new deal, any foreign company will not have to declare name of its Indian partner. It can set up its factory in India under new offset rules without declaring FDI and value of machines installed there," Mandot said. Moreover, vendors can give mandatory details at the time of offset credit under the revised offset rules, he said.

"Defence secretary (procurement) and not the defence minister—as in the previous offset policy—will be the final word on any changes within an offset proposal," Mandot said. "There is, however, no change in rules of offset amount, which mandates a foreign firm to invest 30% of the contract value in India. The amendment is welcome, but there is an urgent need of a comprehensive policy. India is perhaps the only major arms importer that has a very modest offset percentage. It should be raised to at least 50% to ensure an enhanced flow of offsets to the Indian industry," he said.

But a lot more needs to be done. "The entire conversation around defence manufacturing is limited to the eyecatching categories of aerospace, weapons and naval systems," said Kabir Bogra, associate partner at law firm Khaitan & Co.

"To bolster the manufacturing industry, the tier-I and tier-II vendors need to be included in the conversation. We need to ensure that irrespective of the larger OEMs (original equipment manufacturers), their vendors see value in manufacturing in India. Acquisition programmes are political and fiscal affairs which can take time but the vendors can be encouraged to leverage the cost advantage of manufacturing in India," Bogra said.

Bogra said though it may be difficult to delink the manufacturers of regulated products from their OEM base, the manufacturers of dual use products are easier to attract. "We also need to reduce the burden of taxes. To rejuvenate the industry, transaction taxes need to be lowered to allow improved margins with lowering of costs. And, finally, the states need to play their part and ensure that projects actually take off. Apart from Karnataka, Andhra Pradesh, Telangana and Maharashtra, states have not shown any initiative to attract the defence industry," he said.

While there are ways and means to increase local production, what are the ways to boost defence preparedness? The Make in India mission is a priority for defence procurement but "operational readiness" is the military's primary task as "we don't want people to look at us with big eyes", the *Press Trust of India* quoted Parrikar as saying on 19 March.

"We need adequate equipment and that cannot change. Make in India is in its place, our military preparedness is paramount," the minister said. There have been calls for stepping up the country's defence preparedness after the terror attack on the Pathankot airbase on 2 January.

The opposition Congress had in Parliament criticized the government for its handling of the Pathankot incident in which seven security personnel were killed. "Facilitation of a conducive and pro-investment policy environment should be another focal point for the government, taking into account the best interests of various stakeholders. Currently, the sector is subject to numerous regulations and stringent monitoring, which makes functioning for companies in this space quite difficult. To overcome such challenges, the government must work towards harmonization of the policy environment including the FDI policy, licensing regime, offset policy, etc," Mandot said.

The government must channelize its efforts towards streamlining procurement processes, making them time-effective and unambiguous, he said. "Similarly, the offset policy, which has the potential to stimulate indigenous defence manufacturing should be strengthened and made effective. Currently, these policies lack consis-tency and precision," he said.

Mandot said a fresh look at the operating mechanism of the defence public sector undertakings—Defence Research and Development Organisation (DRDO) and Ordnance Factory Board (OFB)—should be undertaken from the standpoint of productivity, innovation, efficiency and utilization. "The government should analyse the gaps and take corrective action for their redressal. Additional investment should be made towards technological upgradation. Institutions like DRDO should be strengthened to produce leading edge technology," Mandot said.

The government should consider according 'infrastructure' status to the aerospace and defence or A&D industry and providing various concessions/benefits in the form of tax incentives to A&D manufacturers, both from a direct and indirect tax perspective, so as to augment domestic defence production, Mandot said. "While the government has significantly enhanced the FDI cap in the defence sector (from the erstwhile 26% to 49%), such policy initiatives have not yielded the desired results. The government could reconsider enhancing the FDI cap to

74%," Mandot argued. But how serious is the government about modernizing the defence forces? Finance minister Arun Jaitley mentioned the word 'defence' only five times in his budget 2016-17 speech, and surprisingly made no mention of India's defence allocation for 2016-17.

As part of incentivizing domestic value addition to help Make in India, Jaitley did propose some changes in customs and excise duty rates on certain inputs, raw materials, intermediaries and components, including those required for defence production.

For instance, the government has proposed to withdraw customs duties exemption on direct imports of specified goods for defence purposes by the centre or state governments with effect from 1 April. Also, the government has withdrawn basic customs duty exemption on specified goods imported by contractors of public sector undertakings (PSUs) or sub-contractors of such PSUs for defence purposes, with effect from 1 April.

The defence budget estimate for 2016-17 is Rs.3.4 trillion, about 10% more than the previous year's estimate, which is broadly consistent with past increases. "With the increasing threat from the neighbouring countries—Pakistan and China—modernization of Indian armed forces has become the need of the hour. China is developing infrastructure on Indian border and flexing muscle in the South China Sea. Growing Sino-Pak defence cooperation is worrying. Pakistan's continued military-terrorist nexus is hitting India where it hurts," Mandot said.

He pointed out that the Indian armed forces have long suffered due to delayed acquisition processes, failure to take timely decisions, deficiency in qualitative requirements formulation and lack of future planning. "The weakness of planning and budgeting has further been aggravated by the deficiencies in the procurement system that the defence ministry has been desperately trying to overcome since the early '90s. The result is a depleting fleet of combat fighter platforms, submarines, guns, tanks, helicopters, night-vision devices and other critical defence equipment," he said.

INDIGENISATION TO CATALYSE, TRANSFORM INDIA'S DEFENCE SECTOR

As India has celebrated its 68th Independence Day, the induction of the first of three Project-15 (Alpha) "Kolkata" class multi-role destroyers in the Indian Navy on August 16 has marked a giant leap for the country in shipbuilding technology. Christened INS Kolkata, it is the biggest warship ever built in India and boasts of enhanced stealth features and land-attack capabilities over its predecessor — the Delhi-class destroyers. Armed with modern sensors and weapons, including the BRAHMOS supersonic cruise missile system, it also has new look exteriors for improved stealth capability.

The commissioning of INS Kolkata symbolises another landmark achievement for India in successfully designing, developing and producing indigenous military platforms and systems for its armed forces. Even after decades of restrictive technology denial regime imposed on it by the rich, powerful nations, India has successfully elevated its stature to a dignified level by acquiring critical military technology.

This is clearly evident from the fact that today India is listed as one among the few elite countries with the capability to build a nuclear submarine (Arihant), an aircraft carrier (Vikrant), a fourth-generation light combat aircraft (Tejas), an intercontinental ballistic missile (Agni), a submarine-launched ballistic missile (K-4/K-15), a supersonic cruise missile (BRAHMOS), a main battle tank (Arjun), a ballistic missile defence system and many other critical military systems and sub-systems including electronic warfare systems, radar systems, unmanned systems, laser technology and underwater sensors.

Even though faltered on several occasions with project delays, whopping costs, and technological shortcomings, (which are no exceptions and evident in many critical military projects undertaken even by leading military powers such as the US, Europe or Russia), indigenisation in Defence Technology has nevertheless steadily and surely witnessed the dawn in India.

With an all-round, comprehensive modernisation drive outlined for its armed forces, India targets to spend over $150 billion over the next five years on defence procurements, offering a lucrative market to the global military firms to grab a pie. This also offers a great opportunity for India's domestic defence sector to get a fair share of the huge money.

But the question here is: Is the Indian defence industry actually ready for its big share? The provision in this year's Union Budget to raise the Foreign Direct Investment (FDI) limit in the Defence Sector from 26% to 49% surely paves the way and expands the scope for further increasing the indigenous content in the defence hardware which India plans to procure in the coming years.

Such a provision promises to woo the domestic private sector enterprises to come forth in a big way in not only partnering with global military firms, but also in establishing a strong manufacturing base in the country to produce state-of-the-art, high-end defence equipment. Many Indian private sector companies keen to make a foray into India's strategic sphere have already tied up with some of the leading international defence and aerospace firms to produce platforms and systems for the Indian armed forces.

Amidst all the euphoria, however, it would be pertinent to note that an increased investment in Defence Research undertaken by India would be equally essential to realise self-reliance in defence design and production. The dynamics of indigenisation would work well only when India also becomes a source of inventing and producing cutting-edge military technology of tomorrow rather than just relying on foreign firms to give access to their technology. Also important would be to nurture and retain the human resources talent pool within the country.

A welcome step in this direction is the Defence Research and Development Organisation's (DRDO) plans to set up R&D centres in universities and leading academic institutions located in different parts of the country to create a strong defence knowledge base. The knowledge base available in various academic institutions and industrial sector could be used for polarising the defence research and also for designing, testing, and developing defence and related items.

So far, India's defence research work has remained within the exclusive purview of DRDO even though the premier research agency has tied up with about 40 academic institutions, 15national Science and Technology agencies, 50 public sector undertakings and over 250 private sector enterprises to carry out R&D work. Similarly, the Transfer of Technology (ToT) clause as highlighted by India's official Defence Procurement Procedure (DPP) needs to be leveraged on so as to gain maximum benefit while clinching any new arms procurement deal with a foreign country/firm. To sum it up all, since its independence 67 years ago, India has charted a long, arduous path in giving a well-defined, dignified shape to its defence development and production sector. Starting almost from scratch and overcoming many challenges, today the country stands tall as one of the major Asian powers with an indigenous defence industry base.

In fact, with a right spirit and energy, India certainly holds the potential to catalyse and transform itself into a vibrant hub of world-class design, development, manufacturing and export hub of high-end defence products in the next two to three decades.

INDIGENOUS DEFENCE RESEARCH AND DRDO PRODUCTS

Indian Armed Forces are used to import Defence systems from abroad and use them mostly for training and during operations whenever necessity rises. Most of these systems are in free flow production in their respective countries and sometimes inducted by their Services. These systems, therefore, have got the maturity in terms of engineering, production and maintenance. This provides the comfort zone for the three Services to induct, operationalise and maintain these weapons.

The most important aspect is that these weapons, are not designed keeping Indian environment, tactics, operational doctrines or user' preferences in mind. They are not customized for the convenience of the Indian Armed Forces. Even then, they are accepted by the Services based on their maturity level. Even in those cases where partial quantities are produced in the country, mostly in Indian Ordnance factories (OFB) and Defence Public Sector Units (DPSUs), there is hardly any technology transfer taking place. These items would already have been produced in large quantities in their respective countries and would have reached end of production life for their own use. Many times, the tooling will be transferred to Indian production line accordingly. Though the products are subsequently made in India, most of the raw materials and components still have to come from the parent country and the value addition by Indian Industry is very small, varying from 10% to 30%. Even then, this is a preferred route for the OFB's and DPSUs as there is no risk for them. They have assured product line and order quantities from the Armed Forces. Most of time, the critical high end system's technology is not passed to India. It is a form of "Technology Apartheid." India ends up paying exorbitant prices and foreign exchange.

The international arms market runs with political and monetary diplomacy. The arms majors adopt all tricks of trade to push their wares. India is one of the largest importers of arms in the world, hence these issues imply to India too.

With this background, it is natural that the Indian Armed forces hesitate to accept Defence Research and Development Organisation (DRDO) developed items as they know that even after DRDO successfully develops, there would be a reasonable time gap before a smooth free flow production gets established by the Indian Industry. There is also pressure from import lobbies and vested interest which cultivate the sensation seeking mass media for defaming Indian indigenous research.

It is to be noted that all countries which develops a complex defence system has gone through the same pains and problems as DRDO before serial production gets established.

Frontier India Defence and Strategic News Service interacted with Dr. VK Atre who has held the position of

Scientific Advisor to Minister of Defence. There are 4 state actors when it comes to indigenization of weapons.

1) The Ministry of Defence (MoD)
2) The Armed Forces
3) The Defence Research and Development Organisation (DRDO)
4) The Public sector defence production units (DPSU)

There are 3 non state actors which influence the outcomes

1) Foreign Vendors
2) The Mass Media.
3) The Import Lobby

THE MINISTRY OF DEFENCE

Ideally the MoD should act as the bridge between the scientific & technical community and the armed forces.

On the role of MoD in indigenization Dr. Atre say's "Variable. There are occasions when MoD has supported DRDO strongly and there are occasions when they have not. It depends on the pressure by the User Service and the projection of Operational Requirement put forward by the User."

The MoD is the hub for the arms import lobby. One must also study pressure from import lobby; we will deal with this subject later.

The central purchase committee is major contributor of delays too. Dr. Atre says "The laboratories can order equipment once the basic project is cleared. There are set purchase procedures. Our (governmental) procedures themselves cause some delay and require to be seriously looked into to reduce the purchase delays."

The Armed Forces

Indian Armed Forces have 3 main wings

a) Imported Army or Indian Army (IA)
b) Imported Air Force or Indian Air Force (IAF)
c) Ingenious Navy or Indian Navy (IN)

It is not just the IA, IAF and IN have to work with DRDO. A host of private industries and PSU's like Bharat Electronics Limited (BEL) work with DRDO and are happy. This year, BEL has decided to give research and development projects worth 120 Crores to DRDO.

IA and IAF do not have a positive research attitude. Dr. Atre say's "In my opinion IN is more interested in indigenous systems than the other two. Even in non-NPOL and sonar projects (for example in EW projects), IN has showed this attitude. DRDO and BEL have very good working relationship; but the latter being a production agency has obviously caters to customer's demands."

The IA and IAF representatives are not helpful too. Dr. Atre say's "IA and IAF representatives are indeed participating in some of the projects. But, in my opinion, most of them remain as representatives and not an integral part of the development team. Naval reps were indeed active participants in the design, development, testing and trails of the equipment and hence were deeply emotionally involved with the systems."

The main project of IA with DRDO is Arjun MBT. The representatives of IA were not helpful. A recent parliamentary committee told "once these officers are posted to the DRDO units, they forget their uniform." Now these representatives have to report to Indian Army every 3 months.

On being asked on IA representative's role in Arjun Tank development, Dr. Atre said "I do not know the answer to this question as I was not involved with Arjun during its developmental phase. Lot has already been written about Arjun."

The other service which has a major project with DRDO is IAF. Let us take a look at the IAF's representative in the project. Dr. Atre say's "Most of the times I felt that they were genuinely interested in seeing the most important and major technology of designing combat aircrafts in India. But at times I felt that they were not genuinely interested in LCA and acted as auditors rather than players. This ambivalent attitude reflected somewhat in the interest shown by HAL. If IAFs attitude was more positive and proactive, the project would (in my opinion) have gained more momentum."

By now it is general knowledge that IA and IAF are partial towards equipment import. It lowers GSQR standards for import equipment while it does not do the same for DRDO. Another issue is IA drags its feet for giving dates for trials for months resulting in project delays.

Say's Dr. Atre "I honestly believe that all our services are partial to 'equipment import' – some are more so. This seems to be a general problem in India. As I indicated earlier, Navy is more ready to be a part of DRDO and look for indigenous equipment while the others are less so. When one import's any equipment, one perhaps has to identify the equipment that nearly meets the GSQR, as otherwise even the foreign companies have to get into R&D mode, which costs time and money. Hence it some times happens that the GSQRs given to DRDO are more demanding than those given to the foreign vendors. This is OK. However, what used to bother me were the acceptance criterion and trials of the imported equipment to verify the same. We at DRDO always felt that the DRDO equipments went through much more demanding User trials than the imported ones. This was generally true and certainly caused further delays. Our scientists often felt that the imported equipment did not perform all that well in the trials and later on in use also. There is some truth in this."

DRDO

For a self assessment of DRDO, I asked Dr. Atre the success rate of DRDO projects, he said "Difficult to put a number. Sonar programs for Navy have the best success rate. Navy accepted the equipment in spite of PDC slippages. EW programs success rate is also high – all the three Services have accepted the equipment designed by DRDO (again in spite of slippages in PDC). Of late, success rate in Radar systems is also high. There are several radars, which have gone into production. The problems of PDC slippages in these have been reduced. (All in all in highly electronic oriented projects we have technologically done well). There have been several successes in Armaments, including torpedoes. For example Pinaka is a success but there was delay in meeting the specifications in user trials. Prithvi and Agni are clearly successes. So you see there are many successes in DRDO development and that is why I had initially indicated basing it only on Arjun and LCA, Akash, Trishul and Nag is not just right."

That is modest statement by Dr. Atre. The fact is the country has achieved 40 percent indigenisation using DRDO products. DRDO. The 70 percent target is not for DRDO to achieve alone. The users too need to co-operate. All major powers in the world use or strive to induct indigenous product when ever available. These products pass through mark 1, mark 2 ... stages in service of these countries before the product matures.

On a rough estimate DRDO has produced more than 1000 critical products and technologies in just 20 years which has brought us on par with the developed countries.

THE PUBLIC SECTOR DEFENCE PRODUCTION UNITS (DPSU)

As mentioned earlier, the OFB and DPSU's have a comfort level when producing an imported system which has a maturity in production cycle. There is very high resistance in technology transfer, when it comes from DRDO, as these systems need to be absorbed, machinery bought, processes created, fine tuned and updated as per the user feed back. Most of the quality problems that has arisen in INSAS, Arjun Tank etc have been due to the OFB and DPSU's.

Say's Dr. Atre "No DRDO should not be blamed for the production in efficiency. I want to elaborate on this so that you understand the scenario correctly and in the right perspective. Our Public Sector Undertakings are much more used to and comfortable with licensed production (most industries in India are, though the scenario is fast changing) which they called technology transfer.

No technological know-how comes through such production except production processes. Of course, we can and did learn from this also. What is interesting to note is that under licensed production, technology transfer takes place from industry to industry on processes already well established in the other country. As the technology transfer from DRDO to PSU is based on lab models and prototypes, the amount of work that has to be put in by the PSUs is much more. This not only adds to the delay but demands much more (conversion) effort from them. When they do not invest this time and effort, clearly there would be quality problems."

Foreign Vendors

The foreign vendors were critical when India achieved independence. They are still critical in terms of key technology or off the shelf product imports. Even DRDO imports from them in order to speed up a project or bring down the project cost. However, these foreign vendors play dirty tricks when the order value is huge. They are represented by Indian agents. These agents have their positive and negative aspects. There have been times, when these agents have supported the imported equipments in critical times. But these agents are too responsible for attacks on the Indian indigenous research as it stops their line of business.

There have been non deliveries and wrong deliveries by these foreign vendors. But due to good relationship with media and the yellow journalist, this news does not get reported.

Due to non delivery by these foreign vendors, DRDO projects get delayed. Foreign vendors are subject to laws of their own country. These government's have policies where in they can hold the exports to India at will.

The Media

The media has been vociferous in criticizing DRDO. Media did the same when ISRO was struggling to launch SLV's in 1980's. Today ISRO successes have put the media on the back foot. As of today most budding journalist, retired armed forces personnel has found it convenient to bash DRDO, as they do not expect the DRDO to retort back. Imagine if the budding journalists write on the mafias or the retired armed forces officers report on their own organisations. It is not just convenience in attacking DRDO, a large number of the officials have openly spoken about the deliberate attempt to malign DRDO. Yellow journalism is naturally at play on behest of foreign agencies and vested interests in India. Dr. Atre quips "The media stories cover the same theme: ARJUN, LCA, Akash and Trishul. The main attack in on the delays and resulting effect on the operational and staff requirements. There is some truth in this. There have been delays of several years, from the original PDCs, in some these projects. This is some thing none of us can deny. But picking on only the delays not talking about DRDO's successes is what bothers me most."

On being asked on the recent attack by media on DRDO, Dr. Atre say's "I am not sure what triggered the most recent attacks on DRDO. As far as I can gather, the situation on Arjun has improved and several tanks were ready (the problem of weight and import content haven't changed in the last several years), Akash had cleared some of its technical problems and several prototypes of LCA were flying and getting ready for the IOC (404 engines were cleared for the first two squadrons and most recent status of MMR is not known to me)."

Import Lobby

This is the bane of Indian defence procurements and detrimental to Indian indigenous research. They are in the Government departments, they are in the armed forces, they are in the Indian import agents and of course the yellow journalist who are apologists for imports. A lot of retired armed forces personnel are found hobnobbing with serving officers, as the serving officers are not supposed to interact with the vendors. These corrupt personnel try to influence the results of the arms tests. The Indian media often quotes them for bashing DRDO.

The controversies over arms deals, that now are normal in India, has led to frustration not only in the defence force but also the general public. The main problem is corruption. The corruption percolates from the middle men to political bosses/ bureaucrats and uniformed personnel.

Endgame

Indigenisation has same connotations as gaining independence. Look at what history has taught us. India has been time and again attacked by the outsiders as we lacked advanced arms and ammunition. The situation is no different today. The physical colonization has been replaced with mental colonization.

It is clear that total Indigenisation cannot happen without firm user commitment. Barring The Indian Navy, other services are not willing to go through the process. A thought that passes is if the imported systems are better than indigenous system, then, the country should import military officers too. Why do we need Indian officers who cannot make their own weapons and doctrines?

MOD SIDELINES PVT SECTOR IN CRUCIAL DEFENCE PROJECT

The Policy turnaround will give BEL Rs 10,000-cr project without tendering. The Ministry of Defence is poised to deliver a disheartening blow to India's nascent private defence industry. After inviting private companies into the Rs 10,000-crore project for developing the Indian Army's futuristic Tactical Communications System (TCS), the ministry is abandoning competitive bidding and handing over the project to a defence public sector undertaking, Bharat Electronics Ltd (BEL). The reason cited by the ministry: Secrecy.

Left in the lurch are six private companies — Wipro, Mahindra Defence Systems, Tata Power, L&T, Rolta and HCL — which the defence ministry had vetted in detail before categorising the TCS project as "Make — High Tech". In this category, the government funds 80 per cent of the R&D cost, while the selected vendor contributes 20 per cent. Also sidelined for the TCS are two non-defence PSUs (DPSUs), ECIL and

ITI.The TCS will be a fully mobile network, which can be transported anywhere during war, even into enemy territory, providing the military with a backbone network on which it can communicate and transfer data. The TCS operates much like a cellular phone network, but with two major differences. While cellular phone transmission towers are fixed onto buildings, the TCS's exchanges and switches will be installed in high-mobility vehicles, allowing them to be transported and set up anywhere. Second, messages sent out over the TCS cannot be easily intercepted or jammed since they will not remain on a single frequency; instead, transmissions will hop frequencies, dozens of times every second, in a pre-programmed sequence.

It is to maintain the secrecy of this "hopping algorithm", or the sequence in which the TCS hops frequencies, that BEL is being handed over the project. The defence ministry is citing a new cyber policy formulated by the apex National Technical Research Organisation (NTRO) — a secretive body that functions under the Cabinet Secretariat, overseeing electronic intelligence. The NTRO had mandated that the "hopping algorithm" must remain the exclusive preserve of the government.

The NTRO's interpretation has been shaped by guidelines issued by Shekhar Dutt, while he was deputy national security advisor. Now the governor of Chhattisgarh, Dutt had earlier served as defence secretary and as secretary of defence production, with close and longstanding links to BEL.

Now, based on that NTRO interpretation, a special defence ministry committee is about to recommend that the TCS procurement be categorised as, "Make — Strategic, Complex and Security Sensitive Systems". Under the Defence Procurement Policy, this will automatically gift the TCS project to DRDO and BEL.

The six private sector rivals for the TCS project are fighting back against what they consider an unfair proposal. Last Wednesday and Thursday, they huddled with industry bodies, Ficci and CII, formulating their response to the defence ministry. Their argument: If the ministry ignores the private sector's world-acknowledged competence in software, IT and communications, and continues sidelining them to benefit DPSUs, it will be hard to convince shareholders to continue investing into defence.

"We fully agree with the need for security," explains a senior executive from one of the TCS contenders, "but secrecy can be fully preserved by reserving the 'hopping algorithm' for DRDO and BEL. To safeguard the secrecy of a Rs 20,000-microchip, which contains the 'hopping algorithm', the ministry is handing them an entire Rs 10,000 crore project."

A defence ministry Feasibility Study Group for the TCS has already discussed the issue of secrecy last year. It was decided that top-secret algorithms in the TCS would be developed by the DRDO's Centre for Artificial Intelligence and Robotics (CAIR), but the private sector could develop the rest of the project.

Indian private companies have played pivotal roles in some of India's most secret defence projects. Larsen & Toubro, one of the companies being sidelined in the TCS project, built most of India's nuclear submarine, INS Arihant, and will have a similar role in building successors to the Arihant. Another private company, Tata Power, which built crucial command systems for the Arihant, also designed the core of the top secret Samyukta Electronic Warfare system.

The Kelkar Committee had recommended that such companies, with a track record and potential in defence production, should be designated Raksha Udyog Ratnas (RURs) and treated at par with DPSUs in the award of projects like the TCS. But, in an inexplicable volte-face after preparing a short list of candidate companies, the defence ministry decided against nominating RURs.

If BEL is awarded the TCS project, that windfall will lead to many more. Applying the NTRO's logic to other command and control projects in the pipeline — such as the Battlefield Management System (BMS); the Operational Data Link (ODL); and the Net-Centric Operations (NCO) system — BEL seems likely to be awarded all of these on a single-vendor basis.

The Ministry of Defence has not responded to an emailed questionnaire from Business Standard on the TCS. "It is particularly ironic that BEL is expected to safeguard security, when it is well known that BEL systems are built mainly from foreign components," points out an official from a private company that is bidding for the TCS. "BEL's Artillery Combat Command and Control System (ACCCS), a system similar to the TCS, has computers and software from Israeli company, Elbit. Whether these have come with malware or switches to render the entire system inoperable will only be known in the future."

Parliament's Standing Committee on Defence, too, has raised concerns about such "false indigenization", where DPSUs have allegedly fronted for foreign companies. The Standing Committee's report of December 2009 notes that, "a sizeable proportion of procurement takes place through the ordnance factories and DPSUs, which are indigenous sources, but have to depend on imports for manufacturing the finished product."

INDIGENISATION FOR INDIAN AIR FORCE

It is also considered reasonable to inform vendors that the requirements of IAF are maintenance requirements. Also there are no technology transfers/original designs.

All the information available in the maintenance/overhaul manuals as also available with the experienced personnel of the Base Repair Depots will be made available to the vendors along with the samples. These details may be inadequate and detailed studies by a knowledgeable person from the concerned field to derive some more information will be required. Special test rigs may have to be developed for the extensive testing required.

Thus, for complex items, vendors are expected to be familiar with design and testing aspects of products. To ascertain this, two bid system is followed. The vendors are expected to develop engineering drawing/circuit diagrams, select appropriate materials and come out with a design. This along with the test schedules is to be approved by appropriate airworthiness approval authority. Ability to achieve this, is in fact one of the yardstick for IAF to assess vendors capabilities. However, in last few years IAF has taken up numerous studies, which have brought out details on ranges of spares. We willingly share all these details and whatever information is available.

Vendor Identification

No formal registration is required for participation in indigensation development activities of IAF.

Potential vendors identified form the following sources :-

(a) Proven and prospective vendors list of BRDs for different categories of spares for development/indigenisation.

(b) Vendor base of HAL, st1:City u1:st="on">ADA and few other DRDO Labs, LCSO, SIATI, CEMILAC and many others, for wider competition.

(c) Internet search to find capable vendor in desired field.

(d) Capable and potential vendors approaching BRDs/HQ MC and expressing their interest.

Vendor Selection

Request for proposal floated to potential vendor for bids is two part i.e., technical and commercial bid. Technical evaluation done against laid down qualitative requirements to enable evaluation of all vendors on a common base. This is done to ensure that all vendors have understood the requirements of tender in the intended sense. TEC report brings all tenders at par to help identify the product and service likely to be made available from selected vendors. Price alone is criteria once the TEC clearance is given to determine award of the tender. Price negotiation is done with tender awardee for negotiation of price.

Conclusion

The aim of the above elaborations was to give an insight of technology intensiveness of the IAF. The Indian Industry is certainly very capable. Our aim is only to prepare you for what you are in for. The requirements of airworthiness cannot be diluted. Nor can the fact, that aviation and aerospace are the most technologically advanced industries.

Our efforts are continuously on to simplify our procedures and share the hardships with our partners in the industry. We invite those of you, who have the capabilities, expertise, infrastructure and the willingness to contribute and prosper with us. For venturing into the complex spares, you have to be tough because as they say "WHEN THE GOING GETS TOUGH, THE TOUGH GETS GOING".

ITEMS DISPLAYED DURING AERO INDIA 2009

The indigenisation requirements of IAF are wide and varied technologically. Though the requirements of BRDs are much larger, items displayed during Aero India 2009 have been based on reasonable order quantities and attractive economics. The items displayed were broadly grouped under five heads as follows :-

- Metallic
- Non – Metallic
- Electrical/Electronics
- Avionics
- Tools, Testers and Ground Equipments

The mechanical items comprise wide range of structural items both metallic as well as non metallic. They include items like pumps, valves, gears, bearings cylinders, shafts, and windshield/windows.

The aero engine items include items like combustion chamber nozzle, ducts, casing, and shaft assembly and spray rings. The major electrical items are inverter, motor, spark plug while the items under avionics group are subassemblies of trans-receivers, radar and flight data recorder. The testers consist of test equipment to carry out ground test of airborne items to ascertain system functionality in air.

The IAF requirement is not limited to items displayed during Aero India 2009 as there are even more items in the pipeline to be indigenised. Interested and capable vendors could contact any of our BRDs for more details. Fresh requirements invariably keep emerging.

PILLARS OF INDIAN DEFENCE SYSTEM

The first decade of the 21st century has made it increasingly evident that security threats are unconstrained by borders. Each of India's neighbours is undergoing a transition, giving rise to varied political experiences and experiments. The menace of terrorism and proliferation of arms, drugs and nuclear technology pose dangers that merit constant attention.

The developments in 2008, particularly the challenges confronting the global financial system, created unprecedented strains in the global security environment.

The continuing links of extremist and terrorist organisations with organs of the Pakistan State adds greater complexities and dangers to the evolving situation confronting us. Strengthening of our security apparatus both internally and on our frontiers is, therefore, a national priority of the highest order.

China's stated objectives, in their White Paper, of developing strategic missile and space-based assets and of rapidly enhancing its blue-water navy to conduct operations in distant waters, as well as the systematic upgrading of infrastructure, reconnaissance and surveillance, quick response and operational capabilities in the border areas, need to be monitored carefully in the foreseeable future for the implications that it can have on the security and defence of India. Similarly, its military assistance and cooperation with Pakistan, including the possibility of enhancing connectivity with Pakistan through the territory illegally occupied by Pakistan in the state of Jammu and Kashmir, will also have direct military implications for India.

India's credible minimum deterrence plays an important role in the regional security calculus. While maintaining a posture of minimum deterrence, India has announced a policy of no-first-use and a policy of non-use against non-nuclear weapon states. India also continues to maintain a voluntary, unilateral moratorium on nuclear testing.

The need for enhanced maritime security has to be seen in the backdrop of a long coastline facing the Arabian Sea on the West, the Bay of Bengal to the east and the vast Indian Ocean in the South. Increased economic activity along the coast and the growth of major towns has heightened this necessity. Over the recent years, maritime issues like the security of sea-lanes, piracy on the high seas, energy security, WMD, terrorism etc. have become important elements in India's security. The Indian Navy has played an outstanding role in curbing piracy in parts of Indian Ocean. The Mumbai terror attacks have once again highlighted the importance of the maritime dimension in India's security.

Army

The Indian Army stands vigil along the border-watchful, prepared for any sacrifice so that the people of the country may live in peace and with honour. The infusion of high technology based precision weaponry has enhanced the lethality of future warfare manifold.

The spectrum of threat ranges from the nuclear to the conventional and the asymmetric, with terrorism emerging like a hydra-headed monster. The rigours of climate i.e., the glacial heights and extreme cold, dense mountainous jungles and the heat and simoom of the deserts also need to be factored.

A pragmatic vision of the shape, size and role of the Army in the long term perspective makes the modernization process of the Army dynamic and the technology process more towards development of a 'Threat Cum Capability Based Force'. The Army has to be prepared for multi spectrum orientation changes and be always a 'Ready and Relevant Army' as per anticipated challenges of the future.

The Mechanised Forces constitute a significant and essential segment of Defence Forces with a formidable combat potential and operational worth. The effort to modernize Mechanised Forces continues, wherein additional quantities of ATGMs for

BMP-2 and T-90 tank have been contracted. The artillery is acquiring an array of guns, missiles and rocket systems with long ranges and superior firepower as also state-of-the-art surveillance systems. Weapon System of the Army include BrahMos Weapon System, Smerch Multi Rocket Launcher System (MLRS) and Pinaka Multi Barrel Rocket Launcher System (MBRLS).

The present situation in the region warrants state-of-the-art systems for the Infantry. This is being achieved through endeavour for better quality personal weapons, thermal imaging devices, mine protected vehicles and improved radio communication systems. A contract has been signed for supply of Boot Anti Mines for use by Infantry. Bullet proof vehicles and shot guns are being procured for counter insurgency operations.

8

Indian Defence Policy in Major Transition

Recently the US journal Defence News reported that the Indian government is working on a program whereby Israel would replace Russia as India's largest supplier of weapons and defence equipment by 2008. Since Russia now supplies some 70 percent of India's weapons imports, this report, if true, would mark a major transformation in Indian defence policy. Under the terms of the program, India would identify the products it wants and ask the Israeli government to negotiate with domestic firms on its behalf as Jerusalem does with regard to its own weapons.

Israel is already the second-largest supplier of military systems to India, so this program could affect a major transformation in India's security relationships. The potential repercussions of this project, which would clearly show a serious break with Moscow's arms salesmen, are immense. Given the deep ties between the US and Israeli defence industries, if this program does materialize it will also probably enhance the United States' competitive position in the Indian defence market and result in further substantial increases in the already rising amount of US arms sales and security cooperation with India. Those sales could either be bilateral or brokered through Israel, such as weapons made jointly by Israel and the United States, including missile defence systems that India reportedly is interested in acquiring.

This program would then also strengthen the developing tripartite relationship among Israel, India, and the US in regard to defence sales. We can see this already occurring, because the United States has brushed aside Pakistan's objections to India's receiving the Israeli Phalcon radar, made with US technology and thus subject to US veto on its transfer to a third party.

Realization of the projected Indo-Israeli project would also simultaneously symbolize and express India's rising continental Asian status as a great power with interests and capabilities across the continent, allowing it to break free of its confining chains as merely a major South Asian power if not the regional leader, something that both Indian and foreign observers have labeled as a prerequisite for a full partnership with the United States.

Not only would those trends strengthen Indo-Israeli ties, they would provide fuel to the oft-reported desire on the part of at least some US elites to create a tripartite alliance with India and Israel against terrorism (if not for other, broader objectives that would emerge later). Joint Indo-Israeli defence collaboration on a scale envisaged above would also, or so these advocates hope, tie into the US alliance and Israeli partnership with Turkey, creating a kind of pan-Asian bloc. The new program grows out of India's difficulty in negotiating a US$10 billion multi-year defence acquisition program with Russia. Three areas in particular seem to have caused some anxiety in New Delhi.

In March 2002, The Times of India reported that the Parliamentary Standing Committee had urged the government to avoid overdependence on Russia for armaments and spare parts. The committee reportedly acknowledged Russia's previous contributions and reliability as a provider of defence equipment to India but cautioned that the current dependence on Moscow for almost 80 percent of its arms imports is unhealthy. It also observed that Russia was not providing military hardware on the same beneficial financial terms that it had during the Soviet era. Therefore the committee also urged the Indian government to cease making advance payments for weapons acquisitions from Russia, and that in the future it seek to put more defence contracts up for competitive tender. Russia also has come under criticism because of India's difficulty in obtaining and negotiating speedy delivery of spare parts for these weapons systems. At the same time it became clear that given its worsening relations with Pakistan, India is seeking to diversify its foreign purchases and use foreign partners to develop its own defence industrial capability, eg by conditioning purchases on obtaining offsets from the sellers to develop its own indigenous capability. The alliance, if it were to materialize, would build on the already greatly improved Indo-Israeli relationship that has led to large-scale military sales from Israel and to India's rapprochement with the United States as well. As the Phalcon deal suggests, it could become possible to envisage tripartite collaboration among these states on missile defence, especially if India's great goal of securing the end to all US sanctions on the transfer of both civil and military technology is realized.

Moreover, the broadening of India's ties and reach in political-military terms through the acquisition of top-quality defence systems would enable it to play the kind of role that analysts in both India and the US postulate as being essential to any serious strategic partnership with the United States. And that role also accords very much with some of the deepest aspirations of India's foreign and defence policy elites, thus highlighting a congruence of visions concerning India's future international position.

In effect India's aspiration to play a major role "from Socotra to Sumatra" would have been both realized and blessed by the United States, as Secretary of State Colin Powell implicitly suggested in 2001. India would then become not just a South or even Central Asian power but a major player in the Persian Gulf, the Middle East, and Southeast Asia.

At the same time, India's search for new vistas in defence acquisition and production relates very much to its rising economic, technological, and military-industrial capabilities as well as to its desire to strengthen existing long-standing partnerships, eg with Russia. For example, beyond the existing

$10 billion weapons sales from Russia to India, India is collaborating with Russia on joint production of a fifth-generation fighter that Russia feels vital to its military future. Both are also collaborating on research that is probably tied to missile defence and nuclear systems as well. More broadly, India is the only country with whom Russia is collaborating on joint production of sophisticated and futuristic weapons systems. Likewise India, not China, gets the best weapons currently being produced in Russia, systems that not even Russia's armed forces can obtain. Moscow offers offsets in the form of technology transfer of production skills and know-how to India, one of its largest customers. Although India obviously seeks to diversify its sources of foreign procurement, Russian producers have until now been confident of their ability to obtain the bulk of Indian defence contracts. Whether or not this confidence is misplaced, time will tell, but diversification and strengthening of India's own capabilities surely would increase India's scientific-technological and manufacturing capabilities for weapons production. This objective also appears to be a major goal of the deals now being made with Russia, Israel, and presumably the United States. We see similar deals with Italian and French firms for joint manufacture of weapons systems.

India's leading defence firm, Hindustan Aeronautics Ltd (HAL), is also pressing an outsourcing program whereby it would help private Indian companies find and choose foreign partners to undertake such high-tech projects as avionics integration, weapons-system integration, and other related efforts to "lay the foundation for a credible domestic aerospace industry base that could meet the majority of India's military aerospace requirements in the next 10 years". And it is no less logical to assume that India would be thrilled to duplicate this particular kind of relationship with Washington, especially as India already has a large space program with military applications and very much wants US conventional-weapons systems and technology transfer.

Indeed, a Pentagon-commissioned study of Indo-American perceptions reported that on the basis of many interviews, a uniform conclusion was reached that "for Indians, technology transfer from the United States is military cooperation's touchstone". Other Indian assessments confirm the great importance that India attaches to transfer of both civil and defence technology as a critical and essential element in any partnership with the US.

While India's aspirations in the defence industry are common to other countries that seek the capability for indigenous production of most, if not all of their weapons, it is nevertheless clear that this deal, if it materializes, would utterly transform defence relationships among major players in the defence business: India, the US, Israel, and Russia. The major transformations in Asian security that accelerated after September 11, 2001, have clearly not yet run their course. Nor is it clear when the overall Asian situation will stabilize or when also the rising tide of weapons sales will abate. But there can be no doubt that major changes are in the offing and that the future holds many more surprises and jolts for all of those who seek to play a key role in the security and defence of Asia.

INDIA'S DEFENCE POLICY

India inherited some defence industries from Great Britain. They included Hindustan Aeronautics Limited (HAL), which is today India's largest defence public sector undertaking (DPSU), Mazagon Docks Limited (MDL), the largest shipyard in the nation, and more than half a dozen ordnance factories. The growth of the domestic defence industry has, however, been sporadic since Independence. It did not follow any definite plan though emphasis was placed on enhancing indigenous defence production capability.

Some analysts have also traced certain vigorousness in the Indian effort at developing an indigenous defence capability to the early 1960s spawned by the 1962 India-China war. The war is seen as having underscored the urgency of building a domestic defence industry through foreign assistance. It was also in consonance with Nehru's policy of building a strong industrial base patterned on the Soviet model. But while the war with

China has been identified as the catalyst in the effort at developing a domestic defence base, there was no concerted, systematic and well-orchestrated effort towards the achievement of this goal.

There were many factors that stood in the way of India building a strong military-industrial base. India's comparatively easy access to various types of defence equipment from the former Soviet Union (FSU) and their purchase against deferred rupee payments and on "friendship" price were some of them. Sophisticated defence equipment was transferred to India under the favourable rupee-rouble arrangements from FSU. Some license production facilities were also established in India, for instance for the Mig-21 aircraft. The Cold War also ensured that India continued to have a favourable and preferred source of defence systems and equipment from FSU. It did not find the superpower wanting in any critical manner in fulfilling India's defence requirements. However, this had the unintended consequences of dampening any sense of urgency in India to develop an indigenous defence industry. Coupled with this was the reluctance of the US to help in India's effort to develop a domestic defence production base. Nevertheless, trudging along, India was able to develop the largest defence industry among developing nations.

However, with the collapse of the FSU, India lost easy access to sophisticated defence equipment at cheap prices. The problem was compounded by the absence of an alternate source of modern defence equipment. The situation became worse with the almost complete disruption in the supply of services and spare parts necessary to maintain the predominantly Soviet-equipped Indian armed forces. The navy was particularly affected, as it was dependent on Soviet designs and equipment for some of the ships that were under construction in India. This led to huge cost and time overruns in the indigenous construction programme of naval vessels.

Ironically, the need to service and maintain various kinds of equipment imported from FSU compelled India to seek ways and means to develop some level of indigenous capability.

Towards this goal, certain technologies and know-how were obtained, both for the repairs and for the local production of some critical spare parts. These efforts were, however, largely case-specific and were not components of any systematic strategy for the comprehensive development of an indigenous defence industry. They were also service-driven in the absence of any coherent strategy to achieve self-reliance. However, the liberalisation of the Indian economy that almost coincided with the collapse of FSU and promised to unlock India's productive capabilities gave impetus to the goal of developing a domestic military-industrial complex.

It was, however, not until 2005 that India formulated a defence offset policy to contribute to the nation's goal of developing its domestic defence industry. This policy was incorporated in the Defence Procurement Procedure (DPP) 2005. The policy introduced a 30 per cent offset in contracts valued above Rs 3 billion under "buy" and 'buy and make" categories.

Under the policy, foreign vendors had the liberty to discharge their obligations either through the execution of defence exports of Indian items and services or through investments in India's defence infrastructure.

They also had the option of selecting Indian firms in consultation with an industry associate of their choice to implement their offset obligations. The hallmark of this policy was its non-obligatory nature, or in other words, these offsets were non-mandatory.

It was left to the Services Capital Acquisition Plan Categorisation Committee (SCAPCC) to recommend the incorporation of offset obligation in acquisition proposals. The offset policy was, however, in the nascent stage and it lacked clarity in many areas. It also suffered from the absence of any designated agency in the Ministry of Defence (MoD) for guiding, overseeing, executing and monitoring the implementation of the policy. In reality, confusion reigned in equal measure in the corridors of South Block as in the minds of the vendors on how to implement the offset obligations. Consequently, the offset policy did not yield any dividend.

The absence of any offset benefit to the Indian defence industry led the Government of India (GoI) to make significant changes in DPP 2006 and they included the following:

- offset was made mandatory in defence contracts of the size and nature as prescribed in the 2005 policy;
- foreign firms were allowed the flexibility of forming joint ventures (JVs) with Indian firms, and;
- a new organisation called the Defence Offset Facilitation Agency (DOFA) was established comprising of representatives of all stakeholders; the Services, DPSUs, Defence and Research Organisation (DRDO), etc.

Defence Offsets

Offsets have been variously defined. In essence, offsets in defence, as in civil trade, are compensations that a buyer seeks from the seller for the purchase of goods and/or services. The demand for offsets in defence has exhibited an upward trajectory since the 1950s. It gained further momentum in the 1980s and has been growing ever since. From around 20 nations about two decades ago, this practice has now been now adopted by more than 130 nations.

European nations have been able to generate more offsets than others. During the period 1993-2004, European countries were able to obtain offsets valued at 99.1 per cent of their defence imports while non-European countries achieved 46.6 per cent of their imports. Significantly, 72.9 per cent of the offsets obtained by European nations were 100 per cent or more of the value of the weapon systems imported by them. The data on arms sales and offsets show that demands for offsets "are increasing over time in all regions."

India was, however, late in adopting an official offset policy though it had obtained some compensatory benefits since Independence through a series of bilateral arrangements. It was only in 2005 that the nation, through its Defence Procurement Procedure (DPP), announced an official policy to secure offsets for its defence imports. The policy was amended to give it greater clarity and direction in 2006 and again in

2008. Consequently, as a late entrant in the field, India's polices are yet to be fully tested against the complex process of managing offsets and it is yet to traverse the path of achieving its declared objective of creating a vibrant military-industrial base.

Objective of Paper

This paper seeks to critically examine the salient features of India's offset policy and answer the following questions.

- Will the policy outlined in DPP 2008 contribute substantially to the development of a military-industrial base in India?
- What are the shortcomings of the policy?
- What modifications are required in the offset policy and connected government procedures to maximise the benefits that can accrue to the nation from capital acquisition of defence equipment?

In order to understand the basic arguments contained in this paper, a few concepts relating to offsets in general and in defence trade in particular are explained.

Offsets Explained

Offset, as the term implies, is an element that counterbalances or compensates an act. It is a set-off from a development, in this case, military acquisition. However defined, the term offset primarily signifies an element of 'compensation' as the predominant import of the term. It occurs "when a supplier places work to an agreed value with firms in the buying country, over and above what it would have brought in the absence of the offset."

As is commonly understood, in trade, offsets have been classified as direct or indirect offsets. Direct offsets are those that are directly connected with the item being sold by the seller and can take the form of co-production, component production, licensed production, etc. Indirect offsets are those not directly related to the product being imported and here compensations can be secured in any other area with the aim of obtaining for the economy what would otherwise have not been available to the buyer but for the purchase. Though the above two forms characterise the two widely-accepted compensatory strategies, it is necessary to add a new terminology to describe a hybrid form of offsets that is between the direct and indirect offsets that India is seeking to obtain. This may be termed as quasi-direct offsets. It can be defined as compensation given in the sector under which the purchase falls, but is not directly connected with the product that is being imported. For instance, when tanks are imported, and the offset is obtained in the form of assistance for the co-production of a warship, then it will fall within this definition (quasi-direct) as it enhances the defence capability of the importing nation, though the compensatory arrangement is not directly connected with the item being imported. Therefore, though analysts have largely described India's policy as seeking direct offsets, it would be more accurate to describe it as quasi-direct offsets.

INDIA'S DEFENCE INDUSTRIAL POLICY

Defence industrial policy in the initial years after independence was guided by the simple phrase called 'self sufficiency'. This was subsequently modified to 'self reliance' in defence production and has become a matter of varied interpretation. While for some it means the ultimate objective of complete non-dependence on imports for defence hardware, for others it means selective self-sufficiency in certain critical technologies. And for some others it is a simple reduction in the ratio of imports to indigenous sources of supply to the armed forces.

However, one can say that India's defence industrial policy broadly consists of three components: (i) maximisation of indigenous manufacturing and production (ii) License production of what could be obtained from abroad and (iii) direct purchase of those equipment not covered by the other two categories but considered essential for ensuring security. Another important unspoken element was that everything, whether indigenous production, license production or direct purchase, was done within the government set-up in line with the general industrial policy. The recent policy change, of course, demonstrates the intention to involve the private sector in defence R&D and production through licensing and the indirect opening of the defence industrial sector to foreign companies through equity participation and the offset arrangement.

The moot question is: was there something wrong with the past policy objectives? On the face of it, the policy components and objectives appear quite sound and logical for a country like India. In simple terms, it means that indigenous production should be maximised; what could not be produced indigenously should be produced under license arrangement; and those that could not be obtained through these two routes should be acquired by direct purchase. A sound policy indeed. But the soundness of a policy has to be judged from tangible outcomes. Arguably, the problems might not have been in the contents of the policy per se. It is due to the nature defence technology and limitations of vision as embedded in the policy.

The policy objective was essentially to substitute imported equipment with indigenous production in the hope of attaining 'self-sufficiency' or 'self reliance'. Unfortunately, the security imperatives of a country translated into defence equipment are like 'moving targets'. Neither the technological capability of the defence sector nor its policy instrument as highlighted above was able to catch up with the targets.

The increasing quantum of defence imports from year to year, the country's inability to upgrade the imported equipment held for significant period under license production, and, indirectly, insignificant defence exports amply testify to this situation. The general industrial policy wherein defence items and their productions were kept strictly within the government set-up further compounded the problem. In this context, two aspects of the policy – indigenous production and license production, merit detailed analysis.

Maximising indigenous production would imply more than one thing. It would mean meeting the quantitative requirements in terms of the existing demands of the armed forces for equipment or items at any point of time. It would also mean increasing the varieties of items and equipment required by them. Most importantly, it would mean the ability to meet the challenges of supplying their ever-changing demands of technology specific equipment and items. India's defence industrial policy has conspicuously failed in this respect. In fact, the implication of this policy is that the country should be able to indigenously produce the challenging demands made by the armed forces. Its logical extension is that defence research and development efforts have to be strengthened through policy focused research and development and adequate resources allocations thereto. It is a known fact that the defence research and development organisation has 50-odd laboratories and establishments. However, its lack of focused research and development is equally well known, though of late it has been able to achieve break-throughs in certain strategic technologies. Moreover, its budgetary allocation has been quite modest even within the overall defence budget and until recently it was part of 'Army Demand'. In fact, the Parliamentary Standing committee on Defence recommended that defence R&D budgetary allocation should be at least 14 to 15 per cent of the total defence budget so that indigenous production to imports in the ratio of 70:30 could be achieved. This recommendation was in line with the projected target of the report of the self-reliance committee entitled '10 year plan for self reliance in Defence systems'. But the fact remains that there is no evidence of adequate policy back-up to attain this desirable but difficult goal. The DRDO does not seem to be suffering from lack of funds per se since only 8 to 10 per cent of its total budget is reported to be spent on fundamental research. Perhaps, the solution to this issue lies somewhere else.

How about production under license, another important pillar of the policy? The normal assumption is that production under license would enable the country not only to acquire the capability to produce a particular equipment or product but also help it gain the technical know-how for subsequent upgradation and further technological innovations. For the last fifty-odd years, India has been producing a number of defence equipment under license. Good examples in this regard are the Vijayanta tank and the MIG series of fighter aircraft. But this does not seem to have helped in the development of the Arjun Main Battle Tank and the Light Combat Aircraft. Moreover, India has not even been able to upgrade certain fighter aircraft held and operated for a long time by its armed forces. Thus, the above assumption is definitely not correct.

A closer examination of license production arrangements reveals certain interesting features. License production arrangements are more of an 'institutional framework' under which various types of contractual agreements could be entered into between the supplier and the buyer. It is not necessarily a proven mechanism of technology transfer as such. It may envisage the setting up of a simple production line or facilities in the buyer country for assembly of the finished parts and components for the final finished product. In such cases, hardly any technology transfer takes place and the supplier does not part with any technical know-how. In fact, the supplier agrees to sacrifice only a small portion of his economic interest. It is also not possible to discern under these circumstances whether the supplier has compensated itself for this marginal loss by way of increasing the cost of the technology or equipment and components thereof. On the other hand, there could be a situation where license production involves an intensive process of technology transfer within and beyond the physical production of the equipment in the host county. This is rare rather than routine. The truth of the matter is that since technology is know-how, it is the function of human understanding. The focus of active mechanisms, implicitly or explicitly, is people. However, the truth is that no foolproof prescription could be given for the effectiveness of technology transfer. It all depends on the nature of technology to be acquired. Perhaps, India has learnt it by the hard way the limitations of licence production for attaining the objective of self-sufficiency or self-reliance in defence production.

The fact that defence technology needs long term investment, its obsolescence is high and economies of scale are difficult to attain unlike in other areas of civilian technology are well known. This is essentially because higher capability tends to drive downward the scales of production. In the context of a limited number of customers, this trend is more regressive. On top of this, contrary to logical expectation, the production of the next generation of an equipment or of a different variant does not bring down the cost of the equipment. It has been the British experience that a new generation could cost between one and a half times to four times of the previous variant. This is due to the fact that production of the next generation is not a simple straight line trajectory work but involves the integration of various systems, which sometimes may involve a number of companies and agencies, that were not partners earlier.

This leads to the conclusion that the policy of maximising indigenous production without a strong R&D policy back-up would not bring tangible results. License production is more of an economic compromise between the supplier and the buyer, and it does not and cannot bring about significant technology transfer without an inbuilt specific and suitable mechanism. Every country at one point of time or the other will attain a saturation level when it comes to supplying certain categories of equipment for its armed forces. Therefore, the ultimate defence industrial policy goal must be to foster defence exports without which it is difficult to sustain the economic base of a country's defence industry.

India's defence industrial policy seems to be lacking in all these important ingredients. Since the industrial base has to be sustained for technological and economic reasons, exports are an essential element of defence industrial policy. This is why many countries and their companies are aggressively competing in the global defence market for exports under different arrangements including license production. It is reported that way back in 1995, the United States government spent more than $7.6 billion in subsidy to help export defence equipment to sustain the economic base of its defence industry. It is a matter of fact that strategic depth in defence production can be increased only by aiming at being 'internationally competitive' through the policy objective of defence exports. In the absence of such an approach, India's defence industrial policy is unlikely to take off in the foreseeable future.

India on the Path to Vibrant Defence Industry

Every major power aspires to build a vibrant defence industrial base. This status is however not easily attainable. Apart from the United States and to some extent Russia and France, all other countries are in the state of struggling to arrive at such a defence industrial position. Certain countries like the United Kingdom may be able to attain this, but due to strategic or economic preferences may deliberately choose not to consider the enormous costs involved as against the perceived security requirements. India's aspiration for this is well documented wherein it has publicly pronounced its goal of 'self sufficiency' soon after political independence and now graduating it to 'self-reliance'. The unfortunate part is that India is still far from nearing that level even after fifty years of this laudable policy. One of the identified ongoing policy drawbacks is its weak linkage with the civilian sector of industry.

The thrust of the new policy initiative therefore is participation of the private sector in defence industry for both research and development as well as production purposes. It has also opened up the defence sector to foreign equity participation up to 26 per cent, with the government recently expressing its willingness to consider even up to 49 per cent on case-to-case basis. Together with this is the initiation of the 'offset policy' for major foreign procurement of defence equipment of Rs.300 crores and above. The big question is: will all these initiatives contribute to the growth of a vibrant defence industry in India?

The immediate effect of these initiatives is that significant numbers of licenses have been applied for and issued to major Indian companies for production of varied components and systems. In fact, according to CII sources alone, as of date, more than 140 companies are involved in about 345 defence items/ products. Complete systems/platforms/weapons systems constitute the majority of the licenses issued, which demands higher financial investments and technical capability. This reflects the ambition and confidence of the private sector in their new ventures. On the other hand, there is a flurry of partnership agreements/collaborative ventures by these industrial companies with major global defence industrial giants from the United States, Western Europe and Israel. This is of course not to ignore the existing and ongoing collaborative projects of Defence Public Sector Undertakings (DPSUs) and Ordnance Factories (OFs) with companies from these countries at the governmental level. An analysis would reveal that India's defence industrial scene now is moving on two distinct parallel lines. The first is equipment and technology emanating from Russia and Eastern Europe, which represent approximately 70 per cent of the country's defence industrial set-up. The new addition is Western technology or modified/upgraded technology through private sector companies that are poised to enter India's defence market. The moot question is: Will these different technologies eventually strengthen India's defence industrial base or add further complexities through highly mixed inventories?

In this emerging situation, a few logical things are bound to happen. First, due to the emerging competition from Western technology largely through the private sector, the Russians or other traditional suppliers are likely to at least scale down their often-repeated business behaviour of project delays, delay in supply of spares and parts, and unwillingness to transfer technology. Moreover, the tendency to jack up costs midway while implementing agreements may also get tempered with the arrival of new competitors. However, the fact remains that the domination of Russian origin technologies and their grip on the Indian military establishment will sustain for quite some years to come particularly given that they are largely embedded through the defence public sector undertakings and other government agencies. The major positive impact of the new situation is, however, that the government agencies/DPSUs are likely to wake up from their slumber at least in those areas where they are producing items of common use, which can be easily produced at a competitive level by the private sector. This will be the immediate benefit brought in by the private sector.

While the above may be the likely positive impact, it is unlikely that Western technology will be able to easily challenge the existing market structure through the private sector. This is due to the peculiarity of defence technology and its market structure. First, given that control of technology is the essence of the growth and expansion of MNCs, the global Western defence giants may not easily part with high-end technology, whereas the Indian establishment would be looking for sophisticated weapons and equipment to supplement what has already been acquired from existing sources. The private sector's ability to enter the market will depend on its capability to supply the components, parts and sub-systems of the new equipment in the initial period. Secondly, opportunities for the private sector would largely depend on the government decision to opt for higher and complete major systems of Western origin technologies such as the MMRCA. If such a decision goes in favour of any of the fighter aircraft of western origin, the private sector would definitely have significant scope to capture the market through the offset channel or through normal business dealings. Thirdly, the ability and willingness of Western technology to supplement the defence technology requirements of the armed forces would be the decisive factor. As of now, the armed forces are already in possession of a certain level of defence technology. What they are looking for is conceptually of a higher level, which would be supplementary in nature to bridge perceived security gaps. Will the western powers through their MNCs be willing to part with this level of technology to fill the gap, which, though may be lower than the high-end strategic technology that they possess? If the answer is in the affirmative, the prospects of their capturing the Indian market are very bright. So is also the market potential for the myriad private domestic defence companies in the next five to ten years.

The challenge for Indian industry as a whole would be the will and ability to integrate the two major technology streams in the coming years. This demands the need for dedicated and focused research leading to the capability to integrate existing systems with incoming systems. While the major platforms may continue to be of Russian/Soviet origin, the genius of Indian industry would be tested in its capability to build armaments and other sub-systems and integrating them at higher levels. This is the core challenge and the capability to do it would eventually make the defence industry genuinely vibrant. This will usher in the 'Indian brand of defence technology' even for export purposes free from possible objections on accounts of violations of intellectual property rights. The role of the Government of India as patron and principal customer shall be very crucial for success in achieving the above objective.

DEFENCE PLANNING SYSTEM

Before independence, the defence services worked on a system of contract budget. Defence expenditure was pegged at Rs 55 crore per year, which was more than half of the Central Government's revenue. There was no serious threat from outside (except during World War II, when a fresh agreement was signed) and this amount was more than adequate to maintain the establishment.

The savings were not allowed to lapse but put away in the Defence Reserve Fund that was utilised to finance measures for re-equipment of the Defence Services, thus freeing the Government from having to provide fund money greater than the contract amount. Expenditure on defence rose steeply soon after independence. However, there was no planned effort and defence programmes consisted mainly of outright purchases from abroad, drawing heavily on available Sterling reserves. In the late 1950s, some efforts were made to initiate domestic weapons production by the Ministry of Defence when Mr. Krishna Menon was the Defence Minister. The Sino-Indian conflict in 1962 aroused a new defence consciousness in the country. After taking care of immediate postwar requirements, systematic defence planning started in 1964. Defence requirements were assessed on a five-year basis and the First Five Year Defence Plan (1964-69) was drawn up. This plan took into account the resources available and assistance which could be expected from friendly foreign countries.

The plan was primarily based on an expansion and modernisation programme considered necessary by each Service in the light of the respective threat perception assessed. It also proposed a defence production base that would gradually reduce the country's external dependence, provide for improvements in border roads and communications, and a modest expansion of DRDO. The Government recognised the imperative need to synergise 'defence' and 'development' instead of planning each on a separate and unrelated level. The MoD emphasised the "inevitable need to harness all resources of the country for the country's defence and for the defence effort to derive full sustenance from the country's economic development plans".

Thereafter, the National Development Council authorised the Chairman of the Planning Commission to review the needs of both development and defence. A Planning Cell was established in 1965 in the Ministry of Defence 'to deal with the wider aspects of defence planning'. The new system was intended to facilitate medium and long-term defence planning and to maintain constant liaison with the Planning Commission and other ministries.

It was expected that the MoD would derive maximum advantage from the development effort by being able to place its priorities for consideration along with the overall economic and industrial plans drawn up by the Planning Commission. The experience of the First Five Year Defence Plan showed that the development of weapons and equipment was a long drawn out process. The Government realised that there could be no forward movement in attaining self-sufficiency in weapons and equipment unless these requirements were planned over a reasonably long period, long enough to cover the span of development and production of new weapons systems and other fighting tools.

The inadequacy of foreign exchange reserves was another hindrance in planning and implementation. In order to mitigate some of these drawbacks, the Second Five Year Defence Plan (1969-74) was instituted on a "roll-on" basis. After a year, an additional year was added so that the Defence Services would have before them a revised and updated five-year plan. In this context, the MoD commented: "Opportunity is taken by this annual exercise to take note of and reflect the change in priorities, the shifts in emphasis and the latest concepts and programmes to reorient the plan within the scheme of resources so that the aims and means are most effectively balanced." This system was expected to facilitate the planning of projects that took five years or more and to revise or eliminate projects, depending on the prevailing foreign exchange situation and availability of domestic resources. For a period of five years, firm assurances were to be given on the availability of resources. This, unfortunately, never happened. In 1971, it was impossible to adhere to the discipline and the pattern of the roll-on plan. Instead of roll-on annual revisions, immediate requirements dominated the Government's attention that pre-empted plan efforts. In its 1971-72 Annual Report, the MoD acknowledged that having a Planning Cell in the ministry was an insufficient and unsatisfactory method of meeting a crisis.

The Planning Cell was not taken seriously in the crucial stages of economic planning and the argument that defence needs would be adjusted in the over-all allocation of resources was proved wrong. In 1974, an Apex Group headed by the Union Minister for Planning again suggested that steady long-term defence programmes would be more cost effective and economical rather than fluctuating allocations due to periodic economic and security crises. In order to integrate defence planning with the overall economic planning effort, defence and economic development plans were made co-terminus.

Planning Machinery

Most of the defence planning machinery and planning methodology was developed in the decade 1964-74. The Joint

Intelligence Committee (JIC) was established in the Cabinet Secretariat to provide external and internal threat assessments. Inputs for this purpose were to be provided by all Intelligence agencies of the Government. The Service Chiefs were to assess the broad military aims and a strategy, coordinated in the Chiefs of Staff Committee, was to be approved by the Defence Minister. However, this was seldom done. Each Service ended up planning its own force level, choice of weapons and equipment, and build-up of infrastructure. In 1977, the Government formed a Committee for Defence Planning (CDP) to "undertake regular assessments relevant to defence planning in the light of all factors having a bearing on national security and defence". However, this committee could not function smoothly nor meet the desired goals.

Planning units were also established in the Department of Defence Production and DRDO. A Planning and Coordination Cell was created in the MoD to coordinate and compile various plans into a 'Defence Plan' for Cabinet approval. As the bureaucrats in the ministry had no professional knowledge or background, this cell could only compile different requirements without any analysis. In Army Headquarters, the Deputy Chief of Army Staff was made responsible for preparing the Army plan. A Perspective Planning Directorate was established in the late 1970s. Naval and Air plans were prepared in the respective Planning Directorates. Financial considerations, nonexistent at this level earlier, were introduced through Finance Planning Sections attached to these Directorates. In 1986, the Directorate General of Defence Planning Staff (DGDPS), comprising officers from the three Services, DRDO, and Ministries of Defence and External Affairs, was established under the Chiefs of Staff Committee (COSC) to coordinate and harmonise defence planning. Civilian officers from the Ministries probably did not find the job professionally satisfying and were gradually withdrawn, thus leaving the DGDPS a tri-Service set up.

All these measures enabled each Service headquarters to prepare defence plans in a more rational manner. But due to lack of clear political direction and each Service primarily planning for itself, joint planning, coordination between Services and other departmental plans of the MoD, were largely ignored. After the Kargil conflict in 1999, the Group of Ministers (GoM) and later the Cabinet Committee on Security (CCS) approved several reforms. An Integrated Defence Headquarters (IDH) was established and the DGDPS was merged with it. The creation of the post of Chief of Defence Staff (CDS), whose tasks would include ensuring intra and inter-Services prioritisation of defence plans and improvement in joint functioning of the Defence Services, was recommended. The reforms also included establishment of a Defence Intelligence Agency and creation of Defence Equipment Production, Research and Planning councils in the IDH and MoD, respectively. Unfortunately, the CDS, who would be the cornerstone of integrated operational planning for defence, has not been appointed.

Analysis of the System

Despite several years of planning efforts, defence planning in India is characterised by seesaw bouts of frenzied activity followed by long periods of relative inaction. Five-year defence plans have rarely been formally approved before commencement. The Tenth Defence Plan, now in its third year, is yet to be accorded formal government approval. Adhocism is the order of the day, leading to knee-jerk responses and haphazard planning, making India a reactive rather than proactive nation in matters pertaining to national security. Whenever India's major adversaries plan a big defence purchase, there is an outcry for similar acquisitions, resulting in piecemeal decisions regardless of long-term impact and overall requirements.

The Defence Forces are forced to follow "a case-by-case" approach to modernisation and procurement of arms, ammunition and equipment to replace obsolescent items, in many cases long after their life cycle is over and they cannot be maintained in a cost effective manner. The Army's Vijayanta tanks, MiG-21s of the IAF, and IL-38 maritime reconnaissance aircraft of the Navy are some examples. Weapons development, procurement and absorption are complex processes. A lead-time of 15-20 years is required to plan and execute major projects. Despite this, for several years, a large amount of the capital acquisition budget has been surrendered. In the prevailing era of strategic uncertainty, the changing nature of warfare demands a judicious mix of threat and capabilities-based forces that can operate efficiently as combined arms, joint Services teams and components of multinational coalition forces.

INDO-U.S. ENGAGEMENT ON MISSILE DEFENCE

In one of its swiftest diplomatic moves ever, within hours of the U.S. declaration that it intends to pursue its plans to deploy the first phase of BMD by the fall of 2004, India became one of the few nations in the world to extend its support for the new security architecture being proposed by the United States.

India hailed the U.S. proposals for deep cuts in nuclear arsenals as well as building missile defences as a significant and far-reaching effort to move away from the adversarial legacy of the cold war. India went on to say that it believes "there is a strategic and technological inevitability in stepping away from a world that is held hostage by the doctrine of Mutual Assured Destruction (MAD) to a cooperative, defensive transition that is underpinned by further cuts and a de-alert of nuclear forces."

This was in sharp contrast to the Indian government's position just one year before when in June 2000 the then Indian foreign minister, Jaswant Singh, had made a case against supporting BMD on grounds that it would undermine international strategic stability, adversely affect the global movement towards nuclear disarmament, and might lead to the militarization of outer space. Not unexpectedly, India's dramatic change of stance generated a vigourous discussion in the country. The opposition parties criticized the government for what they called a hasty and premature reaction to the U.S. proposal with India going ahead with its effusive support even before the traditional U.S. allies had reacted to the decision. Many in the Indian strategic community, the academe and the think tanks also took exception to India's stand. While the debate on a suitable Indian response to the U.S. missile defence programme continues unabated to date, the political fissures generated by the Indian decision in 2001 revealed that, unlike most issues in Indian foreign policy, where there is by and large a political consensus, this issue was highly divisive. The fact that the Indian government of the day apparently did not take other political parties into its confidence did not help matters.

But regardless of the domestic debate, the Indo-U.S. engagement on BMD continued with the visit of U.S. deputy secretary of state Richard Armitage to India a week after India's declaration of support for the U.S. plans. Armitage briefed India on the details of the new strategic framework espoused by the Bush administration via the BMD, and the two sides decided to work together for this new security regime. This visit was also a signal for the United States that India had moved into the orbit of its "friends," who would be consulted on key strategic issues such as missile defence.

This has been followed by various rounds of bilateral and multilateral discussions on missile defence between India and the United States. Moreover, in 2004, as part of a process called "Next Step in Strategic Partnership (NSSP)," India and the United States formally decided to expand their cooperation in the area of civilian nuclear activities, civilian space programmes, and high technology trade as well as agreed to broaden their dialogue on missile defence to promote nonproliferation and ease the transfer of advanced technologies to India. The proposed cooperation under the NSSP progressed through a series of reciprocal steps building on each other, resulting ultimately in the landmark U.S.-India civilian nuclear cooperation pact signed in 2005. Though the United States has also decided to engage Pakistan on missile defence issues, the two states are not involved in cooperation on space and high technology issues.

Most of the Indo-U.S. discussions on missile defence have taken place under the rubric of the Indo-U.S. Defence Policy

Group (DPG), the highest policymaking body that gives shape to Indo-U.S. bilateral cooperation. An Indian team visited Colorado Springs to participate in a missile defence simulation, and India also participated in the missile defence conference in Dallas in 2002. India was a participant in the 2003 multinational missile defence workshop in Japan as well as the 2004 missile defence conference in Germany. India was also invited to the 2005 annual "Roving Sands" air and missile defence exercises in New Mexico.

The Indo-U.S. DPG meetings have continued even after a change of government in India in 2004. This government is led by the Congress Party and is supported from outside by the Left parties, which, while in opposition, have been less than enthusiastic about the Indian support to the U.S. BMD programme, with the Left parties even calling it a renunciation of Indian autonomy in foreign policy. But once in government, the United Progressive Alliance (UPA) government has adopted a cautious attitude towards this issue and has gone beyond the previous government in cultivating its ties with the United States.

As part of the NSSP agreement, the Bush administration gave clearance for a classified technical presentation of the Patriot Advanced Capability (PAC-2) antiballistic missile system to India in February 2005 in response to a request made by India in 2002. This was done after obtaining assurances from India that this technology would not be shared with any other country by India. Patriot, or Phased Array Tracking Intercept of Target, is the foundation of the U.S. Army's integrated air- and missile-defence architecture.

PAC-2 is a long-range, all-altitude, all-weather air defence system to counter tactical ballistic missiles, cruise missiles, and advanced aircraft. The range of the missile is seventy kilometers and it can climb to an altitude of greater than twenty-four kilometers, with minimum and maximum flight times being less than three seconds and three-and-half minutes respectively. While the Indian defence establishment welcomed the U.S. openness with regard to technical details of the PAC-2 system, it views this as an opening towards PAC-3, the latest upgraded version of the antimissile system. PAC-3 was used in Operation Iraqi Freedom, and has a kill rate of more than 95 per cent. There have been reports that the United States might be willing to offer India the advanced version of PAC-2 missiles with the radar system of the latest PAC- 3 so that when Indian is ready, it can upgrade its missile defence capability.

The United States, on its part, made clear that it would welcome continued Indian cooperation on this issue even though the UPA government has been in no hurry to clarify its stand. There is not only a lack of domestic political consensus on this issue, but the Left parties, which constitute a major part of the governing coalition, have been strongly opposed to any Indian entanglement with the U.S. missile defence system. The Indian military, meanwhile, has undertaken a detailed study of the technical, operational, and budgetary aspects of a missile defence system for India and has submitted its recommendations to the government. India has not only signed a defence cooperation framework agreement with the United States in 2005 that commits both sides to expanding "collaboration relating to missile defence," but it has also demonstrated to the world in 2006 its capability to indigenously produce an effective antiballistic missile prototype.

Though India's upgraded Prithvi ABM interceptor has a long way to go before it can be deployed, it has been ranked on par with the U.S. Patriot PAC-3 system, Russia's S-300, and Israel's Arrow in its ability to intercept short- and intermediate-range missile. This has led some to conclude that "India is seriously considering integrating some kind of strategic defensive capabilities into its national military posture."

After successfully testing a hypersonic interceptor missile, which brought India a step closer to developing a full fledged missile defence system, has come the announcement that India should expect to have its home-grown militarily usable missile defence system by 2010.

India's central military research and development facility, the Defence Research and Development Organization (DRDO) claims that it has the technology to develop a potent missile shield for the nation.

The ambition is to eventually develop a two-tier ballistic missile defence system that can intercept missiles at both the mid-course and terminal phases. The Advanced Air Defence (AAD-02), as the new interceptor missile is called, is capable of intercepting M-9 and M-11 class of missiles and compares well with the US PAC-3 (Patriot Advanced Capability). In fact, it is being touted as superior to PAC-3 in interception, range and altitude.

However, with the U.S.-India nuclear pact taking center stage since 2005, discussion of missile defence has taken a backseat in Indian policy discourse but not before exposing the fault lines dividing the Indian foreign policy establishment.

THE GREAT INDIAN NUCLEAR DEBATE

Examining the Indian missile defence debate closely, one should have little difficulty in classifying the various strands of the debate according to the typology that has been offered in the context of the debate on Indian nuclear policy generally. Three schools of thought can be delineated in the realm of Indian nuclear policy. These have been termed as the rejectionists, the pragmatists, and the maximalists. The rejectionists, while holding that nuclear disarmament is both necessary and desirable, argue that India should have nuclear weapons so long as other states with nuclear weapons do not agree to renounce them. Therefore, in the absence of a global and comprehensive nuclear disarmament, India has no option but to have nuclear weapons for deterrence. The pragmatists argue that India should be a part of the global arms control processes, because a comprehensive global nuclear disarmament of the type India wants is neither desirable nor feasible. By agreeing to be a part of the international nuclear arms control regime, which India has traditionally opposed on the grounds it is discriminatory, India should be able to garner several concessions from the international community, and particularly from the United States.

The third viewpoint of the hypernationalists or hyperrealists wants India to go beyond its "credible minimum" deterrent nuclear posture and to equip itself with an entire range of nuclear weapons capability. They want India to acquire the nuclear capability traditionally associated with "great powers." They want India to have nothing to do with global nuclear disarmament. They also would like India to disassociate itself from the nuclear arms control regime, because in their view, it might constrain India's nuclear weapons capability in the future.

The current debate in India on the issue of missile defence is largely along with some subtle differences. In the missile defence debate, the rejectionists and the maximalists have found themselves on the same side, though for very different reasons. Both have expressed strong objections to India's support for the U.S. BMD plans. For the rejectionists, the U.S. missile defence programme would be the beginning of the end of the entire global nuclear arms control and disarmament architecture.

India, with its traditionally supportive stance for the global disarmament movement, should resist supporting the U.S. plans. The maximalists also argue that India should have nothing to do with the U.S. plans, because in their opinion, this is part of the larger global counterproliferation strategy and it will end up constraining the Indian nuclear weapons capabilities in the future, because India would become little more than a U.S. satellite under the U.S. missile defence umbrella.

The pragmatists have supported the Indian government's stance of supporting the U.S. missile defence plans. In their opinion, such a diplomatic posture will not only bring India and the United States closer, but India can also get significant economic and technological benefit from the United States. They also think that while it is inevitable that the United States would go ahead with its missile defence plans anyway, it makes little sense to oppose the U.S. plans when India can benefit from being supportive. There is no doubt that India's support for the missile defence programme has paid dividends, especially leading to greater cooperation in the highly sensitive area of defence technology. Cooperation with the United States is useful, because it meets India's high-tech requirements for the defence sector. The Indian army has initiated as $5 billion fifteen-year programme to equip its infantry with smart, lighter, and more offensive weapons. The navy needs more than a hundred ships over the next fifteen years as replacements and additions as well as maritime patrol aircraft like the P-3 Orion reconnaissance aircraft. And there are major requirements for the air force and civilian space programme. For the pragmatists, Indo-U.S. cooperation on missile defence opens the way for the broader restructuring of the Indian defence sector with U.S. help.

The "Strategic" Direction of Indian Foreign Policy

However, another subtle debate can be delineated in the missile defence discourse in India. And this is a debate about India's larger foreign policy strategy. Many of those who oppose India's support to the U.S. missile defence programme do so on grounds that such a diplomatic posture might end up antagonizing China. China will respond aggressively, they argue, to the U.S. BMD by substantially shoring up its nuclear force posture. China has made its intentions very clear by arguing that "if a country, in addition to its offensive power, seeks to develop advanced TMD [tactical missile defence] or even NMD [nuclear missile defence], in an attempt to obtain absolute security, and unilateral strategic advantage for itself, other countries will be forced to develop more advanced offensive missiles." It might further enhance its nuclear and missile-related cooperation with Pakistan. All this would further endanger India's security.

Conversely, there are those who argue that India should support BMD precisely because it puts China on the defensive. In their opinion, China has done all it could to adversely affect Indian national security interests. India has this one chance to pay China back in the same coin. And if this entails opting for the U.S. missile defence umbrella, so be it.

These two strands in the Indian foreign policy discourse are not clearly defined as of yet. But they reflect the pressures on the Indian foreign policy as a consequence of the global unipolarity and the raising ambitions of India in the last few years. With the end of the cold war, India has increasingly found that its traditional foreign policy posture of nonalignment has become irrelevant.

As a consequence, it has tried to pursue a "multivector, multidimensional" foreign policy, which basically means trying to improve its relations with the major global powers, including the United States, China, the EU, and Russia. But more than any other state, China looms large over the Indian national security landscape. And the larger Indian foreign policy discourse has come to center more and more on China.

It is in this context that China is seen by many as India's rival for geopolitical primacy in Asia. And as China's global profile has risen in recent years, so has India's apprehensions about China's foreign policy goals vis-à-vis India, notwithstanding a substantial improvement in Sino-Indian relations in the last few years. On the one side are those who would like India to improve its bilateral relations with China even further and to do nothing to derail the process of Sino-Indian détente.

They would like India to make a common cause with China in opposing the U.S. attempts at preserving and enhancing its global hegemony. They would like India and China to stand up for a multipolar international political order, which in their view would be more just and peaceful. And therefore the idea of India cooperating with the United States on missile defence is anathema to the advocates of this foreign policy strategy. For them, India's foreign policy should be attuned to the political realities of South Asia's strategic context, rather than serving as a mere extension of U.S. security policy.

On the other side of this debate are those who argue that India can never come out of the straight jacket of being a mere South Asian power unless it starts countering China more proactively. India will have to compete with China for regional dominance in the near term if in the long term it wants to establish itself as a global player of any reckoning. Moreover, they don't see any threat to the U.S. global preponderance in the immediate future. And therefore there is every reason to cooperate with the United States on missile defence, which would greatly enhance India's strategic clout and sideline China. In this context, India's support for the U.S. missile defence plans is viewed as a major factor that has helped in transforming Indo-U.S. ties in the last few years.

It has been pointed out that China can respond to the U.S. BMD plans in a number of ways. It can accelerate its strategic military modernization programme, it can backtrack on its arms control and nonproliferation commitments, and it can reformulate and alter its nuclear weapons doctrine and posture. Whatever course China may adopt in the future, it is clear that it will have a substantial impact on India.

Those who would like India to be opposed to U.S. missile defence plans point to the negative impact the Chinese reaction to the BMD will have on India's security. Whether China decides to upgrade its nuclear arsenal or goes back on its arms control commitments or alters its nuclear doctrine, India's security situation will be adversely affected. However, those who would like India to cast its lot with the United States argue that China's strategic modernization programme has developed and will continue to develop regardless of the U.S. BMD plans, China's dubious nonproliferation record has already hurt India's security, and China's "no-first-use" nuclear doctrine does not apply to India in any case. And therefore supporting the U.S. missile defence plans can only raise India's strategic profile vis-à-vis China.

While there are few who would like India to chart a completely independent route towards its great power status, the debate as it is evolving in the Indian strategic community addresses the larger strategic framework of the Indian foreign policy. Using the typology of the rejectionists, pragmatists, and hyperrealists, the rejectionists are more or less on the side of keeping China in good humour.

Most of the left-liberal Indian political establishment seems at the moment to be supporting this strand. The pro–United States line is taken by the pragmatists and Indian political right. While it is no coincidence that India enthusiastically supported Bush administration's BMD proposals in 2001, when the National Democratic Alliance led by the Hindu nationalist Bharatiya Janata Party (BJP) was in power, the continuing support for strong U.S.-India ties from the centrist Congress Party leading the ruling coalition at the center is a testimony to the growing salience of pragmatists in Indian foreign policy discourse. Though Indians have been berated for not thinking strategically on national security issues, the Indian debate on missile defence is about the larger strategic direction of Indian foreign policy, even though the advocates on both sides might not even realize this themselves. How this debate shapes up and resolves itself will to a large extent decide the strategic direction of the Indian foreign policy in the coming years.

THE NEED FOR A STRATEGIC VISION FOR THE TWENTY FIRST CENTURY

India sadly lacks a 'Strategic Vision'. Vision is defined as 'imaginative insight, statesman like foresight, political sagacity.' 'Strategic Vision' would imply the application of imaginative, statesmanlike foresight and political sagacity by India's political leadership to the nation's national security management and long-range strategic planning to counter both external and internal security threats. Hence 'Strategic Vision' for India would imply the need for :

- Political statesmanship that can have a penetrative foresight of how India can be led to its aspirational goals of being a leading regional and global power.
- Political leadership that can translate India's 'Strategic Vision' into time-bound implementation plans. These implementation plans should incorporate short term, medium term and long term goals.
- Political leadership which is resolute, forceful and determined to direct an integrated national effort

towards achieving strategic goals, cutting through bureaucratic red-tapism and lethargy. National security and strategic implementation should have an over-riding priority over all other national activities.

- Political leadership that is bold and audacious and which will ensure that in the pursuit of India's 'strategic vision', any attempts to thwart it by external or internal threats are met with prompt, decisive and crippling military responses. Power is meant to be used to nip any emerging threats to India's national security.

India's 'Strategic Vision' for the 21st century should incorporate the following goals and components and which should be reflected in appropriate declaratory policies binding across the entire Indian political spectrum:

- India is to be the predominant power in the Indian sub-continent. It already is in terms of size, natural resources and human resources. It has an unbridgeable lead in the sub-continent in terms of economy, industrial development and infrastructure and hi-technology wherewithal. India however is not the pre-dominant military power, as Pakistan has been built up as the 'regional spoiler' state by China in terms of a nuclear weapons and missile arsenal. China has been engaged for the last two decades specifically to arrest India's emergence as the predominant power in South Asia by its proxy efforts through Pakistan.
- India is one of the major powers of Asia, along with China and Japan. To this end India's strategic strengths should be built at an accelerated pace and strategic partnerships evolved to ensure that India becomes a determinant in any regional or global power considerations in political, economic and military terms.

To achieve this ' strategic vision' for the 21st century India needs to develop strategically and in military terms, the following capabilities:

- Military preponderance in both the nuclear and conventional military fields. In terms of levels, it should have an overwhelming military superiority in South Asia and relative parity with China.
- India needs to develop 'force projection' capabilities, especially naval and air. Sizeable air-mobile and naval task forces should be available for rapid deployment in India's area of interest and 'areas of influence'.
- India's naval power should be built to levels which would permit sea-denial if not sea-control in the entire Indian Ocean region.
- Nuclear deterrence strong enough to deter even major powers to attempt political or military coercion i.e., development of an ICBM and SLBM arsenal. India after fifty years of being a 'Soft State' needs to get into a resurgent mode befitting her size and resources. The time has come not only to have the will to build up her power attributes but also to learn and have the will to use power.

Political leadership of a very high order and calibre is required to lead India towards the achievement of the 'strategic vision' thus envisioned.

INDIA'S DEFENCE PREPAREDNESS

India's economic progress has increased it's say in the world order where India is being considered as an emerging superpower. It's the ninth largest country in world in terms of nominal GDP; India has the third largest purchasing power in the world.

This has certainly been reflected its recent imports for the defence industry. In the period 2006 to 2010 India surpassed China as the world's largest importer of weapons systems, indicating India's intention to modernize its military capabilities and efforts toward making its boundaries secure and projecting its capability to outside world. The crucial issue here is that not only weapon & defence technology imports drain country's foreign exchequer but also increases the dependence of our defence technology on other nations.

India's spending on defence as a share of its GDP has remained relatively steady at 2.5 to 3.0 percent. Consequently, India's defence budget has grown by some 64% (in real terms) since 2001 reaching $36.3 billion in the 2011–2012 and $41 billion in 2012-13 (an increase of 17% from the last year). Approximately 40 percent (some $14.5 billion) is allocated to the defence capital outlay budget, which funds for arms procurements, construction and maintenance & installations additional infrastructure, and other military equipment modernizations.

Indian Air Force has experienced a 6 to 7 percent growth in its share of the capital outlay budget over the past decade, while the Indian Army and Navy have seen their shares decrease. The Air Force also receives the major share, some 40 percent of the current capital outlay budget, while the Army and Navy receive 25 and 20 percent, respectively (the remaining is spent on R&D and military production).

Looking at the defence budget one can discern that around 70% of the budget is utilized for paying for imports and the remaining 30% is used for indigenous capability building, defence research and procurement. This is indicative of our dependence on foreign imports and under allocation of resources for indigenous defence technology development. The argument of indigenous R&D in defence technology is Janus faced. R&D in defence technology is predominantly conducted by, and limited to, the government organizations like DRDO, HAL, NAL etc.; but the efficacy and efficiency of these organizations is deplorable, thereby leaving no other alternative but to procure the required technology from abroad. Contesting this it can also be argued that the resource allocation for defence research is very conservative; in fact budget allocation for defence R&D has decreased from 10,539 crores in 2011-12 to 5,995 crore rupees in 2012-13 (43.11% decrease over the last budget) deeply hampering our indigenous R&D. It seems that indigenous R&D

in defence technology is a low priority issue for the government; whereas lack of funds could be a pertinent impediment to the ability of the research organizations to deliver.

Boosting indigenous defence research to come up with advanced defence technology with shorter cycle time requires structural reforms. We not only need to spend more on R&D but also need to improve support infrastructure and be more open minded about public-private-partnership (PPP) in the defence sector. There are many important issues which have to be addressed in this context. It's an imperative to build a quality research network for defence research comprising of government research organizations, universities and other research institutes; defence research is too important to be left for government organizations alone. Why not sponsor defence research projects in competent educational institutions in India? Having spent some time with HAL Bangalore, what comes as a critical observation is the extent to which our government research organizations lack professional management. Research organization need to be managed much more professionally than they are; this will require intensive focus on project management, time-bound objectives and performance dependent appraisals.

For these advancements it is critical to invest more in education and research based infrastructure, such as well-equipped labs, operational with high-speed computational computers and testing facilities, and more industry exposure. Analyzing the present scenario, India currently is home to 50 laboratories all over the country predominantly held by government, most of them under Defence & Research Development Organization (DRDO), while others are associated with Indian Space And Research Organization (ISRO). Labs in other educational institutes such as IITs and IISc seem more associated with commercial based research rather than core defence research. This limits the participation from private sector institutions and educational institutions in coming up with innovative ideas in the field of defence technology development.

To boost indigenous defence research India must look forward to partnership with the private sector. To address the security concerns, government can open up the defence sector to private investment gradually or limit private participation to only domestic private players, but private participation is essential. More vigorous private participation in defence research will not only reduce pressure on the government to allocate resources, but will also bring about more ideas, innovative technologies, timely project completion and as a consequence a more robust indigenous defence development.

Currently there are a number of regulatory barriers for entry of private players, making it difficult for small and medium enterprises (SMEs) to enter the market. This is largely due to the high costs of tendering processes, such as in-country trials and obligations for Transfer of Technology. One of the major impediments is the necessity for No Cost No Commitment Trials which can take several years and consequently small players with sophisticated expertise do not have the resilience to survive this risk. Also the tendering process for defence equipment in India is not transparent; and is replete with procedures and red-tapeism. Such entry barriers discourage prospective foreign or domestic private players to invest in defence R&D in India, as this could lead to irrecoverable sunk costs, and might not lead to any returns in future.

There is a shift in policy stance in this matter. Apprehending the gravity of these issues Ministry of Defence (GOI) released the first ever Defence Production Policy in 2011. This document greatly emphasizes on indigenous production and advocates relaxation of norms and policies, which earlier inhibited private small and medium enterprises entering into defence sector, instilling confidence in them so as to foster public-private-partnerships. But a lot remains to be done for indigenous defence sector development by duly prioritizing R&D investment and related infrastructure and opening up possibilities for private sector participation in the same.

9

Indigenization of Defence Technology and Defence Manufacturing

To be a world power one has to be self reliant economically and in the field of Defence manufacturing. Despite all efforts we continue to import 70 percent of our defence equipment. The new Government has instituted numerous measures in terms of Make in India, Defence Technology and Trade Initiative (DTTI) with the United States, a new Defence Procurement Policy (DPP) 2016 and working on a new Defence Procurement Manual, There is also a new approach with the Raksha Mantri listening to suggestions made by various agencies.

Current state of defence equipment

General V P Malik during the Kargil Conflict stated that we will fight with whatever we have, 17 years have elapsed since the conflict and we still have numerous areas where our projects are way behind schedule. A few of them are a rifle and carbine for the Indian Army. Further, the Arjun Mark 2 is being developed for the Indian Army with 89 upgrades with foreign assistance. The anti tank guided missile Nag has yet to clear User Trials. The Active Electronically Scanned Array (AESA) Radar for Tejas has still not been developed and there is a need to deliver 20 Tejas by 2018 to the Indian Air Force. This has to be combined with the proving of the naval version of the Tejas in another two years. Similarly, the AWACs programme for the Air Force is delayed. As regards the Indian Navy, the Arihant has reportedly been inducted. The stealth combat drone Ghatak and the Medium Altitude Long Endurance Rustom II are still under development. The Services depend on the DRDO which is not able to deliver due to limited budgets, technology denials and inability to master the skills of professional organisations like Atomic Energy Commission and Indian Space Research Organisation.

Need for indigenous development and the modus operandi

In operations only indigenous equipment is guaranteed as imported equipment could be difficult to replace due to strategic considerations. At the same time, there is a need for state of the art equipment in combat to win a tactical encounter. Our development agencies cannot produce such weapons with a singular approach. Advanced technologies with regard to defence equipment are available with a few foreign countries. In the present globalised environment with lesser controls it is possible to obtain transfer of technology through negotiations. The major issue even when technology is obtained, is its pace of change. Accordingly, there is a need for speedy negotiation and absorption to avoid the product becoming obsolete prior/ close to its induction. Further, investing in modern defence equipment entails heavy initial expenditure with a long gestation period before income starts flowing in. In the Indian environment, Government agencies have the capability of investing large amounts for developing a product and private industry has the ability to speedily absorb and produce an item, therefore a combination of the Original Equipment Manufacturer (OEM), the Government agency and the private sector would possibly be the pragmatic path to be adopted to enable a high degree of indigenisation. As stated often, public industries have the Know How and private industry provide the Know Why.

The concept stated has to be applied in a judicious manner to facilitate the indigenous manufacture of high technology products. The process can only be effective if a level playing field is provided where each agency can contribute effectively leading to optimisation of resources. The overall coordination of this activity will involve the active participation of the Ministry of Defence. The Ministry has set into motion a Defence Procurement Procedure (DPP) 2016, which has matured considerably and streamlined the acquisition process considerably. The procedure has a highly structured defence acquisition organisation, with the Raksha Mantri at the apex, a second tier under the Defence Secretary, with the Services represented by the Chiefs at the Defence Acquisition Council and the Vice Chiefs at the Defence Procurement Board. The Defence Acquisition Wing with the Technical Managers from the three services as well as the Finance Managers from the Defence Finance is the pivot around whom the acquisition process rolls.

The latest DPP-2016 has added the concept of Indigenously Designed, Developed and Manufactured (IDDM) as also Industry enabled Make procedure with enhanced funding and commitment to placement of orders. Further the Government has permitted defence exports and enhanced Foreign Direct Investment. (FDI). It is also creditable that export of defence equipment is easier.

Need for FDI

Technology does not come in till the foreign partner is assured of his returns. More FDI enables the foreign partner to manufacture defence products in India which enables our companies to work conjointly at close quarters and gradually absorb their technologies. Accordingly, the Government of India has taken a bold step by liberalising the FDI in the Defence sector. This would encourage the Make in India Programme and create a level playing field for the domestic private industry and foreign industry. The step enables automatic FDI up to 49% for Defence product and 100 % with permission of the Government. Under this policy, there is no need for approaching Cabinet Committee on Security. The technology too, need not be exactly state of the art. There is a need for foreign capital to ensure higher investments in the Defence Sector. The infusion of this capital will gradually bring in technology, too.

The current enhancement of FDI would also enable DRDO to form collaborative arrangements for research and co development. DRDO could enhance research in critical technologies in a pragmatic manner with these companies who would be based in India.

The private sector would find it a challenge as well as an opportunity. Collaboration works better with proximity and the private sector would exploit issues to our advantage by having greater interaction with these companies located in our country.

The moot question is will the foreign companies be willing to come to India? The answer is definitely positive as the Government has undertaken numerous measures to encourage foreign companies to invest in India. However, it needs to be ensured that foreign companies operating in India and manufacturing Defence equipment continuing to do so irrespective of Indian geo-political stance vis-a-vis their countries and governments. There has to be adequate assurance of these companies continuing with their business activities and deliveries irrespective of differences that the two sovereign governments may have. Carefully crafted policies would be required to ensure that failsafe procedures are instituted to guard against these companies not honouring their commitments while operating in India.

Projects worthy of Emulation

There are two projects which merit emulation. First of all the Pinaka Multi Barrel Rocket Launcher programme. The project was developed by the Armament Research Development Establishment, Pune and the launchers are being manufactured by Tata and Larsen and Toubro. The ammunition is being manufactured by OFB and as on date two regiments have been operationalised. An additional two more regiments are in the final stages of commencing induction.

The other example is the supersonic Cruise Missile BrahMos. It is a joint venture between India and the Russian federation. The Indian contribution is 50.5 percent and the balance is Russian. The missile is presently being manufactured jointly and gradually all components are being indigenised. While BrahMos is an Indo-Russian joint venture, a number of industries are involved in manufacturing components. The airframe is being made by Godrej, the composites are being made by Larsen & Toubro, the Inertial Navigation System is being made by Hindustan Aeronautics Limited and the on-board Computer System by Data Patterns. As on date, the weapon system has been inducted in the Indian Navy and the Indian Army. Recently, the missile has proved its steep dive capability enabling it to be deployed in the mountains. The air launched and submarine launched version is under development and is undergoing development trials.

What Matters Most

The synergy between the user, the developer and the manufacturer with suitable coordination by the Ministry of Defence will pave the way for indigenisation of defence products. Further, in order to make it commercially more viable, exports must be permitted of selective items.

DEFENCE PROCUREMENT MOVING TOWARDS INDIGENISATION

Urgent Need for Reform

In recent years, successive Defence Ministers have been repeatedly exhorting the armed forces to procure their weapons and equipment from indigenous sources. The NDA government has been pushing "Make in India" as a cardinal principle of its economic policy to enhance manufacture in the private sector.

It is a well-established fact that no nation aspiring to great power status can expect to achieve it without being substantively self-reliant in defence production. However, the armed forces are not the stumbling block to indigenisation. Unless the government drastically reorients its defence procurement policies, the import content of defence acquisitions will continue to remain between 70 to 80 per cent.

India's procurement of weapons platforms and other equipment as part of its plans for defence modernisation, must simultaneously lead to a transformative change in the country's defence technology base and manufacturing prowess. Or else, defence procurement will remain mired in disadvantageous buyer-seller, patron-client relationships like that with the erstwhile Soviet Union and now Russia. While India has been manufacturing Russian fighter aircraft and tanks under license for many years, the Russians never actually transferred weapons technology to India.

Although the country has now diversified its acquisition sources beyond Russia to the West and Israel, recent deals have failed to include transfer-of-technology (ToT) clauses. The much delayed MMRCA deal with Rafale also appears to have run into rough weather on this account. If this trend continues, India's defence technology base will continue to remain low and the country will remain dependent almost solely on imports for major defence acquisitions. Whatever India procures now must be procured with a ToT clause being built into the contract even if it means having to pay a higher price. The aim should be to make India a design, development, manufacturing and export hub for defence equipment in two to three decades.

Defence Research and Development

Though it seeks to encourage public-private partnerships, privately the government continues to retain its monopoly on research and development and defence production through the DRDO, the ordnance factories and the defence PSUs (DPSUs).

Since its inception in 1958, the DRDO has achieved some spectacular successes like the missile development programme, but also has many failures to its name. Programmes like the Light Combat Aircraft (LCA) and the Main Battle Tank (MBT) Arjun have suffered inordinate delays and time and cost overruns. However, to its credit, the DRDO worked under extremely restrictive technology denial regimes and with a rather low indigenous technology base. The DRDO is now in the process of implementing the report of the P Rama Rao committee that had asked it to identify eight to 10 critical areas that best fit its existing human resource pool, technological threshold and established capacity to take up new projects. And, it must scrupulously stay out of production. The private sector has shown its readiness and technological proficiency to take up the production of weapons and equipment designed and developed by the DRDO and must be trusted to deliver.

The DRDO must concentrate its efforts on developing critical cutting edge technologies that no strategic partner is likely to be willing to share; for example, ballistic missile defence (BMD) technology. Other future weapons platforms should be jointly developed, produced and marketed with India's strategic partners in conjunction with the private sector. The development of technologies that are not critical should be outsourced completely to the private sector. Also, the armed forces should be given funding support to undertake research geared towards the improvement of in-service equipment with a view to enhancing operational performance and increasing service life. Gradually, the universities and the IITs should be involved in undertaking defence R&D. This five-pronged approach will help to raise India's technological threshold over the next two decades by an order of magnitude.

Defence Procurement Procedure

The Defence Procurement Procedure (DPP) manual was introduced in 2005. Since then it has been revised and modified several times based on the experience gained during its implementation. The Defence Production Policy was unveiled in 2011. Its objectives are to: achieve substantive self-reliance in design, development and production of equipment, weapon system and platforms required for defence in as early a time frame as possible; create conditions conducive for the private industry to play an active role in this endeavour; enhance the potential of small and medium enterprises (SMEs) in indigenisation; and, broaden the defence research and development base of the country. However, the emphasis on self-reliance remains wishful thinking at present as most weapons and equipment continue to be imported.

The Defence Procurement Procedure (DPP) was amended once again in April 2013 to reflect the current thinking on 'buying Indian'. However, in effect it still favours the defence PSUs over the private sector. MNCs are now allowed to bring in up to 49 per cent FDI as against 74 per cent for non-defence sector joint ventures. FDI in defence JVs beyond 49 per cent is permitted only with prior government approval. Though the procurement of weapons and equipment worth more than Rs 300 crore from MNCs has been linked with 30-50 per cent offsets, it is doubtful whether the economy is ready to absorb such high levels of offsets. For example, the MMRCA contract, which is likely to be worth around $10 billion, will result in an offset obligation of $5 billion or so. This is much more than the Indian defence industry can possibly absorb over 10-12 years.

On May 1, 2015, the Defence Minister, Mr Manohar Parrikar, appointed a 10-member committee headed by former Home Secretary Dhirendra Singh, to review the defence procurement policies and procedures and to recommend fresh guidelines with a view to implementing Prime Minister Narendra Modi's appeal to 'Make in India'. The review was utilised to learn from the experience gained in the implementation of the current version of the DPP and many pragmatic recommendations were made by the committee. The Defence Minister has begun to implement its recommendations in earnest. For example, the policy on offsets has been reviewed and several pragmatic amendments have been made. Approval of necessity (AON) has been accorded to defence acquisition projects worth approximately Rs 100,000 crore, mostly for make in India projects. However, many important issues remain to be resolved. Among others, the DPP document is still too long and must be cut down to not more than 12 to 15 pages.

The offsets policy has not worked to India's advantage. The defence industry's ability to absorb hi-tech offsets is still limited. Absorbing 50 or even 30 per cent offsets is extremely difficult at present. It may be more prudent to consider offsets only in cases where the benefits expected to accrue will outweigh the additional costs and Indian JV partners can absorb the technology that is brought in. In November 2015, the government restored 'services' as eligible offsets for defence contracts, opening up a business potential of over $3 billion in immediate projects. The government also added the development of software and engineering design to the list of eligible offsets, but limited it to 20 per cent of the project cost. This will bring some relief to the maintenance, repair and overhaul (MRO) and software industries, as also companies involved in the upgradation of military systems and life extension projects of defence equipment.

Indigenous Defence Production

The defence production process must provide a level playing field between defence PSUs and Indian private sector companies forming joint ventures with MNCs where necessary. The amount of FDI that MNCs can bring in must be raised to 49 per cent immediately and to 74 per cent in due course to make it attractive for MNCs. However, no MNC that is unable to provide transfer of technology – either due to the home country's restrictive laws or due to proprietary considerations – should be considered for future defence acquisitions.

India cannot leapfrog to a higher defence technology trajectory virtually overnight. Transforming a low technology base to a higher plane will need time, patience and large-scale capital investment. It will also need strong support across the political spectrum. In the interim period, inevitably, there will be a further dip in defence preparedness. This short-term weakness in capacity building will need to be carefully weighed against long-term gains that will be strategic in nature. The risk involved will require fine political judgment backed by sound military advice.

India is a growing economic powerhouse and should no longer be satisfied with a buyer-seller, patron-client relationship in its future defence procurement planning. As the largest importer of arms and equipment in the world, India has the advantage of buyers' clout. This clout must be exploited fully to further India's quest for self-sufficiency in the indigenous production of weapons and equipment.

In all major acquisitions in future, India should insist on joint development, joint testing and trials, joint production, joint marketing and joint product improvement over the life cycle of the equipment. The US and other countries with advanced technologies will surely ask what India can bring to the table to demand participation as a co-equal partner.

Besides capital and a production capacity that is becoming increasingly more sophisticated, India has its huge software pool to offer. Today software already comprises over 50 per cent of the total cost of a modern defence system. In the years ahead, this is expected to go up to almost 70 per cent as software costs increase and hardware production costs decline due to improvements in manufacturing processes. If a new weapons development project needs 500 software engineers, where else but in India can such a high quality work force be found?

The immediate requirement is to think big in keeping with the country's growing economic clout and to plan for the future with a level of confidence that policy planners have not dared to exhibit before. In 10 to 15 years India must begin to acquire most of its defence equipment needs from Indian companies—with or without a joint venture with an MNC. Only then will the era of self-reliance in defence acquisition truly dawn on the country. It will be a difficult quest, but not one that a great nation cannot realise.

Speed and Transparency in Decision Making

The defence procurement decision making process must be speeded up. The army is still without towed and self-propelled 155 mm howitzers for the plains and the mountains and urgently needs to acquire weapons and equipment for counter-insurgency and counter-terrorism operations. The plans of the air force to acquire 126 multi-mission, medium-range combat aircraft in order to maintain its edge over the regional air forces are also stuck in the procurement quagmire. All three Services need a large number of light helicopters. India's nuclear forces require the Agni-III and V missiles and nuclear powered submarines with suitable ballistic missiles to acquire genuine deterrent capability. The armed forces do not have a truly integrated C4I2SR system suitable for modern network-centric warfare, which will allow them to optimise their individual/combined capabilities.

All of these high-priority acquisitions will require extensive budgetary support. With the defence budget languishing at less than two per cent of India's GDP – compared with China's 3.5 per cent and Pakistan's 4.5 per cent plus US military aid – it will not be possible for the armed forces to undertake any meaningful modernisation in the foreseeable future. Leave aside genuine military modernisation that will substantially enhance combat capabilities, the funds available on the capital account at present are inadequate to suffice even for the replacement of obsolete weapons systems and equipment that are still in service well beyond their useful life cycles. The central armed police and para-military forces (CAPFs) also need to be modernised as they are facing increasingly more potent threats while being equipped with obsolescent weapons.

While the need for confidentiality in defence matters is understandable, defence acquisition decision making must be made far more transparent than it is at present, so that the temptation for supplier companies to bank on corrupt practices can be minimised. For example, tenders should be opened in front of the representatives of the companies that have bid for the contract. Before a contract is awarded, the file should be reviewed by the Chief Vigilance Commissioner (CVC). If the CVC continues to have reservations about such scrutiny, either his charter should be amended or an eminent persons group should be appointed to vet large purchases. Surely, many such persons with unimpeachable integrity can be found in India.

In the past, the selective tweaking of the technical requirements during the procurement process has led to one company being favoured over another. All technical requirements must be frozen when a Request for Proposals (RfP) is issued by the MoD. GSQRs must also be frozen when the procurement process begins. Frequent tinkering with GSQRs by the Services is detrimental to the smooth flow of the acquisition process and the indigenous development of weapons systems. It may sound heretical, but the reports of user trials must be made public. This step will not only amount to a huge leap forward in transparency, but also insulate the trials teams of the three Services from being unduly influenced to stage-manage trials in favour of any of the contending parties.

The Way Forward: Systematic Acquisition Planning

During the long history of post-independence conflicts with India's neighbours and prolonged deployment for internal security, the Indian army and its sister Services have held the nation together. Dark clouds can once again be seen on the horizon, but the efforts being made to weather the gathering storm are inadequate. The government must immediately initiate steps to build the capacities that are necessary for defeating future threats and challenges. It must take the opposition parties into confidence as a bipartisan approach must be followed in dealing with major national security issues. In fact, there is a requirement to establish a permanent National Security Commission mandated by an act of Parliament to oversee the development of military and non-military capacities for national security.

A fluid strategic environment, rapid advances in defence technology, the need for judicious allocation of scarce budgetary resources, long lead times required for creating futuristic forces and the requirement of synergising plans for defence and development, make long-term defence planning a demanding exercise. The lack of cohesive national security strategy and a flawed planning process have resulted in inadequate political direction regarding politico-military objectives and military strategy. Consequently, defence planning in India had till recently been marked by ad hoc decision making to tide over immediate national security challenges and long-term planning was neglected. This needs to be corrected and pragmatic measures need to be instituted to improve long-term planning.

It is now being increasingly realised that a tri-Service Defence Plan must be prepared on the basis of a 15-year long-term integrated perspective plan (LTIPP). The first five years of the plan should be very firm (Definitive Plan), the second five years may be relatively less firm but should be clear in direction (Indicative Plan), and the last five years should be tentative (Vision Plan). A reasonably firm allocation of financial resources for the first five years and an indicative allocation for the subsequent five-year periods is a pre-requisite.

India is expected to spend over $150 billion over the 12th and 13th defence five-year plans on military modernisation. As 70 to 80 per cent of weapons and equipment are still imported, there is an urgent need to further refine the defence acquisition process and insulate it from the scourge of corruption that has afflicted all other national endeavours, including major development projects, while simultaneously encouraging self-reliance and indigenisation.

PROBLEMS IN INDIA'S DEFENCE INDIGENISATION

The recycled fashion that is sweeping India is defence indigenisation, a delectable sound byte that allows all who utter it to feel pious without dwelling on what it requires. India's politicians suffer from addiction to this mantra, and journalists don't get the column inches they need to cover it (surely Bollywood gossip is so much more important?). Though the country basks in the glory of Kargil and thumps its chest over an occasional successful missile test, defence development and production remains a joke in India.

The list of failures and shocking delays in the country's defence sector is long. The cloak of secrecy under which research & development in defence operates causes even greater concern about inefficiencies, waste, questionable priorities, and failed or delayed projects the public is not yet aware of. Worse, many heads nod sagely at the mention of foreign direct investment in Indian defence public sector undertakings (DPSU) as if the solution to India's convoluted woes could be so easily imported. The question of what constitutes indigenisation is itself a tricky one. Would producing defence equipment under license be considered indigenisation? Would allowing foreign defence manufacturers to set up shop in India and procure locally be a sufficient condition?

Many have offered technology transfers and manufacture under license as a solution that would help India leapfrog technological generations. This is an unrealistic assessment, for multiple reasons. First, intellectual property rights may remain with original equipment manufacturer. The impact of this was most visible when US sanctions post-Pokhran II hit the Tejas LCA project. Second, domestic industry may not be able to absorb the technology and may have to import components, reducing the Indian role to mere assembly. Third, countries will not be willing to part with their latest technologies or cooperate too closely with Delhi – despite being an attractive market, India remains non-aligned and hence a question mark in geopolitical calculations.

Offsets are also seen as a mechanism to develop indigenous manufacturing capability. They create jobs, enhance scientific and engineering skills, promote small local manufacturers, and could even lead to exports. They are also, as Transparency International warns, opaque and highly susceptible to corruption. More fundamentally, offsets must come in a value-multiplying form – sourcing aluminium and labour from India may serve the technical definition of offsets but does little to enhance indigenisation. As has been seen after every foreign acquisition such as the MiG-21, T-72, T-90, and others, DPSUs have failed to master the acquired technologies and improve upon them, necessitating further ToTs with each purchase. Operationalisation of manufacturing processes has also remained sluggish in India.

FDI is another oft-mentioned and equally illusionary silver bullet. It is unlikely that foreign investors would agree to transfer critical technologies in joint ventures that cap their investment (and control) at 26 per cent, especially when there is no promise of purchase by the Indian military or even access to export markets and they must operate in an environment strongly biased in favour of DPSUs. The cap is usually defended as a national security measure, but it is unclear what prevents foreign concerns, assuming they would even be interested, from simply obstructing projects to put pressure on Delhi when needed. No wonder then, that FDI in India's defence sector so far is less than minuscule.

Modernisation is not the same as procurement or indigenisation, and neither technology transfers not FDI will help with the latter. Five vectors pull the indigenisation project in different directions: 1. the military, which is (understandably) only concerned with fighting effectiveness; 2. the DPSUs, who are too busy protecting their own bureaucratic privileges and sinecures; 3. the private sector, who seems to have little faith in Delhi's long-term vision and therefore is more interested in short-term profits; 4. the political leadership, which remains clueless as ever; and 5. the citizens, who are too jaded to even ask the right questions.

The hard reality is that indigenisation, in the spirit that dependence on foreign sources is nil, is a complex network of operations and dependencies which will take a generation – about 30 years – to achieve fully. Two components of such a project must be human infrastructure and privatisation.

Presently, DPSUs do not feature on the list of dream jobs for most graduates from Caltech, MIT, or Stanford. The bureaucratic environment and the low prioritisation of R&D as evidenced by the paltry budget allocation has resulted in poor facilities and opportunities for employees. In addition, Indian universities have failed spectacularly to produce a rich pool of talent domestically. The shortage of qualified scientists and engineers, something Homi Bhabha had warned about when he put together the nuclear establishment in the late 1940s, has come to haunt Indian R&D and industry. Privatisation is the other leg of indigenisation. Private firms must be allowed easy entry into the defence sector, allowed to research and develop any product they wish, and solicit their wares not just to the Indian military but to buyers abroad as well. Exports may be regulated through a liberal but effective export controls list and end-user agreements. The export market would encourage private firms to enter defence production as they will not be dependent on the whims of the Indian military and Indian defence bureaucracy. Exports will also allow companies to profit from economies of scale. The government must also push the development of skills in design and manufacture across a wide spectrum of products – chips, hydraulics, supercomputers, weapons-grade steels, composites, engines – at home.

The rapid pace of obsolescence has made it difficult for even private firms to keep up with the latest technological advancements. Universities and the corporate sector must be encouraged to work together to complement each other. Universities must be allowed more autonomy and funded better to establish top-notch research laboratories. Military officials, particularly those in engineering and with combat experience, must be given opportunities for short "refresher" stints in corpo-academic research so that the needs of the forces are clearly understood.

The trick will be to ensure military preparedness while indigenous capability develops. On the one hand, as indigenous capability develops, the products initially will probably not be as good as others available on the international market. On the other hand, a fledgling industry needs the support of steady and large-quantity buyers until it overcomes its learning curve. However, the price of this indulgence could be paid in lives of servicemen and women.

The most difficult part of this balance would be ensuring a successful interlocking set of relationships between the military, private sector, universities, and the political leadership at least over the fledgling period. It is a difficult ask, and that is why no one is talking about indigenisation seriously.

INDIGENOUS PRODUCTION: SELF-RELIANCE, THE BEST DEFENCE

Defence manufacturing has been identified as a priority sector in Prime Minister Narendra Modi's flagship 'Make in India' scheme. While the nomenclature has come into vogue last year, indigenous defence manufacturing has been a rather unsuccessful quest for decades.

Notwithstanding some initial steps by the NDA government — such as increasing the FDI limit to 49 per cent — a lack of clarity on policies from the defence ministry has constrained the progress on 'Make in India'. Defence minister Manohar Parrikar had promised the revised Defence Procurement Procedure (DPP) by April but it is now expected to be released in December. A new DPP will be the starting point for any meaningful action on 'Make in India' in defence. In the last five years, India has been the world's top arms importer with a 15 per cent global share of imports. Nearly 50 per cent of the capital acquisition budget is spent on imports. This excludes many "indigenous" items assembled by Ordnance Factories (OFs) and Defence Public Sector Units (DPSUs) where a high percentage of raw materials and sub-systems are imported.

In 1995, a committee under APJ Abdul Kalam, the then scientific advisor to the defence minister, had recommended that India should improve its indigenisation content from 30 per cent to 70 per cent by 2005. Although no official data exists, the self-reliance in defence production is still estimated to be less than 35 per cent.

About 90 per cent of domestic defence manufacturing is currently done in the public sector, by the 9 DPSUs and 39 OFs. Since 2001, when private participation was allowed in defence sector, 222 letters of intents and industrial licences have been issued to around 150 firms. Of these, only 46 firms have commenced production so far.

Globally, 80 per cent of components, aggregates and assemblies of complex weapon systems and aircraft are made by MSMEs. In India, more than 6,000 MSMEs are currently supplying components and sub-assemblies to the DPSUs, OFs, DRDO and private firms. The defence manufacturing sector currently employs more than 2 lakh people in India. This size of military industrial workforce is similar to nations like the UK and France, which are the top defence manufacturers.

India allocated 1.74 per cent of its GDP towards defence spending in FY16 and is among the top 10 countries in the world in terms of military expenditure. Approximately 40 per cent of the defence budget is allocated for capital acquisitions, which mainly goes towards imports from foreign suppliers. Between 2007-08 and 2014-15, defence budget more-than-doubled from Rs 92,000 crore to Rs 2,22,370 crore, growing at an average rate of 12 per cent per annum. The capital budget also more-than-doubled from Rs 37,461 crore in 2007-08 to Rs 81,965 crore in 2014-15.

Despite the sustained expenditure over the last decade, the equipment profile of the armed forces is in an alarming state. While the desirable equipment profile, as per the defence secretary's testimony to Parliamentary Standing Committee, early this year is 30:40:30 (30 per cent state-of-the-art, 40 per cent current and 30 per cent nearing obsolescence), experts estimate the current profile to be 15:45:40. The Defence Acquisition Council (DAC), chaired by the defence minister, has approved procurement of equipment for more than Rs 1,17,830 crore during the UPA-II regime. Another Rs 1,50,000 crore worth of approvals have been given by DAC under the NDA government.

A modelling of 35 selected projects cleared by DAC, along with their likely dates of induction — from 2012 to 2023 — has been done by a foreign manufacturer. It shows that defence ministry will need $40 billion for just these 35 purchases. This translates into a 7 per cent rise in capital budget in real terms. While the capital acquisition budget has risen in absolute terms in the last few years, it has hardly seen any increase in real terms.

The government policy now aims to achieve 70 per cent indigenisation in defence products by 2027. This translates into an Indian defence market of Rs 87,000 crore by 2022 and Rs 1,65,000 crore by 2027. It presents a huge opportunity to the DPSUs, foreign manufacturers, Indian private players and MSMEs. But the question is of resources. Defence production needs heavy investment over a long period, so as to bring in modern technologies with low economies of scale. Unlike other sectors, defence industry is a monopsony in which the single buyer, the government, is also the authority laying down procurement policies. This makes active government support essential for private defence manufacturers, a fact borne out by the experience of countries — the US, Israel, Brazil and France — where private defence industry has flourished.

Under 'Make in India', the government has to actively support the creation of a private defence industrial base. The government will have to fund research and development, provide a low-interest regime to reduce capital costs, provision specific tax benefits, assure consistent sectoral policies, place firm orders and encourage exports to achieve economies of scale.

For policies to create synergies rather than controls, it is essential that the government creates internal capacity for defence acquisition and manufacturing. While the Pentagon has 12,000 cost engineers on its rolls, the defence ministry has none. The structure and the organisation of the ministry, particularly the department of defence production, which is responsible for DPSUs and OFs, puts private sector at a disadvantage. If form has to follow function, the ministry will have to be restructured to promote private players.

Most of these suggestions form part of the deliberations of experts committee chaired by Dhirendra Singh, which submitted its report on amendments to DPP-2013 to the defence minister in August. Of the 43 recommendations made, 15 directly pertain to 'Make in India' while the rest concern the DPP. These recommendations on the DPP also have a direct impact on indigenous defence production. The future trajectory of Make in India in defence will be determined, to a great extent, by the action taken by the Centre on the Dhirendra Singh committee.

INDIA'S UNENDING DEFENCE EXPENDITURE

Despite criticism from various circles that India is not investing more to tackle development issues as millions remain mired in poverty; the Indian government's ambitious modernisation plan for its military is in full swing. In February this year, Indian military procurement units descended on the DefExpo 2010 trade fair in New Delhi. Inaugurating the Indian Defence Exhibition, Defence Minister A.K. Antony said that India's defence expenditure, which is 2.5 percent of its gross domestic product (GDP), is going to increase. He pointed out, "our defence industry is open up to 100 percent for Indian private sector, while foreign direct investment is allowed up to 26 percent." Antony further indicated that our government is committed to rapid modernisation of armed forces. Over the next 12 years, India is set to spend a whopping US$200 billion on defence acquisitions to replace its outdated inventory. In this regard, on February 15, 2010, a report of the Indian strategic defence magazine (India Strategic's DefExpo) revealed that 70 per cent of the inventory of the Indian armed forces is 20-plus years old, and needs to be replaced with the modern technology.

It explained that nearly half of this funding ($100b) will go to the Indian Air Force (IAF), which would need to replace more than half of its combat jet fleet as well as the entire transport aircraft and helicopter fleet. The army needs new guns, tanks, rocket launchers, multi-terrain vehicles, while the navy needs ships, aircraft carriers and new range of nuclear submarines.

In three from 1994 to 1997 India's defence budget was increased from 20 percent to 24.4 percent. For the financial year 2001-2002 defence has been allocated Rs 620,000.00 million. This amount shows an increase of Rs 75,000 million as compared to previous year's revised estimates of Rs 544,610 million. In 2009, India increased its defence budget by a whopping 28.2 percent or Rs 130,000.00 million. Some experts estimate that military spending will increase further, totalling as much as 200 billion dollars over the period to 2022.

India's military has planned a massive upgrade of its mainly 1990s-era weapons systems which is mostly from the former Russia. The plans include the purchase of 126 new combat aircraft to replace an ageing fleet of MiG-21s..The US has emerged as a potential military supplier to India since the two countries signed a deal of civil energy technology in 2008, which lifted sanctions on New Delhi in order to import nuclear technology. India is likely to become a major customer for the US military-industrial complex over the next few years. During the recent visit of the US Secretary of State Robert Gates to New Delhi, American Defence officials, however, have said that US weapons sales to India would not be a focus of the trip. Regardless of such denials, the key reason for the Gates' visit can be found in the fact that India is planning to raise its military budget by 50% to almost $40 billion, making military expenditure 3% of the annual GDP. In contrast to India's planned defence expenditures, Pakistan's entire 2009-10 budget amounts to little over $30 billion.

India, the largest arms buyer among emerging nations, accounted for 7.5 per cent of all international arms sales between 2000 and 2007. It has spent billions of dollars in the past few years on purchases of planes, radars and ships from Britain, France, Germany and Russia and Israel.

In recent years, India has bought reconnaissance aircraft from US aerospace major Boeing worth 2.1 billion-dollars, medium range missiles for 1.4 billion dollars from Israeli Aerospace Industries, and signed an upgrade service contract with the Russian Aircraft Corporation to upgrade its MiG 29 squadrons for 965 million dollars. Several deals are planned for the near future including one of the largest arms contracts of recent times—a 11-billion-dollar project to acquire 126 multi-role combat aircraft.

It is mentionable that after 9/11, both India and Israel which had openly jumped on Bush's anti-terrorism enterprise are acting upon a secret diplomacy, targeting Pakistan China, Iran and Syria. In this context, Indo-Israeli secret diplomacy could be assessed from the interview of Israel's ambassador to

India, Mark Sofer published in the Indian weekly Outlook on February 18, 2008. Regarding India's defence arrangements with Tel Aviv, Sofer had surprisingly disclosed "We do have a defence relationship with India, which is no secret" and "with all due respect, the secret part will remain a secret." As regards joint exercises, Sofer replied, "Certain issues need to remain under wraps for whatever reason."

Notably, India's 'The Tribune' wrote on September 10, 2003, "India and Israel took giant leaps forward in bolstering the existing strategic ties", and Tel Aviv has "agreed to share its expertise with India in various fields such as anti-fidayeen operations, surveillance satellites, intelligence sharing and space exploration." With the support of Israel, New Delhi has been acquiring an element of strategic depth by setting up logistical bases in the Indian Ocean for its navy. In fact, India wants to become a mini-superpower of the region and hence it uses the pretext of deterrence against Pakistan and China. In this context, New Delhi with the support of US and Israel has presumed peace-loving Pakistan and China as their arch enemies, but it does not admit officially.

In May, 1998, when India detonated five nuclear tests, Islamabad was compelled to follow the suit through its own atomic experiments. But Pakistan which so far relied upon the minimum nuclear deterrence has again been forced by India's unending spending on arms purchases to counterbalance the former. In this regard, Pakistan has signed a number of agreements with China. Nevertheless, currently, more than half of India's budget is allocated for military, paramilitary, various security forces and debt servicing. That leaves less than half for everything else including infrastructure development projects, education, healthcare, poverty alleviation, and various human services. New Delhi' s latest arms buildup will leave even less for what India needs most to lift hundreds of millions of its citizens from abject poverty, hunger illiteracy and disease.

Indian civil society organisations, while complaining of excessive defence spending indicated that the government spends 2.35 per cent of GDP on defence, but only 1.72 per cent on the social sector. The defence budget for 2009-2010 is 29 billion dollars, up 34 percent over the previous one. Indian defence analyst Ravinder Pal Singh, while calling New Delhi's unending defence spending at the cost of poverty-alleviation—with security requirements competing with socioeconomic concerns for money calls it guns-versus-butter question.

Even some of Indian officials are surprised in relation to Indian defence expenditure which has no bounds. For example, an official of the country's finance ministry remarked, "There is a dilemma...poverty needs to be eradicated to prevent men from taking to the guns...but more funds for security means less money for poverty alleviation." Meanwhile, a report of United Nations pointed out that India ranks 134th of 182 countries on the United Nations Development Programme's Human Development Index. It estimated that 50 per cent of the world's undernourished population lives in India. Nearly 31 per cent of the billion-plus Indians earn less than a dollar a day.

Secretary General of the Control Arms Foundation of India Binalakshmi Nepram said, "When people are dying of poverty and bad sanitation, what protection will arms provide them?" On the one hand, international community has been making strenuous efforts for world peace in wake of global financial crisis and war against terrorism, on the other, India has initiated deadly nuclear arms in South Asia where people are already facing multiple problems of grave nature. Majority of South Asian people are living below the poverty level, lacking basic facilities like fresh food and clean water. While yielding to acute poverty, every day, some persons commit suicide in India, Pakistan, Sri Lanka etc.

Setting aside regional problems, and resolution of Indo-Pak issues-especially thorny dispute of Kashmir, Indian rulers state that they don't have any aggressive designs. But it becomes a big joke of the 21st century, reminding a maxim, "armed to the teeth, but no enemy", if we take cognisance of India's unending defence expenditure. Sajjad Shaukat writes on international affairs and is author of the book: US vs Islamic Militants, Invisible Balance of Power: Dangerous Shift in International Relations.

DEFENCE EXPENDITURE AND FINANCE COMMISSION OF INDIA

The Finance Commission of India, a statutory body under the Constitution, plays an important role in providing fscal recommendations to the Government. The body is tasked, among others, to review the state of fnances of the government, assess the requirements of the various sectors of the State and provide guidelines for distributing the State's resources among the Centre and States. The recommendations of the Commission provide the basic foundation for restoring 'budgetary balance, bringing macro-economic stability and equitable growth.'

The 11th Finance Commission, after reviewing the broad requirements of the economy, acknowledged the need for steady growth in Defence Capital expenditure, and accepted the need for overall Defence budget to grow by 15 per cent per year during the Commission's forecast period (2000-01 to 2004-05). Based on the projected 'fiscal profile' of the Central Government, the Commission assumed the Defence budget to reach the level of 3 per cent of the GDP by 2004-05, to meet the increased requirements of the Capital expenditure. However, at the end of the Commission's forecast period, Defence spending increased by only 10 per cent per year, while its share in GDP was much lower than the Commission's estimate of 3 per cent. As regards the growth of Revenue expenditure, the Commission also accepted a 10 per cent growth rate per year for the period from 2000-01 to 2004-05. Against this projected growth rate, the actual growth rate of Revenue expenditure during this period was 4.6 per cent. The corresponding growth figure for the Capital expenditure during this period was 21.4 per cent.

Unlike the 11th Finance Commission, its successor, the 12th Finance Commission, allowed for a relatively moderate growth rate of 6.5 per cent per year for the Revenue expenditure for the five-year period from 2005-06 to 2009-10. In three years

– from 2005-06 to 2007-08 – the annual growth rate on this account stood at 6.6 per cent, which was close to the forecast range provided by the Commission. However, unlike its predecessor, the Commission did not link the Capital expenditure directly with GDP, which grew by 14.5 per cent per year, in nominal prices, between 2005-06 and 2007-08. Compared to this, the Defence Capital expenditure during this period was increased by annual average of less than 8 per cent.

If the recommendations of the past two Finance Commissions of India are taken into consideration, Defence spending has largely remained within the Commissions' projected range and within the country's macro-economic framework. The lesser percentage growth of Defence spending, when compared to its projected figures, suggests that the Defence expenditure has remained within the government's desired objectives of budgetary balance, economic stability and equitable growth.

Defence Projection and Allocation

India's defence spending in current prices has increased substantially over the years, from nearly Rs. 1200 crore in 1970-71 to Rs. 1,05,600 crore in 2008-09 (this represents a five-and-a-half fold increase in constant prices, from nearly Rs. 13,418 crore to Rs 73,360 crore). In the last one decade, it has increased by an average of nearly 10 per cent per year from Rs. 47,070.63 crore in 1999-2000. A fgure depicting India's Defence spending since 1980-81. Notwithstanding the growth in Defence spending, the Defence outlays do not necessarily match the demands of the Defence establishment. For instance, in the last five years, the unmet demand by the Services/ Departments varies between some Rs. 5,880 crore and Rs. 26,150.7 crore, which is nearly 6-27 per cent of the total projected demands. The shortfall on the Revenue side ranges between 4 per cent and 13 per cent, and that on the Capital side varies from as low as 6.9 per cent to over 49 per cent.

The lesser percentage of 'shortfalls' in Revenue expenditure compared to that of Capital expenditure shows that while the former is more or less fixed, the latter is relatively flexible. At the same time, the 'shortfalls' both in absolute and percentage terms indicate that all the demands made by the Defence sector are not fully in conformity with the resources available with the government. However, over the past five years, the percentage 'shortfalls' are coming down, indicating that the government has found the wherewithal to afford and meet the increasing requirements projected by the Defence establishment over the past five years.

Defence Expenditure and Gross Domestic Product

The percentage share of Defence in GDP is considered as a common measure of a country's Defence expenditure and gives a fair idea about its affordability. On the basis of this, comparison is often made to see where a country stands vis-à-vis other countries, and also to arrive at a 'norm' by looking at a particular country's own past trends. Going by this indicator, India's current Defence affordability at around 2 per cent of GDP is less than its neighbours, especially Pakistan's nearly 3.5 per cent and China's over four per cent. Regarding the affordability 'norm' from the past trends, India's Defence spending as a proportion of GDP is fluctuating and more specifically, on a declining path in the recent past. Compared to the seventies and eighties, when the percentage share of Defence in GDP averaged 2.74 per cent and 2.95 per cent respectively, in the last one decade (1999-2000 to 2008-09), the average has come down to 2.18 per cent. Moreover, if the present growth rates of GDP and Defence spending continue, in the next one decade the share of the latter in the former will remain within 2 per cent of GDP. A matrix of projected GDP-Defence spending, at different growth rates.

The declining share of Defence in GDP can be ascribed, among others, to the strong performance of Indian economy in the recent years. For instance, the Indian economy in the last 5 years (2003-04 to 2007-08) grew by an average of more than 14 per cent per year, in current prices, compared to less than 9 per cent per year during the previous five years. The strong performance of the GDP over the years means an enhancement of the country's economic ability to afford more on various sectors including Defence. However, Defence, which earlier received a larger share of the national resources, is now receiving a declining share, and is consequently more affordable, in the relative terms.

Central Government Expenditure

Unlike GDP, which gives the value of national resources generated in an economy in a given year, government expenditure gives the total resources available to the Government for allocation among different sectors. The pattern of allocations from the government expenditures suggests the priority attached on each allocation for each sector. Though this priority is best explained when Defence spending is expressed in terms of its share in Central Government expenditure, yet the analysis can further be extended to that of 'General Government' expenditure (central and state together) to see the priority at the national level.

During the past one decade (1997-98 to 2006-07), total 'General Government' spending and total Central Government spending have increased significantly, by nearly 188 per cent and 168 per cent, respectively. On the other hand, the Defence spending has grown relatively lower at 142 per cent, suggesting that allocation for other sectors have increased at a faster pace. Over the last 5 years Defence spending as a percentage of total Central Government expenditure has been reduced from the peak of 15.9 per cent during 2005-06 to the low of 13.0 per cent during 2007-08 (RE).

The faster growth of both central government and total 'General Government' expenditure compared to Defence expenditure suggests that despite increased level of Defence spending, the government has been able to spend more on the non-Defence sectors. In relative terms and from the point of view of resource allocation, the decreasing share of Defence shows that the allocation for it is easily provided (affordable) over the years.

FISCAL RESPONSIBILITY AND DEFENCE EXPENDITURE

The 'persistent fscal problems' of the country led the Government to pass the Fiscal Responsibility and Budget Management (FRBM) Act, 2003. The Act required eliminating the revenue deficit and bringing it below 3 per cent of GDP by 2008-09. A Task Force, which was constituted to ensure this fscal responsibility of the government, recommended a number of policy proposals pertaining to reforms in tax, and government expenditure.

The 'fscal projections under the reforms scenario', as estimated by the expert group, was expected to accelerate the GDP growth to 13.0 per cent per year, in nominal prices, by 2008-09. The higher growth of the economy along with the proposals under 'reforms scenario' was also expected to take Defence expenditure to a higher level and 'stabilise' it at 2.3 per cent of the GDP from 2006-07 to 2008-09.

However, during this period, the growth of the economy though marginally outpaced the estimates of the Task Force, yet the percentage share of Defence in GDP fell short of 2.3 per cent of the GDP. If Defence were allowed to receive 2.3 per cent of the GDP, as projected by the Task Force, then between 2006-07 and 2008-09, it would have received nearly Rs. 95,000 crore, Rs. 1,08,000 crore, and Rs. 1,21,000 respectively. The Defence budgets for these three years are Rs. 89,000 crore, Rs. 96,000 crore, and Rs. 1,05,600 crores, respectively.

The higher growth of GDP and the reduced share of Defence in it means some of the funds meant for Defence are, in fact, transferred to other sectors (especially towards interest payments and subsidies) so as to keep the FRBM targets under control.

From the Defence point of view, the increased allocations that were expected to accrue to it due to the proposed reforms, have not fully materialised while its own spending remaining well within the estimated range of the country's fscal responsibilities, as outlined by the Task Force.

Government Expenditure and Defence Expenditure

The major heads of government expenditure can broadly be classified into Developmental expenditure and non-Developmental expenditure. During the 10-year period since 1997-98, the annual average growth of Developmental expenditure of both the 'General Government' and Central Government has been more than on the non-Developmental heads. Among the 10 largest heads of the general Government expenditure, Defence has recorded the lowest annual growth rate after Administrative Services. For the same major heads of the Central Government expenditure, Defence, though, has exceeded the overall growth of non-Developmental expenditure, yet compared to the major heads under Developmental expenditure, it has recorded the lowest growth rate after that of Power, and Irrigation & Flood Control.

The relatively faster growth of major heads of Developmental expenditure compared to that of Defence expenditure during the past decade shows that the growth of the latter has not hindered the government's priority in terms of higher percentage allocation on major developmental goals. In other words, Defence, from the resource allocation point of view, has remained within the affordable limit, in the sense that it has not hampered the growth prospects of the economy.

Economic Parameters Examined

All the economic parameters examined in the article show that the allocations for Defence over the years have remained affordable, though, in some cases, in a relative sense. From the point of view of Defence requirements, the decreasing percentage shortfalls (between Defence projections and allocations to Defence) over the past five years indicate that the Government could increasingly afford the requirements projected by the Defence establishment. As far as the objectives of budgetary balance and fscal stability are concerned, the Defence expenditure has largely remained within acceptable limits set by various Finance Commissions and the Task Force on FRBM and therefore, could not be blamed for the budgetary or fscal imbalances, if any, in the economy. While the robust growth of the GDP and the consequent rise of Government revenues have significantly enhanced the country's spending ability, the decreasing share of Defence in these resources indicates that the burden of Defence has reduced significantly. In terms of resource allocation and its priorities, the growth of Defence spending has not caused retardation in growth of spending in other sectors of the economy, especially in the developmental sectors.

Financing Defence Expenditure and Government Expenditure

Financing of government expenditure, including Defence expenditure, constitutes an important aspect of public finance, considering the role of various sources of government earnings and their impact on the economy. Over the last 10 years (1997-98 to 2006-07), the government's total revenue earning has increased by nearly 216 per cent and, as a result, its share in the total government expenditure has increased from 68 per cent to nearly 75 per cent.

The increase in revenue earning, which is mainly on account of increases in both tax and non-tax revenue, has helped the government in reducing the fscal deficit and lessen the debt burden on the economy. While the tax and non-tax revenue have increased by 228 per cent and 172 per cent, the debt burden and fscal deficits, measured by their percentage share in GDP, have decreased from 24 per cent to 16 per cent and from 4.81 per cent to 3.61 per cent, respectively. From the Defence point of view, the increase in the revenue earnings has lessened its percentage dependence on the latter, from 13.81 per cent to nearly 11 per cent. Besides, the surge in revenue earnings, which has reduced government's dependence on the debt financing, has also reduced the share of the Defence debt on India's "external outstanding debt". In other words, in last 10 years, the financing of the Defence spending has become relatively easier on account of the government's increasing earnings.

Measuring Military Expenditure

The SIPRI military expenditure project was initiated in 1967 to study developments in worldmilitary expenditure. The current SIPRI database on military expenditure covers 172 countries and contains consistent data for the period since 1988. Data for the most recent 10-year period are published annually in the SIPRI Yearbook. Data from 1988 is available in the SIPRI military expenditure database on-line. SIPRI provides the only long-term, historically consistent series of military expenditure data with global coverage available today.

Defining Military Expenditure

There is no generally agreed definition of military expenditure worldwide. SIPRI seeks to include in its definition of military expenditure all costs incurred as a result of current military activities. The guideline definition used by SIPRI includes expenditure on the following actors and activities: (a) the armed forces, including peacekeeping forces; (b) defence ministries and other government agencies engaged in defence projects; (c) paramilitary forces, when judged to be trained and equipped for military operations; and (d) military space activities. It includes all current and capital expenditure on: (a) military and civil personnel, including retirement pensions of military personnel and social services for personnel; (b) operations and maintenance; (c) procurement; (d) military research and development; and (e) military aid (in the military expenditure of the donor country). It does not include civil defence and current expenditure for pastmilitary activities, such as for veterans' benefits, demobilization, conversion and weapon destruction.

Other organizations and countries employ varying definitions of military expenditure. Media reports on military expenditure, including in specialist publications, tend to report simply the defence budget of the country in question, although many countries have significant military expenditure in other budget lines. (Sometimes, a defence budget may also include items not included in the SIPRI definition, such as demobilization costs). The International Monetary Fund's *Government Financial Statistics Yearbook (GFSY)* collects expenditure data according to a functional classification; functional classifications typically place military pensions within the social security function, military healthcare within the health function, etc. Many countries likewise report military expenditure according to a functional definition. The NATO definition of military expenditure is similar to the SIPRI definition; however since 2004 NATO has changed its definition so as to exclude expenditure on paramilitary forces (even those with a national defence function in times of war) if they are not "realistically deployable". Meanwhile a number of governments, of which the UK was the first, have moved to a system of 'Resource Account Budgeting' across all areas of government, which involves accounting for expenditure on an accrual rather than a cash basis—whereby costs are accounted for when they are incurred rather than when they are paid—and including items such as a charge for capital employed (based on an assumed return that could be obtained were the capital otherwise employed). This is not included in the SIPRI definition. (The UK does however provide an alternative cash-based measure close to the SIPRI definition.)

Why Measure Military Expenditure?

Military expenditure information is used by a wide variety of users, including governments, diplomats, academic researchers and students, non-governmental organizations, international organizations such as the World Bank and IMF, journalists, and interested members of the general public. Military expenditure data are for a variety of purposes, including;

- To assess the economic burden of a country's military forces on their economy.
- To assess a governments priorities, possibly by comparing spending on the military with spending on other sectors such as health and education, and changes in their relative levels over time.
- To assess a country's orientation as relatively peaceful or 'militaristic' (although one should be cautious in such

an assessment, as this also depends on a country's security situation), or as a measure of how they view the various security threats and challenges they may face. Rapid increases in military expenditure over a short period of time may for example be a warning sign of possible internal or external conflict, although the connection is far from direct.

- To give a rough indication of the relative level of military capability or power of different countries – such a use is rather problematic, as there is no direct relationship between military expenditure – an input measure – and military capability or power, which are output measures.
- To conduct statistical research relating military expenditure across countries and/or over time to other economic, political and security variables. Such research may include:
  1. The impact of military expenditure on economic growth and development, or on other economic variables such as international debt or corruption.
  2. The existence or otherwise of 'trade-offs' between spending on the military and other areas such as health and education.
  3. The determinants of military expenditure, such as a country's economic wealth, armed conflict, political systems, and the military expenditure of neighbours and rivals.
  4. The effect of military expenditure (along with other variables) on the risk of armed conflict.

SIPRI regards military expenditure as a measure of the economic resources devoted to the military. SIPRI presents military expenditure data for each country in three forms: first, in current-price, local currency terms, as this represents the primary raw data from which all others are calculated. Secondly, in constant price dollar terms. Constant prices allow meaningful comparisons of the resources consumed by the military over time, allowing for inflation, while conversion to a common currency allows some measure of cross-country comparison, although this is problematic as the market exchange rates used for conversion may not accurately represent the purchasing power of a currency, while alternative purchasing power parity rates are also subject to numerous difficulties. Conversion to a common currency also allows military expenditure to be aggregated globally or regionally, to gain a sense of the total volume of resources devoted to the military worldwide. Thirdly, SIPRI reports military expenditure as a proportion of each country's GDP (based on figures for each in current local currency). This figure, the 'military burden' is the most direct measure of the economic burden of the military sector. It may also give an indication of the degree of 'militarisation' of a country, although this should be treated with caution.

THE INDIGENISATION OF THE INDIAN DEFENCE INDUSTRY: ANALYSING THE BOTTLENECKS

Sixty nine years of independence, four major battle engagements, 38,000 sq. km unresolved borders dispute with China, regular proxy wars with Pakistan, porous borders and a coastal line of 7,517 kms to be defended. The vulnerable geopolitical location of India demands India to embolden and put thrust on its defence sector. No doubt Indian defence sector has seen epochal times recently with nearly 2 lakh crore ($ 40 billion) on defence procurements in last three years. In the same breath India is also preparing to invest $ 100 billion for the defence procurements in the next decade. Since India ranks 8th in the world in military spending and counts for 14% of the world's arms import with a projected defence expenditure of approximately $65.4 billion by 2020, this clearly manifests the necessity of its own home grown industries and capability mustering for a major indigenisation of the defence sector in the coming years.

However, this ambitious responsibility will definitely be challenged in reality against various prevailing and prospective bottlenecks. This paper attempts to analyse and explore the various bottlenecks in the road to indigenisation of India's defence sector.

The transitions in the geopolitics of the world and the conspicuous turning points in the international politics, demands self-reliance and comprehensive indigenous capabilities of its armed forces. A noteworthy case from history was during the disintegration of Soviet Union which caused a precarious situation for India as 70% of Indian defence equipment were of Soviet origin and the spares, tech-support, supplements etc. were not available owing to the Soviet crisis, thereby making it even more challenging. Currently India imports 70% of its defence requirements, which demands an imperative introspection into the Indian defence system, suggestive of indigenous manufacturing of equipment. This would ensure reduction in its acute dependency on foreign products. The biggest defence markets that are feeding India are USA, France, UK, Russia and Germany today, from which approximately 44% recipients are South Asia and Asia Pacific countries. India accounts for 15% of arms import in last five years according to SIPRI report. The report also claims India to be the world's top arms importer today. Moreover, the comparison by SIPRI data (which compared for two consecutive slots of five years each i.e. 2005-2009 and 2010-2014) projected that the Indian arms import has shown a surge as high as by 140%. In 2010 -2014 India's import rate was three times that of China which clearly indicates the urgency of requirement of indigenous market for her defence sector. The Prime Minister Modi's recent commitment poses for 70% of hardware to be manufactured domestically by the turn of the decade. This declared objective, however will be tested against the complex bottlenecks of *inter alia* formulation of QR (Qualitative Requirements), limited knowledge in the defence market intelligence and technology, insufficient availability of information about testing facility, trial and evaluation methodology etc.

Besides making a self-reliant, India by the indigenisation policies to develop her defence sector, has a certain chance to venture into the green field of exports of the arms and equipment to other South Asian countries like Bangladesh, Myanmar, Srilanka, which currently imports a large chunk from China.

The current defence allocations comes in the wake of high octane call for "Make in India" initiative. Bringing the indigenisation of this sector into reality requires a pragmatic and approachable combination of OEM (Original Equipment Manufacturer), Government agencies and the private sectors. Further, the intensive interaction between domestic representatives and OEM's are very important to establish a robust self-sufficient and profit bearing industry. Apart from this, the major concerns and complex issues that lie ahead are IPR (Intellectual Property Rights) and ToT (Transfer of Technology) matters.

Bottlenecks

What is indigenisation? The ability to design, create and manufacture defence equipment within a country utilising skills and resources (raw and capital) available and to repair and maintain them independently explains the concept of indigenisation.

Defence industrialisation mainly involves technology. And one of the major feature of technology is its speed of change. This involves speedy negotiations to overcome threat of product being obsolete prior to its introduction.

The Indian defence sector accounts for 2.5% of total GDP and 13% of central government expenditure. LTIPP (Long Term Integrated Perspective Plan) 2012-27 however demands for about 3% of the GDP which may be viewed as a serious short coming. The inadequate investment in research and development (approx. 0.85%) which is significantly lower than advanced countries is also a perpetuating weakness towards the serious business of being indigenous. All the defence expenditures sum up to a very modest amount, which is somehow managing the show as of day. The Defence Procurement Policy 2016 advocates preference to buy from India and make in India, giving full opportunity to private as well as public sectors to delve into and invest. The hierarchy of categorization for current DPP (Defence Procurement Policy) to facilitate the policy and encourage self-reliance via prioritization has been provided and may be seen as below: This hierarchy is self-explanatory about a significant transition towards indigenous equipment, and has been done to foster and encourage the role of private sectors in the huge defence industry, awaiting serious (Indian) private players.

In this way the government has projected its policy to encourage development of a systematic self-reliant defence industrial base with a focus on manufacturing. Following their commitment the FDI (Foreign Direct Investment) cap has been raised to 49%. Although according to the specialists this figure is not sufficient enough for steady flow of capital for OEMs and their suppliers with transfer of technology, at least [a] 74% FDI is the desirable figure.

One of the major bane of Indian defence sector is single vendor acquisition. This serves aa a major bottleneck in eclipsing the required transparency which is much needed for steady and successful operation of the sector. The single vendor process is a prospective trigger to scams in acquisition procedures. The scams in deals like Bofors, Singapore Technologies Kinetics (STK), Augusta-Westland, Israel Military Industries to name a few. Many others were debarred in the mired process.

Yet another area which is of great importance is issues relating to and emanating from IPR (Intellectual Property Rights) of the R&D organizations. IPR plays a very significant role in defence sector. In defence manufacturing, IPR includes protection of inventions, industrial designs and the technology via Patent, Copyright, Trade Secret and such other laws. The main motive behind is to provide protection for the investment in the research and development of new technology so as to cover the commercial risks involved. The Indian contracts under technology transfer and manufacture under license [does not] supports technology absorption and innovations. The rights always remains with the OEMs who are reluctant to dispense with their innovative technological information. Therefore, even for the simple need of up-gradations of the available equipment, the resultant dependency on the seller always looms large, making it impossible, thereby rendering the same redundant and un-useable. The OEMs strictly restrict their IP from sharing with their Indian counterparts for their cutting edge technology in fear of losing the commercial monopoly in the market.

It is often seen that there is a very little guideline(s) that are present on IPRs on technological issues, on the contracts that are received by Indian manufacturers. However, according to the new *defence offset policy* higher multipliers are allowed in case of DRDO (Defence Research and Development Organisation), but then the sub-clause contains no guidelines on further [ToT] transfer of these technologies.

The ToT involves approvals from the foreign government and sometimes they demand enormous prices for disseminating the information, as "Know how" does not forms the part of the contract. However, the possible solutions which can be sought may be such as:

- Co-development and Co- production
- Sub-contracting
- Joint ventures
- Licensed Production etc.

Since, the defence procurement is an extremely significant process for the army and its preparedness for any future armed conflict, red tape culture which forms another draconian bottleneck in the indigenisation of this sector, needs immediate remedy and must be reduced significantly if not completely abolished overnight.

The lack of clarity in rules and their implementation in the defence offset policies and absence of proper guidelines in the formulation of offset partnership also sometimes creates long term bottlenecks in harnessing a robust defence procurement process. Such deals often gets aborted or hangs for indefinite long period of time and are sabotaged eventually.

Sometimes the lack of interaction between MoD (Ministry of Defence), Defence service headquarters and Industries creates long term delays or even closure of projects. Moreover, "Play Safe" and "Push Files" are some other root causes of inefficient implementation of the defence policies. No costs, no commitment trial, plays as another hindrance in the indigenisation for this sector as it attempts to discourage SMEs (Small and Medium Enterprises), as all manufacturer will bring technology from a foreign partner spending exuberant amount to produce trial samples and will also bear huge cost for initial set up but in the end only the L1 (Lowest bidder) will be able to recover his investment, [and the] rest will be losing their investment.

Apart from all the above discussed bottlenecks a major area of improvement is the monopolistic domination by the PSUs (Public Sector Undertakings) over the private players. A conducive environment, trust and discipline among various organisations related to this sector is a must to enable organizations to work together on a collaborative platform to achieve the larger fruit.

PRIVATE SECTOR IN DEFENCE PRODUCTION

The Government of India has been reiterating its commitment to achieve the much-publicised target of procuring 70 per cent of its defence requirements from indigenous sources by 2010. Despite its best efforts over the last two decades, India is nowhere near that figure as yet. The Government is well aware of the emergence of private sector as a vibrant and dynamic force, especially in information technology, service sector and manufacturing fields. It has come to realise that self reliance would remain a pipe dream if it continued to bank on public sector alone. One of the objectives mentioned in the new defence procurement procedure is to achieve self-reliance in defence equipment. But the whole procedure is silent about the role of the private sector and no worthwhile initiatives have been proposed to integrate its potential in India's quest for self reliance.

In addition to economic factors, defence industry is generally considered to be an instrument of national sovereignty and pride. Defence industry comprises of all industrial undertakings engaged in the production of hardware and services for use by the defence forces. The origin of the Indian defence industry can be traced to the establishment of Gun and Shell Factory at Cossipore in 1801. At the time of the Independence, India had 16 Ordnance Factories, established by the British to produce low tech items. Bharat Electronics Ltd was the first Defence Public Sector Undertaking (DPSU) established in 1954 to manufacture electronic equipment for the forces. Today, India has 39 Ordnance Factories and eight DPSU.

The Industrial Policy Resolution of 1956 divided industry into three parts:-

- Schedule A: Basic industries which are the preserve of the state, including defence and heavy engineering.
- Schedule B: Industries in which private industry was allowed to operate.
- Schedule C: All other industries.

Manufacture of components, assemblies and sub-assemblies was thrown open to the private sector in 1991. With a view to promote defence-industry partnership, the Ministry of Defence (MoD) constituted six Joint Task Forces in collaboration with Confederation of Indian Industry in 1998. Consequent to their recommendations, the Government opened defence production to the private sector in January 2002. It allowed 100 percent private equity with 26 percent Foreign Direct Investment (FDI). It was a major policy change. Subsequently, the Department of Industrial Policy and Promotion issued detailed guidelines for the issuance of licence for the production of arms and ammunition.

The Kelkar Committee, constituted in 2004, made many radical recommendations. The Government has accepted a majority of them but their implementation has lacked earnestness and focus. The Department of Industrial Policy & Promotion (DIPP), in consultation with Ministry of Defence, has so far issued 37 letters of intent for the manufacture of various types of defence hardware which include armoured and combat vehicles, radars, electronic warfare equipment, warships, submarines, avionics, military aircraft, safety and ballistic products, armaments and ammunition.

Despite the above measures, there has been no discernible change in the ground situation. Only a handful of India's top companies are involved in small value defence contracts. The private sector has to remain content with the supply of some low-tech items to the public sector. Its supplies to DPSU and Ordnance Factories grossed over Rs. 1200 crores and Rs. 1900 crores respectively last year. Whereas these figures signify the contribution made by the private sector, they also highlight the fact that the private sector continues to be merely an outsourcing base for the public sector.

CONTINUED NON-PARTICIPATION OF THE PRIVATE SECTOR

A number of defence-industry seminars, conferences and exhibitions have been held in the recent years. Given decades of insulation and prejudices, this was no small achievement. But old mindsets, complexity of procurement procedures and clout wielded by the public sector have been acting as major deterrents to any meaningful participation of the private sector. New aspirants, in particular, find the whole regime to be highly forbidding.

Policy and Procedural Issues

Decisions are taken by the Defence Acquisition Council to categorise a proposal as 'Buy' or 'Buy and Make' or 'Make' based on the advice given by Defence Research and Development Organisation and the public sector. No inputs are sought from the private sector. Its competence and potential are given no consideration. In all deals where transfer of technology is negotiated, the nominated recipient is always a DPSU, even if a private sector company is better placed in terms of infrastructure and know-how to absorb the technology. A DPSU may have to establish complete facilities ab initio, whereas a private sector company may need only incremental technology.

Requirements of the armed forces are not made known to the private sector sufficiently in advance, with the result that it does not get adequate time, either to scout for foreign tie-ups or to establish the necessary facilities. The time given for the submission of technical and commercial proposals is grossly inadequate for a new entrant in the field. Parameters for the equipment to be procured are formulated with foreign equipment in mind, after reading manufacturers' brochures. Private sector is not consulted in this process, whereas minor acceptable changes in parameters may make the Indian equipment eligible for consideration. As Requests for Proposals (RFP) are issued to foreign original equipment manufacturers as well, they prefer direct bidding. They decline joint ventures with Indian companies as it helps them to guard their technology and perpetuate their monopoly with consequent financial gains. All trials are carried out on 'No Cost No Commitment' basis. Whereas foreign vendors can incur the expenditure involved, many upcoming indigenous companies do not possess the necessary financial strength. This acts as a major disincentive.

Functional Issues

Due to the very nature of its usage, defence equipment has to meet highly exacting standards. There can be no failure in the face of the enemy. Regrettably, many Indian vendors have not fully grasped the import of this requirement and find the quality control regime to be extremely irksome. Every producer seeks economies of scale and assured continuous orders. Unfortunately, Indian procurement regime precludes both. RFPs are issued for one-time piecemeal quantities without indicating the envisaged total requirement over a period of time. Additionally, no long term commitment is made regarding regular flow of orders. This deters Indian companies from committing resources for establishing production facilities as the venture can prove both expensive and risky.

Lack of Mutual Confidence

The Indian public sector has got used to a position of pre-eminence. Its hold over defence orders is total. It thrives because of its monopolistic clout and not because of any displayed excellence. It is fully aware of its weaknesses and knows that it cannot survive an open competition with the private sector. This sense of insecurity makes it wary of any move to facilitate the entry of the private sector and it tries all stratagems to block it. On the other hand, many functionaries feel that the private sector is out to make a quick buck and lacks required perseverance. They tend to view the private sector as traders rather than committed manufacturers who can endure the travails of long drawn procurement procedure. According to them, anyone desirous of entering defence industry has to be fully aware of the fact that defence orders take inordinately long to materialise and vacillation invariably proves unproductive.

The Communication Gap

There is a total absence of an effective institutionalised interface between the MoD, the services and the private sector for regular interaction at the policy making level. There are a number of 'groups' or 'partnership forums' in place, but their utility is limited to exchange of views only.

Procurement Agencies are Unaware of Industry's Potential : The procurement agencies are extremely keen to encourage indigenous production and limit imports to the minimum inescapable requirements. They, however, are unaware of the capabilities and potential of different private sector companies, as the competence of Indian companies has not been authentically catalogued as yet. They do not know whom to invite for submission of proposals. It is much easier to acquire details of numerous foreign producers.

There is no data bank of Indian industries available with the MoD. Requests for Proposals (RFPs) are issued only to a few highly visible companies, while many others lose by default. Although, the Acquisition Wing has been tasked to create the necessary data bank, the process has hardly taken off as yet.

Industry Lacks Knowledge of Defence Requirements and Procedures : On the other hand, many private sector companies have the capability to manufacture the whole range of defence requirements but do not know whom to approach to ascertain details. They are ignorant of the procurement agencies, their policies and procedures. This ignorance makes them wary of dealing with the defence.

To compound the problem, there are over 150 different defence procurement agencies with different procedures. There is no system of centralised notification of requirements and vendor registration. Due to this lacuna, a new entrant finds the whole environment highly dissuasive.

Structural Reforms

A representative of the designated industry association should be a permanent invitee to the Defence Acquisition Council, depending on the security sensitivity of agenda points. His inputs as regards the technical prowess of the private sector will prove invaluable while deciding whether to import technology or not. Similarly, selected agenda points of Defence Procurement Board, Defence Production Board and Defence Development Board should be circulated to the industry association for advice. These steps will go a long way in integrating the private sector.

Bibliography

Alexander, J : *Military Technology and Equipment Technology*, Omega Pub, Delhi, 2008.

Anil, K.C.: *Military and Democracy in India: Challenges, Politics and Power*, Sumit Enterprises, Delhi, 2009.

Banerjee, Sumanta: *In the Wake of Naxalbari: A History of the Naxalite Movement in India,* Calcutta: Subarnarekha, 1980.

Budge I: *The New Challenge of Direct Democracy*, Oxford, Polity Press, 1996.

Deepak, B R : *India and China : 1904-2004 : A Century of Peace and Conflict*, Manak, Delhi, 2005.

Gaur, Mahendra : *Indian Policy of Neighbour*, Delhi, Kalpaz Pub., 2006.

Hoffman, Bruce, *Inside Terrorism in Afghanistan*, New York: Columbia University Press, 1998.

Huntington, S.P.: *The China Modernisation Military and the State*, N.Y., Vintage Books, 1964.

James Campbell: *Excursions, Adventures and Field-Sports in Ceylon : Its Commercial and Military Importance*, AES, Delhi, 2006.

Jones, W.H.: *Government and Politics of India Military*, London, Hutchinson, 1971.

Kala, G.K. : *Demystifying Military Leadership*, Manas Pub, Delhi, 2003.

Kumar, Raj : *Weapons and Military Technology*, Sumit Enterprises, Delhi, 2009.

Mary, W.: *Asian Power and Politics: the Cultural Dimensions of Authority*, Cambridge, Belknap Press, 1985.

Nayyar, K K : *National Security : Military Aspects*, Rupa, Delhi, 2003.

Peter G. Tsouras: *Dictionary of Military Quotations*, Manas, Delhi, 2006.

Posen, B.R.: *The Sources of Military Doctrine*, Ithaca, 1984, Cornell Univ. Press.

Prabir De: *Pak and China in an Era of Globalisation : Essays on Economic Cooperation*, Bookwell, Delhi, 2005.

Radhakrishna: *Military Ethics: Guidelines for Peace and War*, Sumit Enterprises, Delhi, 2009.

Raj Kumar: *Weapons and Military Technology*, Sumit Enterprises, Delhi, 2009.

Rita Raj: *Global Encyclopaedia of Military Education and Training*, Global Vision, Delhi, 2010.

Robert M Cassidy: *Counterinsurgency and the Global War on Terror : Military Culture and Irregular War*, Pentagon Press, Delhi, 2008.

Sali, M L : *Military Geography*, Manas, Delhi, 2009.

Samuel P. Huntington: *The Soldier and the State : The Theory and Politics of Civil-Military Relations*, Natraj Pub, Delhi, 2005.

Sharma, G.K. and M.S. Jaswal: *Study and Practice of Military Law*, Deep and Deep, Delhi, 2006.

Singh, R.S.N. : *Asian Strategic and Military Perspective*, Lancer, Delhi, 2005.

Singhal, D. P.: *India and Afghanistan: 1876-1907. A Study in Diplomatic Relations*, St. Lucia, University of Queensland, 1963.

Strange, Susan: *The Retreat of the State: The Diffusion of Power in the World Economy*, Cambridge: Cambridge University, 1996.

Index

❑❑❑